Posttraumatic Stress Disorders in Children and Adolescents

More Advance Praise for
*Posttraumatic Stress Disorders in Children
and Adolescents: Handbook*

"Dr. Silva and his colleagues describe the concepts underlying current approaches to the diagnosis and treatment of PTSD in children and adolescents, review the available evidence and its limitations, and illuminate the many facets of this complex disorder with well-chosen clinical examples. Timely and thorough, this book is a welcome addition to the clinical literature regarding the responses of children and adolescents to severe trauma."

–A. Reese Abright, M.D., Chief, Child and
Adolescent Psychiatry Service, Saint Vincent
Catholic Medical Centers of Manhattan

"This is a timely volume and it will be particularly useful for the researcher or clinician looking for a developmentally-sensitive, research-based discussion of posttraumatic stress in children and adolescents. Silva's collection covers a broad range of issues important to understanding and treating children's traumatic stress responses."

–Juliet M. Vogel, Ph.D., Director of Child
Psychology Training, Department of Psychiatry,
North Shore University Hospital

A NORTON PROFESSIONAL BOOK

Posttraumatic Stress Disorders in Children and Adolescents: Handbook

Edited by
Raul R. Silva, M.D.

W. W. Norton & Company
New York   London

For information about permission to reproduce selections from this book,
write to Permissions, W. W. Norton & Company, Inc., 500 Fifth Avenue,
New York, NY 10110

Prodution Manager: Leeann Graham
Manufacturing by Haddon Craftsmen, Inc.

Library of Congress Cataloging-in-Publication Data

Posttraumatic stress disorders in children and
adolescents : handbook / [edited by] Raul R. Silva.
p.   cm.
"A Norton professional book."
Includes bibliographical references and index.
ISBN 0-393-70412-2 (pbk.)
1. Post-traumatic stress disorder in children—Handbooks, manuals, etc.
2. Teenagers—Mental health—Handbooks, manuals, etc. I. Silva, Raul R.

RJ506.P55675 2003
618.92'8521—dc22   2003059715

W. W. Norton & Company, Inc., 500 Fifth Avenue, New York, N.Y. 10110
www.wwnorton.com

W. W. Norton & Company Ltd., Castle House, 75/76 Wells St.,
London W1T 3QT

1 3 5 7 9 0 8 6 4 2

Contents

110133

Contributors

Patricia Karen Abanilla, M.D., Unit Chief, Bellevue Child Inpatient Unit, Clinical Assistant Professor of Psychiatry, NYU School of Medicine.

Ava Albrecht, M.D., Associate Director of The Adolescent Day Hospital Program at Bellevue Hospital Center, Clinical Assistant Professor of Psychiatry, NYU School of Medicine.

Carmen M. Alonso, M.D., Director of Residency Training—Division of Child & Adolescent Psychiatry, Assistant Clinical Professor of Psychiatry at NYU School of Medicine, NYU School of Medicine.

Elissa J. Brown, Ph.D., Assistant Professor of Psychiatry, NYU School of Medicine.

Marylene Cloitre, Ph.D., Director of The Institute for Trauma & Stress at the NYU Child Study Center, Kathy & Stephen Graham Professor of Child & Adolescent Psychiatry, Child Study Center.

Barbara Farkas, M.D., Director of Psychiatric Services at the New York Institute for Special Education, Assistant Clinical Professor of Psychiatry at NYU, Bellevue & NYU School of Medicine.

John Fayyad, M.D., Child and Adolescent Psychiatrist, Assistant Professor, Dept. of Psychiatry & Psychology, St. George University Hospital and Balamand University, Faculty of Medicine, Beirut, Lebanon.

Vilma Gabbay, M.D., L.L.B., Child & Adolescent Resident, Clinical Instructor of Psychiatry, NYU School of Medicine.

Michela Bou Ghosn, B.A., Research Assistant, IDRAC (Institute for Development Research & Applied Care), Beirut, Lebanon.

Glenn S. Hirsch, M.D., Medical Director, Division of Child and Adolescent Psychiatry and Child Study Center, Assistant Professor of Psychiatry, NYU School of Medicine.

Aimée Nasser Karam, Ph.D., Attending Psychologist, St. George University Hospital, Clinical Instructor, Balamand University Faculty of Medicine and St. Joseph, University Medical School, Beirut, Lebanon.

Elie Karam, M.D., Professor & Head, Dept. of Psychiatry and Psychology, St. George University Hospital, Balamand University, Faculty of Medicine, Beirut, Lebanon.

Lena Kessler, B.A., Project Director of The National Child Traumatic Stress Network, NYU School of Medicine.

Sharon Christina Kowalik, M.D., Ph.D., Director of Child and Adolescent Psychiatry Clinic at Bellevue Hospital Center, Assistant Professor in Clinical Psychiatry, NYU School of Medicine and Bellevue Hospital Center, NYU Child Study Center.

Tal N. Lee, C.S.W., CSW, & Doctoral Candidate for Clinical Psychology, NYU School of Medicine.

L. Oriana Linares, Ph.D., Director of Foster Care Mental Health Program, Associate (pending) Professor of Psychiatry, Child Study Center.

Jennifer McQuaid, M.A., Project Coordinator for the Partner's Program at the NYU Child Study Center, Assistant Research Scientist, NYU Child Study Center.

Zeina Mniemneh, MPH, Epidemiologist, Senior researcher, IDRAC (Institute for Development Research & Applied Care), Beirut, Lebanon.

Dinohra M. Munoz-Silva, M.D., Private Practice.

Melvin D. Oatis, M.D., Director of Pediatric Consultation Liaison Service, Assistant Professor of Clinical Psychiatry, NYU School of Medicine.

Richard A. Oberfield, M.D., Unit Chief of The Pediatric Consultation Liaison Unit at Bellevue Hospital Center, Clinical Associate Professor of Psychiatry, NYU School of Medicine.

Mia Pappagallo, M.D., Associate/Assistant Unit Chief, Bellevue Child Inpatient Unit, Clinical Assistant Professor of Psychiatry, NYU School of Medicine.

Veronica M. Rojas, M.D., Clinical Director of ACS Bellevue, NYU Mental Health Service, Clinical Instructor of Child & Adolescent Psychiatry, NYU School of Medicine.

Philip A. Saigh, Ph.D., Professor of Health and Behavioral Studies, Teacher's College, Columbia University.

Raul R. Silva, M.D., Deputy Director of Child & Adolescent Psychiatry at NYU School of Medicine and Bellevue Hospital Center, Associate Professor of Clinical Psychiatry NYU School of Medicine.

Kenneth Spitalny, M.D., Child & Adolescent Resident, NYU School of Medicine.

Caroline Cordahi Tabet, DEA, Attending Psychologist, St. George University Hospital, Clinical Instructor, Balamand University, Faculty of Medicine, Beirut, Lebanon.

Anastasia F. Yasik, Ph.D., Psychologist (Does not have a Bellevue title), Assistant Professor in the Psychology Department at Pace University, Pace University.

Preface

This handbook is intended to provide clinicians with a reference guide to the most salient issues of posttraumatic stress disorder (PTSD), stress, trauma, and the concurrent conditions that affect children and adolescents. The primary, though not exclusive, concern is addressing the findings of childhood trauma rather than attempting to deal with childhood PTSD by extrapolating from the clinical and research work with adults. Clinicians of different backgrounds and disciplines will find this book a useful resource comprised of and supported by a mixture of both clinical experience and research findings.

Trauma and stress are part and parcel of human existence. Despite the fact that it was only recently recognized as a formal diagnostic category in 1984, the characteristics of PTSD are as old as the human race. The current classification system (*Diagnosic and Statistical Manual IV*) requires two essential events to occur in order to classify a traumatic reaction as PTSD—a notable stressor is followed by a marked emotional or behavioral response. Without these two *sin equa non* conditions, the diagnosis cannot be considered. The ensuing clinical symptom development dictates if the response meets formal criteria for PTSD. These additional criteria will be reviewed throughout this book.

Despite the fact that the current criteria to establish a diagnosis of PTSD is widely accepted in adults, the criteria may be less useful for clinicians when seeking to identify cases in children and adolescents. Despite the relative simplicity of the DSM description, PTSD is polymorphous. This is particularly apparent when considering the wide array of causal stressors to which persons are exposed as well as each person's individual abilities to develop the syndrome. We have included chapters that address some of these risk factors as well as the epidemiologic aspects of different classes of stressors. (In particular, we have included an entire chapter on the negative effects of war, the ravages of which having been endured by children and adolescents throughout the centuries.) Biological conditions and development are also critical to individual variances in susceptibility to PTSD and are critical to clinical diagnosis. In view of this, we have dedicated a number of chapters to current research and clinical practice bearing on the biological and etiologic underpinnings of this disorder.

We have dedicated a number of chapters to the identification of issues that complicate the cookbook approach of the DSM with regards to the diagnosis of PTSD in children and adolescents. For clinicians who work with these age groups, it is easier to understand how language, vocabulary, age appropriate repertoires as well as cognitive levels modify presentation and confound clear communication in cases of traumatized youth. To this end, there are chapters dedicated to the consideration of human development, matters of the clinical course of illness, and issues of differential diagnosis. The authors have also provided readers with a number of composite cases, each of which highlights features that are seminal to clinical practice. With respect to understanding the intricacies of establishing a diagnosis, we have also included a chapter that is specifically focused on the assessment of children and adolescents. Irrespective of the stressor and the biological constitution of the affected individual, we have found that a number of vulnerability and or resiliency factors can mediate a child's response to a given stressor. As a result, two other chapters were included to address issues related to vulnerability and gender differences. Finally, because many of the cases of traumatized children involve the legal system coupled with the fact that many clinicians are not experts in the intricacies of the law, we have included a chapter to address some of the more important legal aspects of PTSD.

The effort to advance our knowledge base regarding children and adolescents affected by trauma continues. Through the Substance Abuse and Mental Health Services Administration (SAMHSA), the federal government has established 22 National Centers for Trauma and Stress specifically for children and adolescents. This network is designed to establish the collaborations required to answer many of the questions that still plague us. The authors hope that this book may shed some light on what we know about PTSD and help us to identify the gaps in our knowledge that remain to be filled. Specifically, studies to help comprehend the underlying neurological factors of this illness are required. These investigations could help guide useful pharmacologic interventions, which also require further study. One cannot adequately underscore the significance of further studies that may aid in the identification of individual vulnerability factors that predispose certain children to the development of a maladaptive anxiety response. Knowledge of these factors may in turn help guide the creation of preventive or early interventions for those that need them most. At the same time, learning more about features of children's resiliency may help us to better understand those factors that are protective and which can be applied or taught to those individuals who are exposed to serious stressors and do not fare as well.

The authors of the chapters in this book are from different theoretical backgrounds. Some are academicians who have helped clarify many salient issues in the field, while others are researchers who have received grant funding from various federal, city and state agencies to research and meet the needs of traumatized children. As may be noted in the authors list, many of the contributors are affiliated with the New York University School of Medicine and Bellevue Hospital Center system. Since 1726, well before there was even a United States of America, the Bellevue system has had as its mission the task of rendering assistance to individuals who lack the resources or the ability to seek aid elsewhere. As one of the oldest psychiatric facilities in the country and home of the first child and adolescent inpatient unit in the United States, Bellevue has distinguished itself as the safety net for many of the disenfranchised families living within the largest city in North America. In fulfilling this mission, clinicians at Bellevue are responsible for helping some of the most seriously traumatized children in New York City.

The clinicians who authored the chapters of this book have dedicated much of their professional lives to improving our understanding of trauma, pioneering interventions for the treatment of trauma, and treating with care and respect those who are ill and traumatized. This was never more evident than during the events of September 11th, 2001. Bellevue Hospital and New York University are within a few miles from where the World Trade Center once stood. On that day, and in the days and weeks that followed, many of the clinicians delivered services non-stop to children, families, educators, and caretakers. They left the hospital to deliver services in office buildings, schools, and family centers established for victims and their families. They presented lectures and seminars for other health care specialists concerning much of what is written in this book. Interestingly, the decision to write this book occurred prior to September 11th of 2001 and without any knowledge of the clinical work and increased responsibilities that would follow in the wake of the attack on the World Trade Center. Due to the commitment of the authors to serving the needs of our patients, the book took slightly longer to compose than was anticipated.

Raul R. Silva, M.D.
New York 2003

Acknowledgments

As with any sizeable undertaking, acknowledgements for efforts are essential. I would like to thank my coauthors for their contributions, the time they invested, and their dedication to both clinical and academic quality.

Next, I must acknowledge my family: my wife and children. Without their love, affection, and support, life just would not be the same. I hope the time that I dedicate to work does not considerably detract from your happiness.

I would like to express my gratitude to Harold Koplewicz for his support as well as the long leash that he affords me. May your vision for the New York University Child Study Center continue to expand.

I appreciate the efforts of my coworkers who toil alongside me everyday while taking care of business. The NYU School of Medicine, Bellevue Hospital Center, and the Health and Hospitals Corporation also deserve proper acknowledgement for their continued and unwavering support of child mental health.

Seeing that the theme of this book is PTSD, my friends in the New York State Office of Mental Health and the New York City Department of Mental Health merit acknowledgement for their devotion to serving the children affected by the September 11th Terrorist Attacks.

Last, but not least, I wish to dedicate this book to my father and mother, Carlos and Mary, for all of their efforts. Their courage, love, and commitment to education form the cornerstone of my life. Thank you for everything.

Posttraumatic Stress Disorders in Children and Adolescents

1

■

Epidemiological Aspects of PTSD in Children and Adolescents

Vilma Gabbay, Melvin D. Oatis, Raul R. Silva, and Glenn S. Hirsch

With the ever increasing exposure of children and adolescents to the hostilities of school shootings, terrorist attacks, threats of war, destruction of public property, suicide bombings and natural disasters, posttraumatic stress disorder (PTSD) has become recognized as a major public health problem. The widespread coverage of the September 11th, 2001, terrorist attacks on the United States has underscored the importance of epidemiological research regarding PTSD.

In this chapter, important aspects involving the epidemiology of PTSD in children and adolescents will be discussed. Current research data regarding prevalence of PTSD in the general population will be presented as well as the relation to specific traumatic experiences in the realms of child maltreatment, disasters, car accidents, war zones, medical illness, and violence.

Lifetime Prevalence of PTSD in the General Population

The lifetime prevalence of PTSD in the general adult population is estimated to be 8% (American Psychiatric Association, 2000). Large scale epidemiological studies investigating the lifetime prevalence of PTSD in the general child population have not been published. However, several studies have focused upon the adolescent population. A study that examined a random sample of 1,007 young adults disclosed an estimated lifetime prevalence for PTSD to be 9.2% (Breslau et al., 1991). This group was living in a large urban environment and had a lifetime prevalence rate of 39.1% to exposure to traumatic events. Another large community sample of adolescents was found to have an estimated PTSD lifetime prevalence of 6% (Giaconia et al., 1995). A study with 490 adolescents aged 16 to 22 reported a lifetime prevalence of only 2% (Cuffe et al., 1998). These reports provide us with a range of lifetime prevalence rates that vary from 2% to 9.2%.

Prevalence of PTSD in High-Risk Populations

The very nature of PTSD being linked to a traumatic event underscores the importance of comparing the prevalence of the disorder in high-risk populations to that of the general population. Children and adolescents who have histories of being exposed to traumatic events have higher prevalence rates of PTSD according to a number of research studies. In the following section, we will present the prevalence rates in different high-risk populations. There is considerable variability in the prevalence rates of PTSD in at-risk populations, which range from 3% (Garrison et al., 1995) to 100% (Frederick, 1985). These seemingly discrepant and highly variable rates may be attributable to factors such as: the sample population, the time elapsed between the traumatic exposure and symptom development, the nature of the trauma, as well as the diagnostic or assessment scales used in the studies.

The Prevalence of PTSD and Child Maltreatment

Child maltreatment is a serious health problem in the United States. Maltreatment includes physical, sexual, or emotional abuse and neglect. According to a 1998 estimate by the U.S.

Department of Health and Human Services, each year more than 1 million children are victims of maltreatment. The scientific literature has recognized a strong association between child maltreatment and PTSD as evidenced by the numerous studies that have investigated the psychiatric consequences of abuse (Adam et al., 1992; Deblinger et al., 1989; Hillary & Schare, 1993; Kiser et al., 1988, 1991; McLeer et al., 1988, 1992, 1998; Pelcovitz et al., 1994).

In children evaluated in psychiatric outpatient settings who have had a history of sexual abuse, the documented PTSD prevalence rates ranged from 36.3% to 48.9% (Adam et al., 1992; McLeer et al., 1992, 1994, 1998; Wolfe et al., 1993). In a study where the authors randomly selected 101 children who were involved in court proceedings due to severe maltreatment, 39% of children met criteria for PTSD based on structured diagnostic interviews (Famularo et al., 1993). In another study involving 92 children aged 4 to 16 and selected from various agencies other than psychiatric units, 19.6% of the children met criteria for PTSD while a total of 63.5% were diagnosed with a *Diagnostic and Statistical Manual of Mental Disorders* Axis I disorder (Merry & Andrews, 1994). These diagnoses were made 12 months after the disclosure of child abuse or maltreatment.

Ackerman and associates (1998) reported on 204 children (ages 7 to 13) who had been abused. They divided the sample into three groups. The first group consisted of 127 children who had been sexually abused only. The next group was comprised of 43 patients who only experienced physical abuse, while the last group contained 34 individuals who had been both sexually and physically abused. Using the Diagnostic Interview for Children and Adolescents—Revised (DICA-R), the authors noted an increased risk for developing PTSD in both types of abuse. Thirty-four percent of the children who had a history of either sexual or physical abuse were diagnosed with PTSD, while 58% of those who had experienced both types of abuse met criteria for

PTSD. In summary, patients exposed to maltreatment developed PTSD at rates ranging from approximately 20% to over 63%.

The Prevalence of PTSD in Children and Adolescents Involved in Automobile Accidents

Automobile accidents continue to be the leading cause of death in the adolescent population. Thus, it is not surprising that traffic-related traumas are considered yet another risk factor for the development of PTSD in children and adolescents. Keppel-Benson and colleagues (2002) examined 50 children using structured interviews approximately 9 months following their exposure to a traffic accident. The prevalence of PTSD was estimated to be 14%. Interestingly, a higher degree of physical injury predicted more severe PTSD symptoms while a higher level of social support predicted less severe symptoms.

In a prospective study of children (ages 3 to 18) involved in automobile accidents, patients were evaluated at seven to twelve months after their injuries using validated diagnostic questionnaires. There was a 25% prevalence rate of PTSD in this sample (de Vries et al., 1999). Risk factors associated with the development of PTSD were young age and the parent witnessing the event. Of note, the severity of a child's injury was not reported to predict PTSD. In a cohort of Scottish children who had survived injuries related to automobile accidents and were examined 3 to 4 months after their injuries, the prevalence of mild PTSD symptoms was 35% while 14% of the children had severe PTSD symptoms (Di Gallo et al., 1997). Overall, the reports identified PTSD development for children and adolescents involved in motor vehicle accident at rates ranging from 14% to 35%.

The Prevalence of PTSD in the Medically Ill population

Another group considered to be at substantial risk for the development of PTSD is the medically ill. Pelcovitz and associates

(1998) evaluated a group of 23 adolescents who had a form of cancer and compared them to 27 physically abused adolescents and 23 healthy, nonabused adolescents. The lifetime prevalence of PTSD in the cancer group was 35%, while the prevalence in the abused group was only 7%.

After evaluating 64 pediatric leukemia survivors, ages 7 to 19, by utilizing a self-report measure of posttraumatic stress (the Posttraumatic Stress Disorder Index), Stuber and colleagues (1996) found 12.5% of the leukemia survivors reported a severe level of posttraumatic distress. Stoddard and colleagues (1989) assessed the prevalence of PTSD in a group of 30 children with histories of severe burn injuries that required elective surgical reconstruction. The assessments were done within a mean time interval of 8.9 years after the injury. The lifetime PTSD prevalence was estimated to be 53.3%, while the current prevalence rate was an estimated 6.7%. Depending on when PTSD assessments are conducted, prevalence rates for developing PTSD among the medically ill population range from 12% to 53%.

The Prevalence of PTSD in Children and Adolescents Exposed to Disasters

Over the past 2 decades, there has been a substantial interest in epidemiological research studies examining the psychiatric sequelae of child and adolescent populations exposed to mass disasters. These studies include the investigation of natural disasters such as earthquakes (Galante & Foa, 1986; Pynoos et al., 1993), floods (Green et al., 1991), hurricanes (Shannon et al., 1994), as well as humanly created disasters such as the Oklahoma City bombing (Pfefferbaum et al., 1999), terrorist attacks (Koplewicz et al., 2002), and sniper shootings (Pynoos et al., 1987). The psychiatric manifestations in children and adolescents exposed to such disasters are sometimes delayed in onset, prolonged in nature, and affect children as young as preschool age (Nader et al.,

1990; Pfefferbaum, 1997; Scheeringa et al., 1995; Vogel & Vern-berg, 1993; Yule et al., 1999).

There have been several epidemiological studies that examined the psychiatric sequelae of hurricanes in children. Garrison and colleagues in 1995 examined the rates of PTSD in a random-digit-dialing sample of adolescents 6 months after the occurrence of Hurricane Andrew. The authors reported that approximately 3% of males and 9% of females met criteria for PTSD. In another study, Shannon and associates (1994) focused on the psychiatric effects of Hurricane Hugo. They examined sequelae 3 months after the hurricane by using the Child PTSD Reaction Index. In this study, the estimated PTSD prevalence was 5%. The same prevalence rate of 5% was reported by Garrison and colleagues (1993) in adolescents using the same measurement instrument (Child PTSD Reaction Index) 1 year after the occurrence of Hurricane Hugo. Shaw and colleagues (1995) studied children affected in the high-impact area of Hurricane Andrew using the Child PTSD Reaction Index at 32 weeks after the disaster. The authors found that 51% of children had moderate levels of PTSD and 38% had severe to very severe levels of impairment. At the follow-up interval of 21 months, Shaw and colleagues (1996) reported that 70% of subjects continued to identify moderate to severe levels of impairment secondary to PTSD. Varying prevalence rates were discovered in a recent study by Goenjian and associates (2001), who investigated the effects of Hurricane Mitch that hit Central America in 1998. The hurricane caused massive destruction of property and the death of approximately 10,000 people. One hundred fifty-eight adolescents from three differentially exposed cities were rated 6 months after the traumatic exposure utilizing the Child PTSD Reaction Index. This group found PTSD prevalence rates of 90%, 50%, and 14% in the different sites. Both the level of impact and magnitude of destruction at the three different cities were believed to account for much of the variance in prevalence.

Earthquakes represent another area of epidemiological inter-est related to PTSD. Hsu and colleagues (2002) assessed the PTSD prevalence in a group of 323 adolescents aged 12 to 14 from one of the worst regions affected by a catastrophic earth-quake that occurred in Taiwan during 1999. The children received an evaluation 6 weeks after the earthquake that included a self-rated questionnaire and an independent diagnos-tic evaluation made by a psychiatrist. The authors reported the prevalence rate of PTSD to be 21.1%. Prevalence rates docu-mented in other studies of earthquake victims (Hsu et al., 2002; Goenjian et al., 1995; Najarian et al., 1996; Pynoos et al., 1993) vary widely, ranging from 21.1% to 95% in children. Some of the variance is accounted for by the severity level of the quake and the use of different rating and diagnostic instruments.

The psychiatric sequelae of PTSD in children and adoles-cents in response to terrorist attacks is limited. However, studies began to examine the effects of the terrorist attacks of Septem-ber 11, 2001, and the recurrent suicide bombings in Israel upon children and adolescents. In a study of the 1993 World Trade Center bombing in New York City, Koplewicz and colleagues (2002) followed 22 children who were trapped in the building. Nine children had been trapped in an elevator and 13 had been on the observation deck at the time of the attack. Assessments were done 3 and 9 months after the event, using the PTSD Reac-tion Index and a Fear Inventory. At the 3-month period, only 14% of the group were likely to have met diagnostic criteria for PTSD. At the 9-month mark, this rate dropped to 4.5% (1 of 22 subjects). Other studies that investigated the effects of the Okla-homa City bombing in 1995 found an increased risk of PTSD in relation to television viewing of the event (Pfefferbaum et al., 2001).

The Prevalence of PTSD in War Zones

It is estimated that wars have caused the death of up to 10

million children in the past decade (UNICEF, 1996). Living in refugee camps as a consequence of war represents another traumatic experience. The United Nations High Commissioner for Refugees (UNHCR) estimates that as of 1997, there were 13.2 million refugees in the world (UNHCR, 1997). The appalling events that took place with Cambodian refugees during the years 1975 to 1979 have been well documented and studied (Becker, 1986; Hawk, 1982). Four follow-up studies (Kinzie et al., 1986; Kinzie et al., 1989; Sack et al., 1993; Sack et al., 1999) were conducted in the United States investigating the prevalence rates of PTSD among adolescents who had experienced the horrors of the Pol Pot regime in Cambodia as children (ages 8 to 12) between the years 1975 and 1979. Using structured interviews, these studies have shown the persistence of high prevalence rates of PTSD over a 12-year period. The initial study by Kinzie and colleagues (1986) began in 1984, approximately 5 years after the traumatic exposure and 2.5 years after their immigration to the United States. The estimated prevalence rate of PTSD among the 40 adolescents investigated was 50%. In a follow-up study conducted three years later (Kinzie et al., 1989), the rates of PTSD among the 27 adolescents in the original group was 48%. They also reported that 61.5% of the subjects who were initially diagnosed with PTSD (Kinzie et al., 1986) continued to meet criteria for the disorder (Kinzie et al., 1989). In a 6-year follow-up study, the prevalence rate for 19 adolescents from the original group was 38% (Sack et al., 1993). In a fourth study (Sack et al., 1999), a 12-year follow-up of 27 of the original 40 adolescents took place. The persistence of PTSD in this population was reported as 35%. It should be noted that the onset of PTSD in 18% of subjects developed 5 years after the cessation of the traumatic exposure.

Sack and associates (1994) also examined a random community sample of 209 Khmer youths from two communities. They estimated the lifetime prevalence for PTSD at 21.5%, with a point prevalence of 18.2% in this study. Savin and colleagues (1996) investigated the prevalence rates of PTSD among 99 Cambodians, aged 18 to 25, who lived in the Site II refugee camps along the Thai-Cambodian border. This group had survived the traumatic events of the Pol Pot regime as children in addition to living through more than a decade in a refugee camp. Semi-structured interviews were used for diagnostic purposes. In this sample, 26.3% of subjects met the diagnostic criteria for PTSD, which were related to the traumatic events of the Pol Pot regime and had a lifetime prevalence of 31.3%. Goldstein and associates (1997) conducted a survey of 364 displaced children, 6 to 12 years old, who were in a rural refugee camp in Croatia during the Bosnia-Herzegovina conflict of 1992–1995. The authors found a very high PTSD prevalence rate (93.8%). Another study (Allwood et al., 2002) that examined a sample of 791 children from 6 to 16 years old from Bosnia during the 1994 siege of Sarajevo estimated the prevalence of PTSD to be 41%.

Studies have shown that even brief periods of exposure to war trauma may predispose children to high posttraumatic stress reactions. Nader and colleagues (1993) investigated a group of 51 Kuwaiti children 5 months after the February 1991 withdrawal of Iraqi forces from Kuwait using the Child PTSD Reaction Index. The authors reported that 70% of subjects met the criteria for PTSD. In the same context of historical events related to the Persian Gulf War, several studies looked at the Israeli youth population who had experienced Iraqi missile attacks. In one study (Schwarzwald et al., 1993), which examined stress reactions in 5th through 10th grade children 1 month following their exposure to the SCUD missile attacks, the prevalence rate of PTSD was estimated to be 22.1%. In a follow-up study (Schwarzwald et al., 1994) 1 year after the Gulf war, they reported the point prevalence for PTSD in a group of 6th, 8th, and 11th grade children as 12%. Saigh (1989) conducted a study in the context of the civil war in Lebanon. A group of 840 children were clinically examined. The author reported that 32% of children developed PTSD during and after the serious battles in Beirut, Lebanon. In another study (Saigh et al., 1990) that examined PTSD rates in 200 children who were exposed to the Lebanese war, a PTSD prevalence rate of 46.5% was reported based on ratings from the Children PTSD Inventory.

Prevalence of PTSD among Children and Adolescents Exposed to Violence

Children and adolescents who are exposed to violent acts represent another high-risk group for the development of PTSD. The high prevalence rates of violence in certain inner-city areas have been a major public concern. Research examining the prevalence rates of exposure to violence documented that up to 80% of inner-city adolescents have witnessed an assault, 40% have witnessed a shooting or stabbing, and almost 25% have witnessed a homicide (Bell & Jenkins, 1993; Lorion & Saltzman, 1993; Schubiner et al., 1993; Schwab-Stone et al., 1995). Lipschitz and colleagues (2002) investigated the prevalence rates of PTSD among 90 females who ranged from 12 to 21 years old who presented for a routine medical check-up in an inner-city medical clinic. Diagnostic instruments used included the Child PTSD Checklist and a semistructured diagnostic interview for PTSD. The PTSD prevalence rate was estimated as 14.4% of girls exposed to trauma. Berman and associates (1996) reported a higher PTSD prevalence of 34.5% in a random sample of 96 students at a high school exposed to community violence. Breslau and colleagues (1991) assessed the prevalence rate of PTSD in a random sample of 1,007 youngsters. The lifetime prevalence of exposure to traumatic events was 39.1%, while the prevalence rate of PTSD in those exposed to violence was reported to be 23.6%.

Correctional settings reserved for children exhibiting severe delinquent behaviors are another environment where high prevalence rates of PTSD exist after exposure to violence. Steiner and colleagues (1997) assessed the prevalence of PTSD among 85 incarcerated males, ages 13 to 20, of whom 25% were randomly selected and 75% were referred for psychiatric examinations. Diagnostic tools included a standard psychiatric screen, a semi-structured interview for PTSD, and self-report questionnaires. Prevalence of PTSD was found to be 31.1%, and another 20% of the sample met partial criteria for PTSD. Another study (Ruchkin et al., 2002) looked at 370 Russian male juvenile delinquents. Diagnoses were established by the Schedule for Affective Disorders and Schizophrenia for School-Age Children–Present and Lifetime Version, which is a semistructured diagnostic instrument. Among the 351 subjects who had a history of trauma, 24.8% met criteria for PTSD and 41.6% met partial criteria. Violence-related experiences (witnessing and victimization) were the most common types of trauma. Cauffman and colleagues (1998) examined the rates of PTSD in a sample of 96 female offenders (ages 13 to 22 years). In this study, 65.3% of subjects met PTSD criteria at some time in their lives, with an additional 9.5% expressing partial symptomatology. Current PTSD diagnosis at the time of the study was estimated to be 48.9% with 11.7% meeting partial PTSD criteria.

References

Ackerman PT, Newton JE, McPherson WB, Jones JG, Dykman RA. (1998). Prevalence of post traumatic stress disorder and other psychiatric diagnoses in three groups of abused children (sexual, physical, and both). *Child Abuse Negl.* 22:759–774.

Adam BS, Everett BL, O'Neal E. (1992). PTSD in physically and sexually abused psychiatrically hospitalized children. *Child Psychiatry Hum Dev.* 23:3–8.

Allwood MA, Bell-Dolan D, Husain SA. (2002). Children's trauma and adjustment reactions to violent and nonviolent war experiences. *J Am Acad Child Adolesc Psychiatry.* 41(4):450–457.

American Psychiatric Association. (2000). *Diagnostic and Statistical Manual of Mental Disorders* (4th ed., text rev.). Washington, DC: American Psychiatric Association.

Becker E. (1986). *When the War Was Over: The Voices of Cambodia's Revolution and Its People*. New York: Simon & Schuster.

Bell CC, Jenkins EJ. (1993). Community violence and children on the southside of Chicago. *Psychiatry*. 56:46–54.

Berman SL, Kurtines WM, Silverman WK, Serafini LT. (1996). The impact of exposure to crime and violence on urban youth. *Am J Orthopsychiatry*. 66:329–336.

Breslau N, Davis CG, Andeski P, Peterson E. (1991). Traumatic events and posttraumatic stress disorder in an urban population of young adults. *Arch Gen Psychiatry*. 48:216–222.

Cauffman E, Feldman SS, Waterman J, Steiner H. (1998). Posttraumatic stress disorder among female juvenile offenders. *J Am Acad Child Adolesc Psychiatry*. 37(11):1209–1216.

Cuffe SP, Addy CL, Garrison CZ, et al. (1998). Prevalence of PTSD in a community sample of older adolescents. *J Am Acad Child Adolesc Psychiatry*. 37:147–154.

Daviss WB, Mooney D, Racusin R, Ford JD, Fleischer A, McHugo GJ. (2000). Predicting posttraumatic stress after hospitalization for pediatric injury. *J Am Acad Child Adolesc Psychiatry*. 39(5):576–583.

Deblinger E, McLeer SV, Atkins MS, Ralphe D, Foa E. (1989). Posttraumatic stress in sexually abused, physically abused, and nonabused children. *Child Abuse Negl*. 13:403–408.

de Vries AP, Kassam AN, Cnaan A, Sherman SE, Gallagher PR, Winston FK. (1999). Looking beyond the physical injury: posttraumatic stress disorder in children and parents after pediatric traffic injury. *Pediatrics*. 104(6):1293–1299.

Di Gallo A, Barton J, Parry-Jones WL. (1997). Road traffic accidents: early psychological consequences in children and adolescents. *Br J Psychiatry*. 170:358–362.

Famularo R, Fenton T, Kinscherff R. (1993). Child maltreatment and the development of posttraumatic stress disorder. *Am J Dis Child*. 147(7):755–760.

Foy DW, Goguen CA. (1998). Community violence-related PTSD in children and adolescents. *PTSD Res Q*. 9(4):1–6.

Frederick CJ. (1985). Children traumatized by catastrophic situations. In: Eth S, Pynoos RS, eds. *Posttraumatic Stress Disorder in Children*. Washington, DC: American Psychiatric Press; 71–100.

Galante R, Foa D. (1986). An epidemiological study of psychic trauma and treatment effectiveness after a natural disaster. *J Am Acad Child Adolesc Psychiatry*. 25:357–363.

Garrison CZ, Bryant ES, Addy CL, Spurrier PG, Freedy JR, Kilpatrick DG. (1995). Posttraumatic stress disorder in adolescents after Hurricane Andrew. *J Am Acad Child Adolesc Psychiatry*. 34:1193–1201.

Garrison, CZ, Weinrich, MW, Hardin, JB, Weinrich, S, Wang L. (1993). Posttraumatic stress disorder in adolescents after a hurricane. *Am J Epidemiol*. 138(7): 522–530.

Giaconia R, Reinherz H, Silverman A, Bilge P, Frost A, Cohen E. (1995). Traumas and posttraumatic stress disorder in a community population of older adolescents. *J Am Acad Child Adolesc Psychiatry*. 34:1369–1380.

Goenjian AK, Molina L, Steinberg AM, et al. (2001). Posttraumatic stress and depressive reactions among Nicaraguan adolescents after Hurricane Mitch. *Am J Psychiatry*. 158(5):788–794.

Goldstein RD, Wampler NS, Wise PH. (1997). War experiences and distress symptoms of Bosnian children. *Pediatrics*. 100:873–878.

Green BL, Korol M, Grace MC, et al. (1991). Children and disaster: age, gender, and parental effects on PTSD symptoms. *J Am Acad Child Adolesc Psychiatry*. 30: 945–951.

Hawk D. (1982). The killing of Cambodia. *New Rep* 187:17 21.

Hillary BE, Schare ML. (1993). Sexually and physically abused adolescents: an empirical search for PTSD. *J Clin Psychol*. 49:161–165.

Hsu CC, Chong MY, Yang P, Yen CF. (2002). Posttraumatic stress disorder among adolescent earthquake victims in Taiwan. *J Am Acad Child Adolesc Psychiatry*. 41(7):875–881.

Kazak AE, Barakat LP, Meeske K, et al. (1997). Posttraumatic stress, family functioning and social support in survivors of childhood leukemia and their mothers and fathers. *J Consult Clin Psychol*. 65:120–129.

Keppel-Benson JM, Ollendick TH, Benson MJ. (2002). Post-traumatic stress in children following motor vehicle accidents. *J Child Psychol Psychiatry Allied Disciplines*. 43(2):203–212.

Kinzie JD, Sack WH, Angell RH, Clarke G. (1989). A three-year follow up of Cambodian young people traumatized as children. *J Am Acad Child Adolesc Psychiatry.* 28:501–504

Kinzie JD, Sack WH, Angell RH, Manson S, Ben R. (1986). The psychiatric effects of massive trauma on Cambodian children, I: The children. *J Am Acad Child Psychiatry.* 25:370–376.

Kiser LJ, Ackerman BJ, Brown E, et al. (1988). Post-traumatic stress disorder in young children: a reaction to purported sexual abuse. *J Am Acad Child Adolesc Psychiatry.* 27:645–649.

Kiser LJ, Heston J, Millsap PA, Pruitt DB. (1991). Physical and sexual abuse in childhood: relationship with post-traumatic stress disorder. *J Am Acad Child Adolesc Psychiatry.* 30:776–783.

Koplewicz HS, Vogel JM, Solanto MV, et al. (2002). Child and parent response to the 1993 World Trade Center bombing. *J Trauma Stress.* 15(1):77–85.

Lipschitz DS, Rasmusson AM, Anyan W, Cromwell P, Southwick SM. (2002). Clinical and functional correlates of posttraumatic stress disorder in urban adolescent girls at a primary care clinic. *J Am Acad Child Adolesc Psychiatry.* 39(9):1104–1111.

Lorion RP, Saltzman W. (1993). Children's exposure to community violence: following a path from concern to research to action. *Psychiatry.* 56:55–65.

Manne SL, Du Hamel K, Gallelli K, Sorgen K, Redd WH. (1998). Posttraumatic stress disorder among mothers of pediatric cancer survivors: diagnosis, comorbidity, and utility of the PTSD Checklist as a screening instrument. *J Ped Psychol.* 23:357–366.

McLeer SV, Callaghan M, Henry D, Wallen J. (1994). Psychiatric disorders in sexually abused children. *J Am Acad Child Adolesc Psychiatry.* 33:313–319.

McLeer SV, Deblinger E, Atkins MS, Foa EB, Ralphe DL. (1988). Post-traumatic stress disorder in sexually abused children. *J Am Acad Child Adolesc Psychiatry.* 27:650–654.

McLeer SV, Deblinger E, Henry D, Orvaschel H. (1992). Sexually abused children at high risk for post traumatic stress disorder. *J Am Acad Child Adolesc Psychiatry.* 31:875–879.

McLeer SV, Dixon JF, Henry D, et al. (1998). Psychopathology in non-clinically referred sexually abused children. *J Am Acad Child Adolesc Psychiatry.* 37:1326–1333.

Merry SN, Andrews LK. (1994). Psychiatric status of sexually abused children 12 months after disclosure of abuse. *J Am Acad Child Adolesc Psychiatry*. 33:939–944.

Nader KO, Pynoos RS, Fairbanks LA, Al-Ajeel M, Al-Asfour A. (1993). A preliminary study of PTSD and grief among the children of Kuwait following the Gulf crisis. *Br J Clin Psychol*. 32:407–416.

Nader K, Pynoos RS, Fairbanks L, Frederick C. (1990). Children's PTSD reactions one year after a sniper attack at their school. *Am J Psychiatry*. 147:1526–1530.

Najarian LM, Goenjian AK, Pelcovitz D, Mandel F, Najarian B. (1996). Relocation after a disaster: posttraumatic stress disorder in Armenia after the earthquake. *J Am Acad Child Adolesc Psychiatry*. 35:374–383.

Pelcovitz D, Kaplan S, Goldenberg B, Mandel F, Lehane J, Guarrera J. (1994). Post-traumatic stress disorder in physically abused adolescents. *J Am Acad Child Adolesc Psychiatry*. 33:305–312.

Pelcovitz D, Libov BG, Mandel F, Kaplan S, Weinblatt M, Septimus A. (1998). Posttraumatic stress disorder and family functioning in adolescent cancer. *J Trauma Stress*. 11(2):205–221.

Pfefferbaum B. (1997). Posttraumatic stress disorder in children: a review of the past 10 years. *J Am Acad Child Adolesc Psychiatry*. 36:1503–1511.

Pfefferbaum B, Nixon SJ, Tivis RD, et al. (2001). Television exposure in children after a terrorist incident. *Psychiatry*. 64:202–211.

Pfefferbaum B, Nixon SJ, Tucker PM, et al. (1999). Posttraumatic stress responses in bereaved children after the Oklahoma City bombing. *J Am Acad Child Adolesc Psychiatry*. 38:1372–1379.

Pynoos RS, Frederick C, Nader K, et al. (1987). Life threat and posttraumatic stress in school age children. *Arch Gen Psychiatry*. 44:1057–1063.

Pynoos RS, Goenjian A, Tashjian M, et al. (1993). Posttraumatic stress reactions in children after the 1988 Armenian earthquake. *Br J Psychiatry*. 163:239–247.

Ruchkin VV, Schwab-Stone M, Koposov R, Vermeiren R, Steiner H. (2002). Violence exposure, posttraumatic stress, and personality in juvenile delinquents. *J Am Acad Child Adolesc Psychiatry*. 41(3):322–329.

Sack WH, Clarke G, Him C, et al. (1993). A six-year follow up of Cambodian youth traumatized as children. *J Am Acad Child Adolesc Psychiatry*. 32:431–437.

Sack WH, Him C, Dickason D. (1999). Twelve-year follow-up study of Khmer youths who suffered massive war trauma as children. *J Am Acad Child Adolesc Psychiatry*. 38:1173–1179.

Sack WH, McSharry S, Clarke G, Kinney R, Seeley J, Lewinsohn P. (1994). The Khmer Adolescent Project. I. Epidemiologic findings in two generations of Cambodian refugees. *J Nerv Ment Dis*. 182:387–395.

Saigh PA. (1989). The development and validation of the Chldren's Post-Traumatic Stress Disorder Inventory. *Int J Special Education*. 4:75–84.

Saigh PA, Fairbank JA, Gross A. (1990). *A logit analysis of the symptoms of traumatized adolescents.* International research on childhood posttraumatic stress disorder. Symposium conducted at the meeting of the American Psychological Association, Boston, MA.

Savin D, Sack WH, Clarke GN, Meas N, Richart I. (1996). The Khmer Adolescent Project: III. A study of trauma from Thailand's Site II refugee camp. *J Am Acad Child Adolesc Psychiatry*. 35(3):384–391.

Scheeringa MS, Zeanah CH, Drell MJ, Larrieu JA. (1995). Two approaches to the diagnosis of posttraumatic stress disorder in infancy and early childhood. *J Am Acad Child Adolesc Psychiatry*. 34:191–200.

Schubiner H, Scott R, Tzelepis A. (1993). Exposure to violence among inner-city youth. *J Adolesc Health*. 14:214–219.

Schwab-Stone ME, Ayers TS, Kasprow W, et al. (1995). No safe haven: a study of violence exposure in an urban community. *J Am Acad Child Adolesc Psychiatry*. 34:1343–1352.

Schwarzwald J, Weisenberg M, Solomon Z, Waysman M. (1994). Stress reactions of school-age children to the bombardment by SCUD missiles: a 1-year follow-up. *J Trauma Stress*. 7(4):657–667.

Schwarzwald J, Weisenberg M, Waysman M, Solomon Z, Klingman A. (1993). Stress reaction of school-age children to the bombardment by SCUD missiles. *J Abnorm Psychol*. 102(3):404–410.

Shannon MP, Lonigan CJ, Finch AJ Jr, Taylor CM. (1994). Children exposed to disaster: I. Epidemiology of post-traumatic symptoms and symptom profile. *J Am Acad Child Adolesc Psychiatry*. 33:80–93.

Shaw JA, Applegate B, Schorr C. (1996). Twenty-one-month follow-up study of school-age children exposed to Hurricane Andrew. *J Am Acad Child Adolesc Psychiatry*. 35:359–364.

Shaw JA, Applegate B, Tanner S, et al. (1995). Psychological effects of Hurricane Andrew on an elementary school population. *J Am Acad Child Adolesc Psychiatry*. 34:1185–1192.

Steiner H, Garcia I, Matthews Z. (1997). Posttraumatic stress disorder in incarcerated juvenile delinquents. *J Am Acad Child Adolesc Psychiatry*. 36:357–365.

Stoddard FJ, Norman DK, Murphy JM, Beardslee WR. (1989). A diagnostic outcome study of children and adolescents with severe burns. *J Trauma*. 29:471–477.

Stuber ML, Christakis D, Houskamp BM, Pynoos RS, Kazak AE. (1996). Post trauma symptoms in childhood leukemia survivors and their parents. *Psychosomatics*. 37:254–261

UNICEF. (1996). *The State of the World's Children*. New York: Oxford University.

United Nations High Commissioner for Refugees. (1997). *The State of the World's Refugees 1997–1998*. New York: Oxford University Press.

U.S. Department of Health and Human Services. (1998). *Child Maltreatment 1996: Reports From the States to the National Child Abuse and Neglect Data System*. Washington, DC: US Government Printing Office.

Vogel JM, Vernberg EM. (1993). Children's psychological responses to disasters. *J Clin Child Psychol*. 22:470–484.

Wolfe DA, Sas L, Wekerle C. (1993). Factors associated with the development of posttraumatic stress disorder among child victims of sexual abuse. *Child Abuse Negl*. 18:37–50.

Yule W, Perrin S, Smith P. (1999). Post-traumatic stress reactions in children and adolescents. In: Yule W, ed. *Post-traumatic stress disorders: Concepts and Therapy*. Chichester, UK: John Wiley & Sons, Ltd. 25–50.

2
■

Resiliency and Vulnerability Factors in Childhood PTSD

Raul R. Silva and Lena Kessler

Posttraumatic stress disorder (PTSD) is an illness that officially found its way into the accepted psychiatric nomenclature in the *Diagnostic and Statistical Manual of Mental Disorders*, Third Edition (*DSM-III*; American Psychological Association, 1980). Despite this late formal acknowledgement, the psychological responses to serious stressors had been chronicled in the literature for centuries (for review see Saigh & Bremner, 1999). Additionally, there have been a number of similar psychiatric presentations with various names used to identify them, including the combat specific identifier of *shell shock* and the term *gross stress reaction* used in *DSM-I*.

Since the 1930s (Bender & Blau, 1937; Bodman, 1941), there have been reports describing children with marked emotional manifestations resulting from serious stressors such as sexual abuse and exposure to war. The elements of reexperiencing, avoidance, and hyperarousal are clearly evident in these presentations and seem, at least phenomenologically, similar to the symptoms currently included in the diagnosis of PTSD. However, it was not until 1987 that the *DSM-III-R* included features specific to children in the description of PTSD to account for developmental differences.

Nonetheless, the trials and tribulations endured by many children in today's society provide ample substrate for this illness to develop. The exposure of children and adolescents to many severe stressors, such as domestic violence or physical and sexual abuse, could clearly start the etiological wheels of psychopathology rolling. These events, in addition to many natural disasters, meet the criteria of being "outside the range of normal human experience" as stipulated by the DSM.

Interestingly, the contribution of an obviously negative environment could be further expanded to include the stress and experiences of living in the inner city and high crime neighborhoods across our country. To this end, a number of investigators have taken the opportunity to examine how social adversity may impact youth in the development of PTSD.

In one cohort, Fitzpatrick and Boldizar (1992) identified that 70% of African-American youth in an inner city were exposed to at least one qualifying DSM-III stressor. Silva and colleagues in 2000 reported that 59% of youths in their inner-city clinic were exposed to similar stressors. In the same report by Fitzpatrick and Boldizar, 27% of those exposed developed the symptomatology to meet criteria for PTSD, while a similar percent (22%) did so in the Silva sample. Even across other heterogeneous demographic samples, the rates of development of PTSD in stress-exposed adolescents are remarkably similar (Deykin & Buka, 1997; Giaconia et al., 1995).

Although DSM-IV seems to presume a causal relationship between stress exposure and PTSD development, the findings that only a portion of the children exposed to these stressors go on to develop complete clinical presentations of PTSD provide investigators and clinicians with some evidence that there may be resiliency and vulnerability factors that mediate the development of PTSD.

Although the identification of mediating factors in a predictive model regarding the development of PTSD is in its infancy, such findings represent a crucial step for guiding early and preventative treatment initiatives.

Definitions

The term resiliency derives from the Latin roots *re*, which means *back*, and *salir*, which means to *jump*. This quality of bouncing back, or the ability to recover, is of paramount importance in identifying the positive attributes or characteristics that are protective.

Vulnerability derives from the Latin word *vulnerare* which means to *wound*. Because there are so many very different factors contributing to resiliency and vulnerability in the development of PTSD, determining them requires a number of different perspectives. Although dividing these factors into clusters is based on an initial, arbitrary classification system, it is a useful organizational approach.

Theory

There are a number of different ways of grappling with the issues of resiliency and vulnerability. In order to elaborate on the biological aspects of this examination, a brief review of how the body reacts to stress will be presented. (Further information on this topic is included in this book's chapters on risk and neurobiology, Chapters 3 and 5.)

In the realm of stress, a number of the body's systems interact to assist in mounting a response. The body works on a number of different fronts, but one of the most rapid responses takes place on the neurochemical level. Catecholamines, which are small organic molecules that act on the brain and throughout the body, are one of the earliest and most crucial response substances. Basically, there are three types of catecholamines: dopamine, epinephrine, and norepinephrine. Their secretion has a regulatory role in this response.

Normally these substances keep various systems functioning smoothly in response to demands of the internal and external environment. The body responds to a stressor usually by the activation of the adrenergic neurons in the brain, at the level of the hypothalamus.

It should be kept in mind that neurotransmitter systems frequently respond in tandem with other corporal systems (for review see Friedhoff & Silva, 2002). To this end, there is a close link between the cortisol and adrenergic responses. Both of these substances are produced in the adrenal glands, which are located directly above the kidneys. Stimulation of the adrenergic nervous system yields an increase in secretion of plasma epinephrine and norepinephrine from the nerve cell bodies in the medulla of the adrenals. The release of these substances induces elevation of heart rate as well as blood pressure. This cascade of events is coupled with an increase in norepinephrine that then induces cortisol-releasing hormone production at the level of the hypothalamus. Furthermore, epinephrine stimulates beta adrenergic receptors, located in fatty tissues, which induce lipolysis. This breakdown of fats is geared at producing energy for a corporal response.

Other body systems, such as that involving the pancreas, are also involved in producing the substrate for the body's response. Stimulation of α-adrenergic receptors in the cells of the pancreas decreases insulin secretion, which results in a consequent increase in glucose. Behaviorally speaking, this normal response prepares the organism for the "fight or flight" phenomenon. The increase in glucose and breakdown of fats yield energy for muscular exertion at the time of the response.

Despite the well defined mechanics of this process, the underlying mechanisms that transform a stressful experience into a maladaptive anxiety disorder are not fully understood. It would seem that in the case of those who have developed PTSD, the most substantial response that takes place is neither fight nor flight, but rather fright. This perspective is validated in part by the DSM-IV's definition of PTSD, stating that a person must respond to the stressor in an intensified manner. By definition, the trauma must produce significant arousal, but more speculatively, it appears that in many cases the trauma occurs in a situation in which the individual is deprived of an instrumental response that is reactive to the trauma. Ultimately, the instrumental response may be neurobiological, physical, or behavioral in nature. So, in essence, with the lack of fight or flight venues, fright becomes the only outlet for response. In reviewing the literature, it is possible to divide the reports that address resiliency and vulnerability into a number of factors. These include biological (such as familial/genetic contributants), cognitive, emotional, environmental, predisposing psychopathology, features related to the stressor, and previous experiences.

Biological Factors

In attempting to understand the neurobiological response in terms of deprivation, investigators may wish to focus on the cortisol system. This system is often considered the buffer system in the mediation of both internal and external stress experienced by the organism. As is described in more detail in Chapter 5 on neurobiology , in adults (where most of the research has taken place) plasma cortisol levels tend to be on the low side. Some of the findings in children have revealed that cortisol levels (salivary) may be increased. The discrepancy is difficult to reconcile, but each of these differences (either hyper- or hypocortisol production) seem to represent the deprivation of the normal biologic response to a stressor. An underlying predisposition of this sort of dysregulation, which may be triggered by an unanticipated stressor, may ultimately manifest itself in the posttraumatic symptom cluster. This view is shared by Heim and Nemeroff (2001) who acknowledged that early stressors may ultimately have a protracted effect on the functioning of the cortisol system that may predispose the individual to develop psychiatric symptomatology later. DeBellis (2002) has also speculated that early changes induced by trauma such as maltreatment during childhood may ultimately lead to biological dysregulation with a consequent vulnerability to develop illnesses such as PTSD.

There is also information that may point to a familial or genetic component to the development of PTSD (Krystal et al., 1989). In several studies that have focused on children, the familial influence on symptom generation is hard to ignore. Yehuda's group (Yehuda, Schmeider, Giller et al., 1998; Yehuda, Schmeider, Wainberg et al., 1998) examined a cohort of parents who survived the Holocaust and their offspring. It is important to note that the offspring hadn't been exposed to the Holocaust. Despite this, those offspring who had been exposed to a trauma and also had a parent with PTSD were significantly more prone to develop PTSD themselves. In another study, Laor and associates (1996) investigated families affected by the SCUD missile attacks during the Persian Gulf War. These families had experienced damage to their dwellings. In this sample, younger children whose mothers developed traumatic symptoms were also more likely to develop stress-related symptoms. Two other groups (McFarlane, 1987; Sack et al., 1994) have reported that the development of PTSD in youth who had experienced substantial stressors were also correlated with the occurrence of parental PTSD. Tiet and colleagues (1998), in a large epidemiological sample, found that youths who had been exposed to different serious life events would have significantly worse adjustments if their mothers also suffered from psychopathology. Clearly, the results of these studies could be accounted for by other factors such as observed coping styles, but the idea of familial or genetic influence must also be entertained. The vulnerability to develop PTSD either through assimilation or familial transmission provides an important assessment feature for clinicians to delve into.

Intelligence Factors

The impact of intelligence in the development of PTSD has also received some attention. As we discussed above, Tiet and colleagues (1998), in their sample of 1,285 individuals between the ages of 9 and 17 years, attempted to identify how the 25 different life stressors impacted on their functioning. In this large sample, higher IQ's bolstered the youths' adjustment process. In another study (Silva et al., 2000) of an inner-city clinic population, higher verbal IQ was considered the strongest resiliency measure protecting against the development of PTSD in a sample of 59 consecutively evaluated children and adolescents who had experienced a qualifying *DSM-IV* life stressor.

Orr and Pittman (1999) have suggested that the increased predisposition towards developing PTSD for those with reduced cognition may revolve around the premise that these individuals have a deficit in how they process the event or in their coping attributes. Conversely, Saigh (2000) in an analysis of 24 youths, whose ages ranged from 7 to 17 years old, determined that higher verbal IQ scores on the WISC III were found in the cohort that were PTSD positives than were found in both the PTSD negative group and a nonclinical control group.

It is important to bear in mind that a number of confounding factors could be involved in the observation of lower IQ and PTSD vulnerability. First, there are a number of other conditions that could lead to both lowered IQ and predisposition to psychopathology. Brain damage experienced by abused children can underlie both conditions. Also, as may be evidenced in many cases of abuse and neglect, early maternal deprivation could contribute substantially to both presentations. Additionally, it is hard to absolutely determine if the emotional sequelae of PTSD, in and of themselves, did not have an impact on the IQ results in the samples mentioned above. It would be very helpful in interpreting these results to have had pre-stressor values. Caution should be used in assumptions made along this line until longitudinal studies shed further light on the relationship between IQ and PTSD development.

Trauma-Related Cognitive Attributions

In two different reports, Mannarino and Cohen (1996a, 1996b) investigated predictors of symptom development in a cohort of sexually abused girls. Symptom development was assessed at the time the abuse was disclosed and then again 12 months after. They used the Children's Attributions and Perception Scale, which contains items related to self-blame and decreased trust. Greater scores on this scale predicted more serious presentations at both time points.

In another study, Dougall and colleagues (2001) investigated issues related to resiliency factors that included psychosocial variables such as social support, wishful thinking as a coping style, and the perception of loss of control. They examined 115 individuals injured during motor vehicle accidents. The authors assessed the subjects at three time points (1 month, 6 months, and 1 year) after the accidents. Wishful thinking significantly distinguished those patients who went on to develop PTSD.

It seems that characteristics such as trust, optimism, and lack of guilt, referenced above, are positive attributes that should be investigated as potential indicators of resiliency when assessing children who have been exposed to trauma.

Environmental Factors

In this section, the term *environmental factors* will also be used to subsume exposure. In general, the potential of developing an illness such as PTSD requires exposure, and thus the potential environment and consequent exposure to the precipitating trauma in and of itself represents a serious risk to the development of this condition The exposure to high index stressors seems to increase the risk of the development of PTSD in youth (March, 1993). Kilpatrick and colleagues (1998) believed that those individuals exposed to more high index stressors are at greater peril of developing PTSD.

The literature available in child psychiatry has documented the capacity for a vast array of serious stressors to induce PTSD. These include witnessing criminal assault (Pynoos & Nader, 1988); war related events (see Chapter 15, this volume); hostage scenarios (Terr, 1983); sustaining physical injuries (Stoddard & Saxe, 2001) and severe burns (Saxe et al., 2001); and undergoing life-saving medical procedures (Stuber et al., 1991). Disasters such as dam collapses (Green et al., 1991), train accidents (Milgram et al., 1988), earthquakes (Pynoos et al., 1993), hurricanes (Garrison et al., 1995), and maritime accidents (Yule et al., 2000; Udwin et al., 2000) are often of sufficient magnitude to provoke the development of maladaptive anxiety disorders such as PTSD.

In an effort to identify how children respond to different stressors, our group (Silva et al., 2000) attempted to determine if different traumas varied in their potential to produce PTSD. Full PTSD symptomatology developed in relatively comparable rates for the cohorts that experienced the three major types of trauma (sexual abuse 15%, physical abuse 21%, and domestic violence 17%). The differences were not statistically significant. Despite this, upon examination of the relationship between trauma and severity of symptoms, individuals who had witnessed domestic violence and those who had been physically abused developed statistically greater severity. We highlight this finding not because it is an absolute or definitive result, but because even in samples such as this in which children are exposed to more than one stressor there may be some traumatic events that are more powerful than others in inducing more severe forms of PTSD.

Previous Experience

The long-term impact of stressors, such as childhood abuse, has been studied as a possible predictor for the development of PTSD. In one such report, Carlson and colleagues (2001) investigated the role of features such as neglect, social support, and physical, sexual, and other forms of abuse in the child's environment as predictors of adult psychopathology in 178 inpatients. More specifically, multiple regressions demonstrated that these predictors accounted for 42% of the variance in PTSD symptoms. Patients who have been previously traumatized may, upon retraumatization, have a greater propensity to redevelop PTSD based at least partially on their previous experiences to significant stressors. One must be aware of inquiring about these events for exposed children, and especially for those who have experienced a previous pathological response such as PTSD in the past, because the connection between present reaction and past experience may not always be evident. The other finding by the Carlson group (2001) related to social support also requires commentary. Pine and Cohen (2002) explained that the role of social and familial support cannot be underscored as risk factors for the development of PTSD, especially in this section of previous experience, as the disruption of support cited were previously intact. However, it has been noted that as causal factors go, disruption of social and familial support do play an important role.

Features Related to the Stressor

Johnson and colleagues (2001) undertook an investigation looking at this very question of stressor characteristics. They wanted to identify which characteristics of the stressor (including how the child dealt with the trauma during the experience) were related to the development of PTSD in survivors of child sexual abuse. The study included 89 female survivors of child sexual abuse and used a number of standardized measures, which among others included the current PTSD symptomatology. A number of correlation analyses with statistical corrections demonstrated that a number of abuse features correlated with the development of PTSD. These included dissociation around the time of the abuse, belief that they would be killed, and whether or not the victim sustained injury.

The role of dissociation was also looked at in another sample of 158 adult females who were criminally assaulted or raped (Dancu et al., 1996). They used the Dissociative Experience Scale as their measure of dissociation. Their findings suggest that with certain types of trauma there may be increased vulnerability to develop PTSD in those individuals who dissociate. Finally, in their sample, individuals who reported a history of being sexually abused as a child were significantly more likely to dissociate. Bernat and colleagues (1998) investigated the relationship between peri-traumatic factors and the development of posttraumatic stress symptoms. Their sample included 937 undergraduate students. In this sample, over 70% were freshman and sophomores. While 67% of their sample had experienced what they considered a traumatic event, only 12% of these went on to develop full PTSD criteria. They found that the presence of dissociation and negative emotions as well as fearing they would be killed all predicted the development of PTSD.

LaGreca and colleagues (1996) studied PTSD symptoms in 442 students, who were between 3rd and 5th grades, following Hurricane Andrew. The sample was evaluated at 3, 7, and 10 months following the event. A number of variables were examined in a hierarchical multiple regression to predict those children that would develop more severe PTSD presentations. Symptom severity was measured by the PTSD Reaction Index. The variables examined included demographic characteristics, exposure to traumatic events during and after the disaster, major life stressors during the ensuing 10 months, features related to social support, and coping styles. At the 7-month mark, those children who thought their lives were at risk and had a greater number of life-threatening experiences during the hurricane, as well as the children whose lives were more disrupted by the hurricane, experienced greater PTSD symptom severity. Despite the fact that we chose to group this report in the category of factors related to the actual stressor, it also supports the position of disruption of social supports discussed earlier in this chapter.

Thabet and Vostanis (1999) conducted a study to examine the nature of the relationship between PTSD and wartime trauma factors in a cohort of 239 Palestinian children. The subjects' ages ranged from 6 to 11 years old. The total number of traumas experienced by the children turned out to be the strongest predictor of PTSD severity. Once again, previous trauma and multiple traumas must be issues that clinicians incorporate into their assessment, as individuals with these features represent a heightened risk for the development of PTSD.

In a well designed study, March and colleagues (1997) studied over 1000 children 9 months after an industrial fire. Their ages ranged from 10 to 16 years old. Among other features, the study intended to assess the association between certain factors and PTSD development. About 12% of their sample met DSM-III-R criteria for PTSD. The degree of exposure, both direct and indirect aspects, was the strongest predictor of PTSD based on the Self-Reported Post-Traumatic Symptomatology scale. Lack of self-attributed personal efficacy predicted the development of posttraumatic stress symptoms. Here the issues of self esteem seem to once again resonate as resiliency features in the child.

Saxe and associates (2001) examined how the dose of morphine given for acute burns affected the course of PTSD 6 months after hospital discharge in 24 patients who ranged in age from 6 to 16 years. There was a significant correlation between the dose of morphine and PTSD ratings. In their report, higher doses were related to lower PTSD symptoms, highlighting the role of fear conditioning and experience in traumatic memory development.

Personality and Preexisting Psychopathology

Schnurr and colleagues employed Minnesota Multiphasic Personality Inventory (MMPI) data collected on military subjects prior to enrolling in military service and correlated them to the development of PTSD symptoms (1993). The findings identified that certain personality factors may contribute to the development of PTSD when coupled with the stress of war. Blanchard and associates pursued a similar hypothesis (1996). In their study, they followed a group of 132 individuals who were in motor vehicle accidents (MVA). Patients as young as 17 years of age were included in this study. Assessments were performed initially within 4 months of the MVA and were repeated 6 and 12 months later. At the time of the first assessment, slightly over 36% met full criteria for PTSD. Using a multiple regression analysis, it was seen that the presence of Axis II diagnoses prior to the MVA significantly predicted continued symptoms at 1 year in those patients that developed PTSD within 4 months of the MVA.

In addition to personality factors, the preexistence of other psychiatric disorders may alter the expression of a trauma experience in certain individuals. In the Silva and colleagues study (2000), antecedent anxiety was significantly related to the development of PTSD. Furthermore, in this sample, those patients who had preexisting anxiety and were also sexually abused were more likely to develop more severe PTSD pictures. The authors concluded that antecedent anxiety seemed to amplify the expression of PTSD.

In another study, the authors examined the interaction between familial psychopathology and the development of protracted PTSD (Davidson et al., 1998). The families of 81 female rape victims were examined. A total of 285 individuals were interviewed. Data were analyzed by logistic regression and revealed that the families' propensity for major depressive disorders predisposed the rape victim to develop PTSD.

LaGreca and colleagues (1998) had the opportunity to investigate the behavioral and academic functioning of 92 children 15 months prior to Hurricane Andrew. The investigators wanted to identify potential predictors of PTSD. For this sample of children, a number of self, peer, and teacher ratings as well as measures of academic skills were available prior to the disaster. The occurrence of the hurricane presented the opportunity to repeat these measures at 3 months and thus investigate potentially meaningful correlations. Posttraumatic stress disorder symptoms were assessed at 3 and 7 months after the incident. At 3 months, PTSD severity was predicted by baseline ratings of anxiety, inattention, and academic skills, while at 7 months, of these ratings, only preexisting anxiety scores predicted greater PTSD severity scores.

North and associates (2002) performed a 3-year follow-up on a cohort of 116 individuals who survived a mass shooting. The authors assessed the sample at three distinct time points for issues related to PTSD, paying particular attention to details related to remission and delayed identification of illness spanning the 3 years. It was noted that females and subjects with preexisting psychiatric disorders represented heightened risk for the onset of PTSD.

On the other hand, the presence of certain diagnoses may be less compatible with the development of PTSD symptoms. In the Silva study (2000), those patients with the diagnosis of either oppositional defiant disorder or conduct disorder were significantly less likely to develop more elaborate forms of PTSD. It is conceivable that these patients, by the nature of their existing outwardly directed behavior, are less likely to manifest internalizing symptoms of PTSD. In trying to reconcile these findings, it is possible to say that trauma accentuates features of preexisting psychopathology in some children.

Conclusions

In today's world, the possibilities that a child will be involved in some type of trauma have grown commonplace. Whereas in some foreign countries where wars are fought in people's hometowns, in parts of our own country veritable wars are fought in homes, schools, and city streets. Some children are deeply affected by what they experience, whereas some come out of a situation virtually unscathed. This chapter has highlighted many resiliency and vulnerability factors that play a significant role in informing how a child will react to trauma.

It has been shown that children's and adult's perceptions of their trauma have a large effect on the development and severity of PTSD symptomatology. Studies have shown that feelings of guilt, helplessness, pessimism, and loss of trust are maladaptive and may increase the likelihood of developing PTSD. They are also directly related to the severity of the disorder. It has been stated that when there is no ability or opportunity for a fight or flight response, the only response left is that of fright. This is a way of understanding where PTSD stems from. With many trauma types, children are more prone than adults not only to feel helpless in relation to a trauma, but to actually be helpless. In addition to how a person perceives the trauma, the way he or she copes during the trauma is also important. Those who dissociate during the trauma seem more likely to develop PTSD, and those with previous child abuse are more likely to use dissociation as a coping technique. This is one of the ways that the advent of multiple traumas or the existence of previous trauma also comes to bear significant weight on a person's post-trauma reactions.

Examining preexisting psychopathology has also proven vital in understanding who may or may not develop PTSD. As discussed, the existence of some disorders appears maladaptive in dealing with trauma, while others actual appear to serve as resiliency factors. Preexisting internalizing disorders such as anxiety and depression have been shown to increase the likelihood of PTSD development, while that of externalizing disorders, such as oppositional defiance and conduct disorders, seem to mitigate its development. This, perhaps, is another example of the positive effects of flight or fight (externalizing) reactions and the negative effects of a fright (internalizing) reaction.

It seems that today's world presents many more complexities than that of centuries ago. Historically, lives were more simply about survival, and there was very little to mediate one's innate fight or flight response to a dangerous situation. And so, it seems that as the world becomes more complex, so too does our reaction to it. This, added to the complex nature of a developing child, seems a daunting paradigm. Therefore, we need to continue with our attempts to identify and understand the effects that the complexities of today's world, in close conjunction with the myriad modulating internal factors, have on the types of trauma children experience, the ways in which trauma is experienced, and the differences in PTSD manifestations.

We have come far in gathering the needed information and clustering symptoms to form a diagnosis of PTSD. We are now, however, faced with the vitally important task of looking at the role that resiliency and vulnerability factors play in the preventative care and treatment of traumatized children.

References

American Psychiatric Association. (1980). *Diagnostic and Statistical Manual of Mental Disorders* (3rd ed.). Washington DC, American Psychiatric Association.

Bender L, Blau A. (1937). The reaction of children to sexual relations with adults. *Am J Orthopsychiatry.* 7:500–518.

Bernat JA, Ronfeldt HM, Calhoun KS, Arias I. (1998). Prevalence of traumatic events and peritraumatic predictors of posttraumatic stress symptoms in a nonclinical sample of college students. *J Trauma Stress.* 11(4):645–664.

Blanchard EB, Hickling EJ, Barton KA, Taylor AE, Loos WR, Jones-Alexander J. (1996). One-year prospective follow-up of motor vehicle accident victims. *Behav Res Ther.* 34(10)775–786.

Bodman F. (1941). War conditions and the mental health of the child. *Brit Med J.* 11:486–488.

Carlson EB, Dalenberg C, Armstrong J, Daniels JW, Loewenstein R, Roth D. (2001). Multivariate prediction of posttraumatic symptoms in psychiatric inpatients. *J Trauma Stress.* 14(3):549–567.

Dancu CV, Riggs DS, Hearst-Ikeda D, Shoyer BG, Foa EB. (1996). Dissociative experiences and posttraumatic stress disorder among female victims of criminal assault and rape. *J Trauma Stress.* 9(2) 253–267.

Davidson JR, Tupler LA, Wilson WH, Connor KM. (1998). A family study of chronic post-traumatic stress disorder following rape trauma. *J. Psychiatr Res.* 32(5):301–309.

DeBellis M. (2002). Developmental traumatology: a contributory mechanism for alcohol and substance use disorders. *Psychoneuroendocrinology.* 27:155–170.

Deykin EY, Buka SL. (1997). Prevalence and risk factors for posttraumatic stress disorder among chemically dependent adolescents. *Am J Psychiatry.* 154(6):752–757.

Dougall AL, Ursano RJ, Posluszny DM, Fullerton CS, Baum A. (2001). Predictors of posttraumatic stress among victims of motor vehicle accidents. *Psychosomatic Med.* 63(3):402–411.

Fitzpatrick KM, Boldizar JP. (1992). The prevalence and consequences of exposure to violence among African-American Youth. *J Am Acad Child Adolesc Psychiatry.* 32(2):424–430.

Friedhoff AJ, Silva RR. (2002). Catecholamines. In: Dulbecco R, ed. *Encyclopedia of Human Biology Millennium Edition.* Orlando, Fla: Academic Press; 595–602.

Garrison CZ, Bryant ES, Addy CL, Spurrier PG, Freedy JR, Kilpatrick DG. (1995). Posttraumatic stress disorder in adolescents after Hurricane Andrew. *J Am Acad Child Adolesc Psychiatry.* 34:1193–1201.

Giaconia RM, Reinherz HZ, Silverman AB, Bilge Pakiz BA, Frost AK, Cohen E. (1995). Traumas and posttraumatic stress disorder in a community population of older adolescents. *J. Am Acad Child Adolesc Psychiatry*. 34(10):1369–1380.

Green BL, Korol M, Grace M, et al. (1991). Children and disaster: age, gender, and parental effects on PTSD symptoms. *J Am Acad Child Adolesc Psychiatry*. 30:945–951.

Heim C, Nemeroff CB. (2001). The role of childhood trauma in the neurobiology of mood and anxiety disorders: preclinical and clinical studies. *Biol Psychiatry*. 49(12):1023–1039.

Johnson DM, Pike JL, Chard KM. (2001). Factors predicting PTSD, depression, and dissociative severity in female treatment-seeking childhood sexual abuse survivors. *Child Abuse Negl*. 25(1):179–198.

Kilpatrick DG, Resnick HS, Saunders BE, Best CL. (1998). Rape, other violence against women and posttraumatic stress disorder: critical issues in assessing the adversity-stress-psychopathology relationship. In: Dohrenwend BP, ed. *Adversity, Stress, and Psychopathology*. (New York: Oxford University Press; 161–176.

Krystal JH, Kosten TR, Southwick S, Mason JW, Perry BD, Giller EL. (1989). Neurobiological aspects of PTSD: review of clinical and preclinical studies. *Behav Ther*. 20:177–198.

LaGreca A, Silverman WK, Vernberg EM, Prinstein MJ. (1996). Symptoms of posttraumatic stress in children after Hurricane Andrew: a prospective study. *J Consult and Clin Psych*. 64(4):712–723.

LaGreca AM, Silverman WK, Wasserstein SB. (1998). Children's predisaster functioning as a predictor of posttraumatic stress following Hurricane Andrew. *J Consult and Clin Psych*. 66(6):883–892.

Laor N, Wolmer L, Mayes LC, et al. (1996). Israeli preschoolers under SCUD missile attacks. *Arch Gen Psychiatry*. 53: 416–423.

Mannarino AP, Cohen JA. (1996a). Abused related attributions and perceptions, general attributions and locus of control in sexually abused girls. *J Interpersonal Violence*. 11:162–180.

Mannarino AP, Cohen JA. (1996b). A follow-up study of factors that mediate the development of psychological symptomatology in sexually abused girls. *Child Maltreatment* 1:246–260.

March J. (1993). What constitutes a stressor? The "criterion A" issue. In: Davidson J, Foa E, eds. *Posttraumatic Stress Disorder: DSM-IV and Beyond*. Washington, DC:American Psychiatric Press; 37–54.

March JS, Amaya-Jackson L, Terry R, Costanzo P. (1997). Posttraumatic symptomatology in children and adolescents after an industrial fire. *J Am Acad Child Adolesc Psychiatry.* 36(8):1080–1088.

McFarlane AC. (1987). Posttraumatic phenomena in a longitudinal study of children following a national disaster. *J Am Acad Child and Adolesc Psychiatry.* 26:764–769.

Milgram NA, Toubiana Y, Klingman A, et al. (1988). Situational exposure and personal loss in children's acute and chronic reactions to a school disaster. *J Trauma Stress.* 1: 339–352.

North CS, Tivis L, McMillen JC, et al. (2002). Coping, functioning, and adjustment of rescue workers after the Oklahoma City bombing. *J Trauma Stress.* 15(3):171–175.

Orr SP, Pitman RK. (1999). Neurocognitive risk factors for PTSD. In: Yehuda R, ed. *Risk Factors for Posttraumatic Stress Disorder.* Washington DC: American Psychiatric Press; 125–141.

Pine DS, Cohen JA. (2002). Trauma in children and adolescents: risk and treatment of psychiatric sequelae. *Biol Psychiatry.* 51(7):519–531.

Pynoos RS, Goenjian A, Tashjian M, et al. (1993). Posttraumatic stress reactions in children after the 1988 Armenian earthquake. *Br J Psychiatry.* 163:239–247.

Pynoos RS, Nader K. (1988). Children who witness the sexual assaults of their mothers. *J Am Acad Child Adolesc Psychiatry.* 27:567–572.

Sack WH, McSharry S, Clarke GN, Kinney R, Seeley J, Lewinsohn P. (1994). The Khmer adolescent project I. Epidemiological findings in two generations of Cambodian refugees. *J Nerv and Ment Dis.* 182:387–395.

Saigh, PA. (2000, October). *Intellectual functioning of traumatized and non-traumatized inner-city youth.* Presented at: Symposium: Current Perspectives on Child-Adolescent PTSD Research at 47th Annual Meeting of the American Academy of Child and Adolescent Psychiatry.

Saigh PA, Bremner D. (1999). The history of posttraumatic stress disorder. In: Saigh PA and Bremner JD, eds. *Posttraumatic Stress Disorder: A Comprehensive Text.* Boston, Mass: Allyn & Bacon; 1–17.

Saxe G, Stoddard F, Courtney D, et al. (2001). Relationship between acute morphine and the course of PTSD in children with burns. *J Am Acad Child Adolesc Psychiatry.* 40(8):915–921.

Schnurr PP, Friedman MJ, Rosenberg SD. (1993). Premilitary MMPI scores as predictors of combat-related PTSD symptoms. *Am J Psychiatry*. 150(3):479–483.

Silva RR, Alpert M, Munoz DM, Kim JI, Matzner F, Dummit S. (2000). Posttraumatic stress disorder: stress and vulnerability in children and adolescents. *Am J Psychiatry*. 157(8):1229–1235.

Stoddard FJ, Saxe G. (2001). Ten-year research review of physical injuries. *J Am Acad Child Adolesc Psychiatry*. 40(10):1128–1145.

Stuber ML, Nader K, Yasuda P, Pynoos RS, Cohen S. (1991). Stress responses after pediatric bone marrow transplantation: preliminary results of a prospective longitudinal study. *J Am Acad Child Adolesc Psychiatry*. 30:952–957.

Terr LC. (1983). Chowchilla revisited: the effects of psychic trauma four years after a school bus kidnapping. *Am J Psychiatry*. 140:1543–1550.

Thabet AA, Vostanis P. (1999). Post-traumatic stress reactions in children of war. *J Child Psych Psychiatry and Allied Disciplines*. 40(3):385–391.

Tiet Q, Bird HR, Davies M, et al. (1998). Adverse life events and resilience. *J Am Acad Child Adolesc Psychiatry*. 37:1191–1200.

Udwin O, Boyle S, Yule W, et al. (2000). Risk factors for long term psychological effects of a disaster experienced in adolescence: Predictors of posttraumatic stress disorder. *J Child Psychol Psychiatry*. 41: 969–979.

Yehuda R, Schmeidler J, Giller EL, Siever LJ, Binder Byrnes K. (1998). Relationship between posttraumatic stress disorder characteristics of holocaust survivors and their adult offspring. *Am J Psychiatry*. 155:841–843.

Yehuda R, Schmeider J, Wainberg M, Binder-Byrnes K, Duvdevani T. (1998). Vulnerability to posttraumatic stress disorder in adult offspring of Holocaust survivors. *Am J Psychiatry*. 155:1163–1171.

Yule W, Bolton D, Udwin O, et al. (2000). The long-term psychological effects of a disaster experiences in adolescence: I: The incidence and course of PTSD. *J Child Psychol Psychiatry*. 41:503–511.

3

■

Risk Factors for PTSD in Children and Adolescents

Veronica M. Rojas and Mia Pappagallo

Exposure to traumatic events occurs in the lives of many, yet not all who are exposed to traumatic events develop posttraumatic stress disorder (PTSD) (Perry & Azad, 1999). It is clear that, although a traumatic event is necessary to cause PTSD, it is not, in and of itself, a sufficient condition. Breslau and colleagues in 1999 reported that 20% of subjects will develop PTSD if exposed to a traumatic event, and they believe that this rate will be higher in children.

According to the *Diagnostic and Statistical Manual of Mental Disorders, Fourth Edition, Text Revision (DSM-IV-TR)*, lifetime prevalence rates of PTSD range between 3 to 8% in community-based studies for adults, but no specific prevalence data is available for children. This naturally leads to questions about risk factors: What determines whether a child or adolescent will develop PTSD? What are the risk factors? What factors may contribute to the severity of symptoms in a child or adolescent diagnosed with PTSD? A careful review of these issues may serve as a guide for diagnosis and treatment.

Perry and associates reviewed data and described various traumatic events that induce individuals to react in a singular manner (1999). As we know, each person experiences and copes with stress uniquely. Distinctive internal characteristics of each individual—such as age, gender, past experiences, and immune responses—as well as aspects of the child's external environment are all considered when examining PTSD. Perry further noted that each child will react to a trauma or stress in a very unique manner, which will eventually determine the individual's propensity to develop PTSD symptoms.

As investigators, we should emphasize and always consider the importance of a child's culture, family support, and parents' reaction, as well as the proximity and severity of the stressor as mediating conditions.

It is essential to contemplate each child's personality as well as his or her differing clinical presentations. These tend to vary according to characteristics, such as type of stressors, intensity of experience, and acuteness or chronicity of the traumatic event.

Reviewing the literature on PTSD and risk factors in children and adolescents, we encountered numerous differences among studies, depending on the type and intensity of trauma reported. This may be due to discrepancies in methods used to diagnose PTSD, such as assessment tools and criteria or other confounding variables, making the diagnosis of PTSD exceptionally complex (Saigh, 1999).

It is known that PTSD has been studied more extensively in adult populations. This is primarily due to the complexity and difficulty of conducting research in children. In accordance with their developmental stages, children tend to show a variety of reactions to stress and ones that differ from adults. In addition, there is a paucity of standardized, age-appropriate structured interviews and rating scales.

It is also common that parents or children do not inform clinicians of any previous traumatic event or stressor. Additionally, some clinicians tend to overlook or neglect to ask about details of traumatic events. Thus, PTSD may be misdiagnosed as another psychiatric disorder or not recognized as such at all.

Some authors (Perry & Azad, 1999) have found that a helpful approach is to categorize risk factors for children and adolescents in line with three broad domains: characteristics of the stressor, characteristics of the victim, and characteristics of the family and social milieu. Although most studies involve adults, some studies on children and adolescents address one or more of these broad domains. In this chapter, some of the risk factors for PTSD in children will be reviewed, using these three domains as a reference.

Nature of the Stressors

The *DSM-IV-TR* defines trauma as "a stressor involving direct personal experience of an event that involves actual or threatened death or serious injury, or other threat to one's physical integrity; or witnessing an event that involves death, injury or a threat to the physical integrity of another person; or learning about an unexpected or violent death, serious harm, or threat of death or injury experienced by a family member or other close associate" (Criterion A1, p. 463).

Many authors agree with this view. Nevertheless, this definition is broad and open to a number of interpretations regarding what may qualify as "trauma" for each individual. Our concern stems from the fact that trauma and the perception of trauma can differ radically from one person to another.

Sigmund Freud (1896/1962) believed that the source of neurosis was related to traumatic experiences of the past. A number of current researchers concur with Freud, stating that the child's psychological state at the time of the event can determine whether the event will be perceived as traumatic.

Perry (1999) noted that the manner in which an individual perceives trauma is mediated by different factors. These factors are intertwined with the person's culture, developmental stage, personality, vulnerability, family cohesion or support, previous traumatic event(s), frequency and type of traumatic event, and prior psychiatric disorders or history.

The available literature of PTSD in children could elicit an exhaustive list of risk factors. However, this chapter will focus on natural disasters, kidnapping, war, torture, migration and exile, and sexual and physical abuse.

Natural Disasters

Reactions to natural disasters differ from those incited by other stressors. One possible reason is that natural disasters usually affect a large group of people rather than an individual. We could theorize that affecting a larger group of people at the same time could create a *contagion effect* (Terr, 1981) depending upon the individual, the community, and the type of society. For instance, a family's appraisal of an event as well as a child's age and developmental level at the time of the event, such as with preschoolers, might be related to the parents' response and their symptomatology.

In natural disasters, there is the possibility of multiple losses: family, neighborhood, social support, environment, and society. These factors, in addition to the history and predisposition of an individual, will determine whether an individual, develops PTSD. Following this concept, Green and colleagues (1991) reported that the extent of traumatic stressors contributes to each person's coping mechanisms. These stressors included exposure to dreadful and appalling sights and scenes, witnessing or learning of violence against loved ones, or simply being harmed and injured.

It is vital to take into account the influence of each community's level of immediate versus delayed response and available economic resources. Yet exposure alone to natural stressors can be a risk factor in the development of PTSD even without considering those factors.

In the United States, one natural disaster involves children in communities exposed to hurricanes. Shannon and colleagues (1994) reported that almost 6% of the 5,687 children exposed to

Hurricane Hugo appeared to meet the criteria for PTSD. They also found that girls had more symptoms associated with emotional processing and boys tended to show cognitive or behavioral problems. Likewise, Garrison and colleagues (1995) reported that 3% of males and 9% of females, ages 12 to17 met criteria for PTSD after Hurricane Andrew in Florida.

If we were to compare these rates with those observed following earthquakes, we would find that there is a higher percentage of PTSD in earthquakes than in hurricanes. For example, Bradburn (1991) studied 22 children after the earthquake in San Francisco and found that 63% met criteria for PTSD. Goenjian and associates (1995) reported that 61.5% of children met criteria for PTSD after the 1988 Armenian earthquake.

Rachman (1980) proposed the theory of *emotional processing* with regards to a traumatic event. He explained that a sudden and unpredictable disaster might predispose an individual to have a lesser capacity for emotional processing and that exposure to such an event is a major risk for the development of PTSD. We acknowledge the merit of this concept and believe that this might be one explanation for the discrepancy in PTSD prevalence rates in children exposed to natural disasters.

Kidnapping

Although not very common, kidnapping represents an important risk factor for the development of PTSD. The available literature and data are limited, but the abduction of children and adolescents has been gaining more international attention.

The Chowchilla study became one of the first reports to describe the complexity of the signs and symptoms of PTSD in children during a kidnapping (Terr, 1981). This study looked at children ages 5 to 14 who were kidnapped in a school van for 11 hours and buried alive for 16 hours. Terr found that every child developed symptoms consistent with PTSD and also remained affected for more than 4 years.

Terr (1981) explained that kidnapped children who developed PTSD can present with a misperception of the event. Some children manifest repetition of the trauma during play or in the form of nightmares. Finally, the trauma may have a seriously adverse impact on development.

Another form of kidnapping has not received careful investigation. These kidnappings occurred during "the military process" or political oppression in developing countries. In the 1970s, extreme right and left political forces terrorized Argentina. During that time, the military force took political power and kidnapped more than 9,000 people, including babies, children, and adolescents who came to be called the *missing people (los desaparecidos)*. In 1983, the Argentinean president, Dr. Raul Alfonsin, created the National Commission of Missing People (Comision Nacional sobre la Desaparicion de Personas, CONADEP). The commission's main responsibility was to investigate these kidnappings. The commission identified 172 children and 250 adolescents who were kidnapped between 1973 and 1980. The majority of the school age children were kidnapped simultaneously with their parents. The adolescents were kidnapped in their homes, on the streets, or after leaving school. Only 20 of the kidnapped children were discovered alive. The total population of children and adolescents who were found developed PTSD and other psychiatric disorders (National Commission of Missing People, 1995). Further study of this population became hindered by socioeconomic and political factors in the country.

War

During war, children experience tremendous loss, beginning with the threat to their own personal safety, potential loss of family members, significant disturbance in day-to-day routines, and the loss of a sense of control. Chapter 15 will present more information regarding this particular subject.

Torture

Kinzie and colleagues (1988) reported that, of Cambodian refugee children who suffered "massive trauma" during the years of Pol Pot's regime, 50% developed PTSD. Moreover, a 3-year follow-up study indicated that these children maintained a diagnosis of PTSD. We believe that the percentage of children in this population who suffered from PTSD symptoms was higher than normal because atrocities (such as torture and abuse) were directly committed toward these children. Hubbard and associates (1995) found that 24% of 59 Cambodian young adults who survived childhood trauma during the same regime presented with PTSD 10 years following the traumatic event.

Migration and Exile

Migration varies in its traumatic potential. For some, migration is a unique, intensive, and ongoing *restructuring* of the self, while for others it is related to anxiety and sorrow. In addition, the migration process may be a sudden and definitive alteration in the course of a family or individual's lifetime.

Grinberg and Grinberg (1989) described the migration process as a succession of changes whereby one gradually moves farther from his or her known objects. The experience has components of disorganization that require focus and attention. Thus, the migration process requires a person to re-develop a sense of self/identity. However, when a person considers the migration process to be traumatic, this succession of changes or "renaissance" might not occur. Instead, PTSD symptoms and other symptoms might develop. Children have adjustment requirements different from those of the adults who accompany them. The degree of functioning of preschool children depends more on the functioning of their caregivers than the traumatic event itself.

Exile, in particular, can be considered a traumatic event as it is usually a sudden event—a crisis—that exposes children and their families to a state of disorganization and requires a subsequent reorganization in an unknown land. This process of resettlement may entail the acquisition of a new language, adaptation to unfamiliar academic settings and peers, frequent relocation, economic hardship, and culture shock. Yet, Clarke and associates (1993) reported that school-age children and adolescents from Cambodia had rates of developing PTSD more strongly associated with the *pre-migration* status. He reported that these rates had a direct association with exposure to a traumatic event before being a refugee.

Sexual and Physical Abuse

In the early 1960s Henry Kempe and his colleagues (1962) defined physical abuse as "the battered child syndrome."

When discussing abuse in particular, one should keep in mind that the concept of abuse might have distinct implications in different cultures. There are some countries where corporal punishment or sexual practices that Westerners might feel verge on abuse continue to occur and are accepted as part of the culture. For example, in some countries of Africa, removal of the clitoris is still performed on adolescent females, and young girls are engaged in prearranged marriages with older and unfamiliar males.

Regardless of the culture's definitions, physical and sexual abuses may contribute to long-term and detrimental psychological consequences. These traumatic events are significant risk factors for the development of PTSD and other psychiatric disorders, which may include borderline personality disorder, antisocial personality disorder, major depression, and substance abuse.

Posttraumatic stress disorder has been diagnosed in 20–70% of children who suffered sexual abuse (Wolfe et al., 1989; McLeer et al., 1992). These rates are high and increase the risk of long-term psychological sequelae in the lives of these children. Symptoms related to sexual abuse include reenactment of the event, withdrawal or total avoidance of the place or person related to the abuse, hypervigilance, and flashbacks of the event. Moreover, children can have symptoms such as irritability and behavioral disorganization as well as premature development of sexualized behavior.

Nurcombe (1997) indicated that sexual abuse as a risk factor ought to be divided into categories, such as an antecedent factor, abuse-related stressors, a form of post-disclosure stressor, and even a mediating factor. He holds the belief that the presence and nature of these variables contribute to the outcome of these children.

As antecedent factors, he reinforces the notion that family dynamics and functioning prior to the occurrence of sexual abuse may be directly linked to the final result. If the child has a supportive family environment, the child's outcome might be less traumatic than if a supportive environment were absent.

Even so, Ferguson and colleagues (1996) reported that sexual abuse involving genital penetration was directly related to psychiatric disorders, regardless of the prior family functioning and supportive system.

Nurcombe links abuse-related factors to the type of perpetrator and abuse, as well as its frequency and duration, all of which may impact the course of the outcome. Events subsequent to the abuse may also be connected to the symptomatology that a child will develop. Therefore, it is important to determine the degree of support in a given system surrounding the child.

Regarding mediating factors, Nurcombe elaborates on descriptions of the relationship between a child's feelings towards his or her self and others and the coping mechanisms that the child might establish after the abuse.

Pelcovitz and associates (1994) reported that victims of physical abuse showed social, emotional, and behavioral impairment, yet none of the children were diagnosed with PTSD. Adam and colleagues (1992) supported this concept by reporting that more sexually abused children met criteria for PTSD when compared to physically abused children. It is possible that the lower percentage of PTSD attributed to physical abuse might be due to methodological differences, that is, these children simply act out their physical abuse by being aggressive against themselves or others. This external expression of rage could be explained by identification with the aggressor, through which the child incorporates qualities of the aggressor's personality in an endeavor to master the fear they induce.

It is evident that these forms of abuse not only have a tremendous social, emotional, and cognitive impact in the lives of these children at the time of the event, but that they also have long-term sequelae. For this reason, factors of abuse should be investigated or uncovered prior to deciding upon a diagnosis.

Factors that Mitigate Risks

Several factors can moderate risks for the development of PTSD. We will refer to a few of them.

Physical Versus Emotional Proximity

As Pfefferbaum (1997) proposed in her 10-year review of PTSD in children, the physical proximity of a traumatic event is of significance for the development of PTSD.

Physical proximity refers to the physical distance between the child and the traumatic event. Generally, the closer the exposure to traumatic events, the greater risk of developing PTSD.

Similarly, Pynoos and colleagues (1987) found PTSD in individual children significantly connected to their physical proximity among a group of children who experienced a sniper attack on their school playground. Laor and colleagues (1996) reported that in Laor's developmental perspective on risk-modifying factors the proximity and severity of the traumatic event are directly linked to the development of PTSD.

In line with this concept, after the September 11th, 2001, terrorist attack on the United States, several hypotheses suggested that children who were close to the World Trade Center area in New York City had more PTSD and PTSD-like symptoms than children who were farther away. However, a recent letter to the editor of the American Academy of Child and Adolescent Psychiatry reported that children who viewed the disaster on television also developed PTSD symptoms (Duggal et al., 2002). This question of the role of repeated exposure through viewing television as a risk factor for PTSD remains one to entertain.

Emotional proximity factors include having a loved one (i.e., family member) suffer a trauma or pass away. The *DSM-IV-TR* includes this as part of their definition of trauma. Kiser and associates (1998) reported that the family is the basic unit or system that provides an individual with the concept of cohesion, belonging, and socialization. When this system or unit is destabilized due to a traumatic event, individuals in the family interact differently.

Intensity

It is necessary to consider the intensity of a trauma as a fundamental component of a risk factor. Once again, a traumatic event may be extremely stressful in and of itself. However, intensity may differ according to certain variables such as the degree of threat or the number of threats experienced during an episode.

Bremner and colleagues (1993), in a paper regarding child-hood sexual abuse and combat-related PTSD, described a previous trauma history as creating a *snowballing effect* for the development of future PTSD symptoms, once a victim is reexposed to another traumatic event. Nishith and associates (2000) concurred with this concept and reported that prior interpersonal trauma contributes to current PTSD symptoms in female rape victims.

Characteristics of the Victim

There is generally little that a clinician can do to predict and prevent most traumatic occurrences, since most are by nature unpredictable. This is especially true in cases of natural disaster and events such as the September 11th terrorist attacks. Even when the clinician is aware that children and adolescents live with many external risk factors, such as dwelling in a high-crime neighborhood, having refugee status, or living in a war zone, it is often difficult or impossible to control such variables. It is, there-fore, of particular clinical relevance to examine the set of risk factors related to the characteristics of the victim. These are the factors that may direct us in providing effective interventions following a traumatic event.

A number of studies have attempted to identify characteristics of a victim that may increase or decrease the vulnerability to traumatic events. These characteristics include such demographic factors as gender, ethnicity, and age, as well as individual characteristics, such as prior psychiatric diagnoses, temperament, and coping style. It is important to note that, in the current body of research, results are often inconsistent because study populations and the types of trauma investigated are extremely varied.

Demographic Factors

Demographic variables, although not necessarily risk factors in and of themselves, are likely to interact with other factors to moderate an individual's propensity to develop PTSD when exposed to particular types of stressors.

GENDER

Although it is not clear that gender, per se, is a risk factor for developing posttraumatic stress symptoms, it is likely that gender plays some role in the development and expression of PTSD. Expectations imposed on a child or adolescent may vary with gender, just as gender may influence that person's ability to elicit and utilize social supports. Gender also has a role in shaping the coping style of the individual (Pfefferbaum, 1997).

Several major epidemiological studies of the general adult population have found that women have higher rates of PTSD than men (Breslau et al., 1997). Both the Epidemiological Catchment Area study and the National Comorbidity Survey revealed a lifetime prevalence of PTSD as being twofold higher in women relative to men. Breslau and colleagues (1997) replicates this in the Detroit Area Study of Trauma despite finding an equal prevalence of traumatic events in both men and women. One hypothesis is that this difference may be observed because of the higher prevalence of other disorders in women, such as major depressive disorder and anxiety disorders (Breslau et al., 1997), but individual characteristics and aspects of the trauma may also exert an influence.

Fewer studies have been done with children and adolescents, and results have been inconsistent. Some studies with larger sample sizes show a greater prevalence of PTSD in girls (Shannon et al., 1994; Green et al., 1991), while in others the difference, if any, is not statistically significant. For further review of these studies, the reader may refer to Saigh and colleagues' study from 1999.

While female gender may not necessarily put children and adolescents at greater risk for developing PTSD, it has been observed to affect the manner in which symptomatology is expressed. Shannon and associates (1994) looked at 5,867 children exposed to Hurricane Hugo and found differences in the way boys and girls with PTSD expressed their symptoms. This study revealed that girls tended to show more posttraumatic *internalizing* symptoms (related to emotional processing and reactions to the trauma), while boys tend to show more *externalizing* symptoms. Ackerman and colleagues (1998) provided data that supports this as well. They also note that girls tend to dissociate more in the acute response than do boys. It is possible that girls tend to fit the diagnostic picture of PTSD more readily than boys because of their reporting more specific anxiety symptoms.

ETHNICITY

The role of race or ethnicity influencing the risk in developing PTSD is complex and difficult to study. Caution is required in drawing conclusions. The difficulty in studying race and ethnicity, in part, stems from the fact that the definition of terms such as *race, ethnicity,* and *culture* vary across sources. These terms integrate diverse issues such as the role of multiple hereditary backgrounds, multicultural identities, or the status a specific community confers upon a particular ethnic group, which are not always easily sorted out. These terms, in turn, are broad and difficult to dissect (Yamaguchi et al., 2002). There are also many confounding variables, including socioeconomic status. Thus we must be cautious not to attribute differences to ethnicity alone.

In general, studies of the role of race and ethnicity in PTSD have yielded inconsistent data in both adults and children. LaGreca and associates (1996) reported significantly higher levels of PTSD in Hispanic and black children than white children, while Shannon and colleagues (1994) and Garrison and associates (1993) demonstrated nonsignificant differences between these races. Davidson (1991) and Breslau and colleagues (1991, 1995) showed a statistically nonsignificant higher rate of PTSD in nonwhites.

In spite of these inconsistencies, Pfefferbaum (1997) reviewed the literature and noted that race and ethnicity, at the very least, likely affect the kind of exposure and response to trauma. For instance, as stated earlier in this chapter, refugee populations from a variety of ethnic backgrounds are commonly exposed to many distinct forms of trauma from a number of sources.

People of various cultural backgrounds have different ways of expressing affective states and harbor different beliefs about how to handle emotional disturbances. These differences can influence access to care, as some groups may not present to mental health professionals. When patients do seek care, cultural differences can also determine the manner in which they present symptoms to clinicians.

It appears that cultural and ethnic factors can interact with other factors in determining symptomatology and outcome.

Age and Level of Development

People respond differently to life events according to their developmental status. Nowhere is this more relevant than in the field of child and adolescent psychiatry. We know that children of all ages respond to traumatic events, and even very young children and infants have been documented responding to stress (Scheeringa, 1995).

Children are in a constant state of cognitive, emotional, and developmental flux. The existing literature, once again, yields inconsistent data regarding age of the child as a risk factor for PTSD. Some studies imply that older adolescents are at higher risk, while others indicate that younger children are at higher risk (Saigh, 1999). It would appear that age is not an independent risk factor, but that it interacts with other factors such as familial factors and nature of the trauma to exert its effect on development of PTSD symptoms.

Age and developmental stage can affect individual response style, processing, and memory of a traumatic event. Some data suggests that perhaps older children have the cognitive capacity to recognize the significance of a trauma, and are therefore at higher risk for developing PTSD (Garrison et al., 1995; Schwarz & Kowalski, 1991b). Wolfe and associates (1994) assessed a sample of sexually abused Canadian children and found that children above age 12 had a higher prevalence of PTSD than younger children. Conversely, other data suggests that older children may be protected by their greater affective, cognitive, and behavioral maturity (Pynoos & Nader 1988; Jensen & Shaw, 1993).

Some studies show that specific symptomatology differs with age. One such study (Schwarz & Kowalski, 1991a) examined children after a school shooting and found that younger children had more avoidant symptoms, while older children showed more heightened arousal and reexperiencing symptoms.

Children and adolescents' age and developmental level can also affect their perception of parental distress. Age may also influence the degree to which parental distress affects them, with younger children being more affected. Laor and colleagues (1996) looked at Israeli preschoolers exposed to SCUD missile attacks during the Persian Gulf War. They note that, the younger the child, the more dependent the child is on the immediate supportive environment, including parents and community, which can, in turn, affect the vulnerability of that child. This study found that younger preschoolers (ages 3 and 4) with poor family cohesion had more symptoms than older preschoolers (age 5) with poor family cohesion.

This study suggests that younger children may be more vulnerable to PTSD, at least following this sort of large-scale disaster, because they are more dependent on external protective factors than are school-aged children and adolescents. Even within that younger group, consistent with Jean Piaget's cognitive theories and Sigmund Freud's psychodynamic theories, the 5-year-old children had fewer symptoms than their younger cohort, which could be related to their advanced ability to cognitively process events and regulate affect.

Psychiatric History

There is some evidence that a prior psychiatric history is associated with the development of PTSD in both youth and adults. Boney-McCoy and Finkelhor (1996) reviewed literature about children and adolescents who have been exposed to violent victimization (sexual abuse, physical abuse, kidnapping, and peer physical assaults), which led to questions of whether children with existing psychiatric symptoms (anxiety or otherwise) are, in fact, more likely to be victims than children without psychiatric symptoms because of their augmented risk. In order to address this question, this research group constructed a longitudinal, prospective study, drawing subjects and data from the National Youth Victimization Prevention Study (Boney-McCoy & Finkelhor, 1995a, 1995b). This study consisted of two waves of phone interviews with 1,433 children between the ages of 10 and 16 years and their primary caretakers. This study examined children at two points in time, evaluated such variables as Time 1 PTSD symptoms, depressive symptoms, family relational factors, and history of victimization and Time 2 PTSD symptoms and various forms of victimization since Time 1. When other variables were controlled for, there remained a strong correlation between Time 1 prior symptomatology and PTSD symptoms at Time 2. The authors proposed two hypotheses: prior symptoms may have persisted across both time frames and, in the case of sexual assault, the prior symptoms may have made subjects more vulnerable to victimization. In any case, prior psychiatric symptoms appear to put children at some degree of risk for later development of PTSD.

Conclusions

Risk factors for the development of PTSD vary according to these differing conditions: age; intensity, frequency, and proximity of the stressor; level of development at the time of the traumatic event; personality prior to and during the traumatic event; family cohesion; and of course, cultural characteristics.

While absolute risk factors cannot be clearly delineated, some broad factors have emerged as important risk factors for PTSD in children and adolescents. It appears that interpersonal trauma, such as sexual and physical abuse, and large-scale disasters in which personal trauma is involved (war in Cambodia) yield higher rates of PTSD. With regards to individual characteristics, girls and boys may show their symptoms differently; age and developmental level vastly influence the way children and adolescents perceive and react to trauma.

Further studies of children and adolescents are needed to more definitively determine the relative risk that each factor confers.

References

Ackerman PT, Newton JE, McPherson WB, Jones JG, Dykman RA. (1998). Prevalence of post traumatic stress disorder and other psychiatric diagnoses in three groups of abused children (sexual, physical, and both). *Child Abuse Neglect.* 22(8):759–774.

Adam BS, Everett BL, O'Neal E. (1992). PTSD in physically and sexually abused psychiatrically hospitalized children. *Child Psychiatry Hum Dev.* 23:3–8.

Boney-McCoy S, Finkelhor D. (1995a). Psychosocial sequelae of violent victimization in a national youth sample. *J Consult Clin Psychol.* 63(5):726–736.

Boney-McCoy S, Finkelhor D. (1995b). Prior victimization: a risk factor for child sexual abuse and for PTSD-related symptomatology among sexually abused youth. *Child Abuse Neglect.* 19(12):1401–1421.

Boney-McCoy S, Finkelhor D. (1996). Is youth victimization related to trauma symptoms and depression after controlling for prior symptoms and family relationships? A longitudinal prospective study. *J Consult Clin Psychol.* 64(6):1406–1416.

Bradburn, IS. (1991). After the earth shook: children's stress symptoms 6-8 months after a disaster. *Adv Behav Res Ther.* 13:173–179.

Bremner JD, Southwick SM, Johnson SB, Yehuda R, Charney DS. (1993). Childhood physical abuse and combat-related posttraumatic stress disorder in Vietnam veterans. *Am J Psychiatry.* 150(2):253–259.

Breslau N, Chilcoat HD, Kessler RC, Davis GC. (1999). Previous exposure to trauma and PTSD effects of subsequent trauma: results from the Detroit Area Survey of Trauma. *Am J Psychiatry.* 156(6):902–907.

Breslau N, Davis GC, Andreski P. (1991). Traumatic events and posttraumatic stress disorder in an urban population of young adults. *Arch Gen Psychiatry.* 48:216–222.

Breslau N, Davis GC, Andreski P. (1995). Risk factors for PTSD-related traumatic events: a prospective analysis. *Am J Psychiatry.* 152:529–535.

Breslau N, Davis GC, Andreski P, Peterson EL, Schultz LR. (1997). Sex differences in posttraumatic stress disorder. *Arch Gen Psychiatry.* 54(11):1044–1048.

Bromet E, Sonnega A, Kessler RC. (1998). Risk factors for *DSM-III-R* PTSD findings from the National Comorbidity Survey. *Am J Epidemiol.* 147:343–361.

Clarke GN, Sack WH, Ben R. (1993). English language skills in a group of previously traumatized Khmer adolescent refugees. *J Nerv Mental Dis.* 181:454–456.

Davidson JRT, Hughes D, Blazer DG. (1991). Posttraumatic stress disorder in the community: an epidemiological study. *Psychol Med.* 21:713–772.

Duggal H, Gennady B, Vineeth J. (2002). PTSD and TV viewing of the World Trade Center. *J Am Acad Child Adolesc Psychiatry.* 41(5):494–495.

Fergusson DM, Horwood LJ, Lynskey MT. (1996). Childhood sexual abuse and psychiatric disorder in young adulthood. *J Am Acad Child Adolesc Psychiatry.* 35:1365–1374.

Freud S. (1955). Studies in hysteria. In J Strachey, trans. & ed., *The Standard Edition of the Complete Psychological Works of Sigmund Freud;* vol. 2, 3–311). London: Hogarth Press (Original publication 1893–1895)

Freud S. (1962). Further remarks on the neuro-psychoses of defense. In J Strachey, trans. & ed., *The Standard Edition of the Complete Psychological Works of Sigmund Freud* (vol. 3, 162–185). London: Hogarth Press. (Original publication 1896)

Garrison CZ, Bryant ES, Addy CL, Spurrier PG, Freedy JR, Kilpatrick DG. (1995). Posttraumatic stress disorder in adolescents after Hurricane Andrew. *J Am Acad Child Adolesc Psychology.* 34(9):1193–1201.

Garrison CZ, Weinrich MW, Hardin SB, Wienrich S, Wang L. (1993). Post traumatic stress disorder in adolescents after a hurricane. *Am J Epidemiol.* 138:522–530.

Goenjian AD, Pynoos RS, Steinberg AM, et al. (1995). Psychiatric comorbidity in children after the 1998 earthquake in Armenia. *J Am Acad Child Adolesc Psychiatry.* 30:945–951.

Green BL, Korol M, Grace MC. (1991). Children and disaster: age, gender and parental effects on PTSD symptoms. *J Am Acad Child Adolesc Psychiatry.* 30:945–951.

Grinberg L, Grinberg R. (1989). *Psychoanalytic Perspectives on Migration and Exile.* New Haven, Conn: Yale University Press.

Hidalgo RB, Davidson JRT. (2000). Post traumatic stress disorder: epidemiology and health-related considerations. *J Clin Psychiatry.* 61(suppl 7):5–13.

Hubbard J, Realmuto G, Northwood A, Masten A. (1995). Comorbidity of psychiatric diagnoses with PTSD in survivors of childhood trauma. *J Am Acad Child Adolesc Psychiatry.* 34(9):1167–1173.

Jensen PS, Shaw J. (1993). Children as victims of war. current knowledge and future research needs. *J Am Acad Child Adolesc Psychiatry.* 32:697–708.

Kempe CH, Silverman FN, Steele BF, Droegemueller W, Silver HK. (1962). The battered child syndrome. *JAMA.* 181:4–11.

Kinzie JD, Sack W, Angell R. (1988). A three-year follow up of Cambodian young people traumatized as children. *J Am Acad Child Adolesc Psychiatry.* 28:501–504.

Kinzie JD, Sack W, Angell R, et al. (1985). The psychiatric effects of massive trauma on Cambodian children. *J Am Acad Child Adolesc Psychiatry.* 25:370–376.

Kiser LJ, Ostoja E, Pruitt DB. (1998). Dealing with stress and trauma in families. *Child Adolesc Psychiatric Clin North Am.* 1:87–101.

LaGreca AM, Silverman WK, Vernberg EM, Prinstein MJ. (1996). Symptoms of posttraumatic stress in children after Hurricane Andrew: a prospective study. *J Cons Clin Psychol.* 64:712–723.

Laor N, Wolmer L, Mayes LC, et al. (1996). Israeli preschoolers under Scud missile atttacks: A developmental perspective on risk-modifying factors. *Arch Gen Psychiatry.* 53:416–423.

Lonigan CJ, Shannon MP, Taylor CM, Finch AJ Jr, Sallee FR. (1994). Children exposed to disaster: II. Risk factors for the development of posttraumatic symptomatology. *J Am Acad Child Adolesc Psychiatry.* 33(1):94–105.

McCloskey LA, Walker M. (2000). Post traumatic stress in children exposed to family violence and single-event trauma. *J Am Acad Child Adolesc Psychiatry.* 39(1):108–115.

McLeer SV, Deblinger EB, Esther B. (1992). Sexually abused children at high risk for PTSD. *J Am Acad Child Adolesc Psychiatry.* 31:875–879.

National Commission of Missing People. (1995). *Nunca Mas.* Buenos Aires: Eudeba.

Nishith P, Mechanic MB, Resick PA. (2000). Prior interpersonal trauma: the contribution to current PTSD symptoms in female rape victims. *J Abnorm Psychol.* 109(1):20–25.

Nurcombe B. (1997). *Child Sexual Abuse: Part I: Psychopathology* (Beattie-Smith Lecture). University of Melbourne, Australia.

Pelcovitz D, Kaplan S, Goldenberg B. (1994). Posttraumatic stress disorder in physically abused adolescents. *J Am Acad Child Adolesc Psychiatry.* 33:305–312.

Perry BD, Azad I. (1999). Posttraumatic stress disorders in children and adolescents. *Curr Opinion Pediatr.* 11:310–316.

Pfefferbaum B. (1997). Posttraumatic stress disorder in children: a review of the past 10 years. *J Am Acad Child Adolesc Psychiatry.* 36(11):1503–1511.

Pynoos RS, Frederick C, Nader K, et al. (1987). Life threat and posttraumatic stress in school-age children. *Arch Gen Psychiatry.* 44:1057–1063.

Pynoos RS, Nader K. (1988). Children who witness the sexual assaults of their mothers. *J Am Acad Child Adolesc Psychiatry.* 27:567–572.

Rachman S. (1980). Emotional processing. *Behav Res Ther.* 18:51–60.

Saigh PA, Yasik AE, Sack WH, Koplewicz HS. (1999). Child-adolescent posttraumatic stress disorder: prevalence, risk factors and comorbidity. In: PA Saigh & JD Bremner, eds. *Posttraumatic Stress Disorder: A Comprehensive Text.* Boston: Allyn & Bacon; 18–43.

Scheeringa MS, Zeanah CH, Drell MJ, Larrieu JA. (1995). Two approaches to the diagnosis of posttraumatic stress disorder in infancy and early childhood. *J Am Acad Child Adolesc Psychiatry.* 34(2):191–200.

Schwarz ED, Kowalski JM. (1991a). Malignant memories: PTSD in children and adults after a school shooting. *J Am Acad Child Adolesc Psychiatry.* 30:936–944.

Schwarz ED, Kowalski JM. (1991b). Posttraumatic stress disorder after a school shooting effects of symptom threshold selection and diagnosis by *DSM-III, DSM III-R,* or proposed *DSM-IV. Am J Psychiatry.* 148:592–597.

Shannon MP, Lonigan CJ, Finch AJ Jr, Taylor CM. (1994). Children exposed to disaster: I. Epidemiology of post-traumatic symptoms and symptoms profiles. *JAACAP.* 33(1):80–93.

Terr LC. (1981). Psychic trauma in children: observation following the Chowchilla bus kidnapping. *Am J Psychiatry.* 138:14–19.

Uemoto M, Shioyama A, Koide K, et al. (2000). The mental health of school children after the Great Hanshin-Awaji Earthquake: I. Epidemiological study and risk factors for mental distress [Japanese]. *Seishin Shinkeigaku Zasshi—Psychiatria et Neurologia Japonica.* 102 (5):459–480.

Wolfe DA, Sas L, Wekerle C. (1994). Factors associated with the development of posttraumatic stress disorder among child victims of sexual abuse. *Child Abuse Negl.* 18.37–50.

Wolfe VV, Gentile C, Wolfe DA. (1989). The impact of sexual abuse on children: a PTSD formulation. *Behav Ther.* 20:215–228.

Yamaguchi W, Kino J, Goebert D, et al. (2002). A conceptual model of cultural predictors of anxiety among Japanese American and Part-Japanese American adolescents. *Cultur Divers Ethni Minor Psychol.* 8(4):320–333.

4
■

Legal Aspects Related to PTSD in Children and Adolescents

Vilma Gabbay and Carmen M. Alonso

Posttraumatic stress disorder (PTSD) has been increasingly introduced to the courts in causes of actions involving minors. The significance of the disorder in the legal arena is well reflected by Stone's (1993) frequently quoted statement: "No diagnosis in the history of American Psychiatry has had a more dramatic and pervasive impact on law and social justice than posttraumatic stress disorder." It is, therefore, not uncommon for child psychiatrists to be required to deal with the forensic aspects of PTSD and often to be called upon to enter the unfamiliar culture of the legal arena. In this chapter, we will review the legal issues concerning PTSD in children and adolescents, their application in civil and criminal proceedings, specific litigation rules, and some aspects of a forensic evaluation. Our goal is to familiarize child psychiatrists with their possible roles involving minors with PTSD claims.

General Issues Concerning PTSD and Litigation

Posttraumatic stress disorder is a common form of psychiatric injury that follows extreme stress. It is classified under anxiety disorders in *Diagnostic and Statistical Manual of Mental Disorders, Fourth Edition* (DSM-IV; American Psychiatric Association, 1994) and in *International Classification of Diseases* (World Health Organization, 2003) as a reaction to severe distress or an adjustment disorder. The disorder was historically named railway spine, Erichsen's disease, traumatic neurosis, accident neurosis, compensation neurosis, litigation neurosis, or chronic or delayed PTSD (Tyndel, 1999). The law, which values objective proof, has viewed psychiatric disorders with some suspicion due to their vagueness and subjective qualities. Courts have long faced the dilemma of whether or not to permit recovery of damages that are purely psychic in nature (Louise, 1999). The lack of a scientific tool to unequivocally prove the diagnosis of PTSD, the risk of fraudulent claims, and concern about "hired-gun" court experts are ongoing issues (Taylor & Buchanan, 1998). This problem was demonstrated in a study comparing psychiatric reports between treating practitioners and experts, where treating practitioners and plaintiffs' experts were more likely to diagnose PTSD and depression, while defendants' experts were more likely to find no psychiatric disorder (Large & Nielssen, 2001). However, neuroscience has enhanced our understanding of the pathophysiology of PTSD, suggesting hypothalamic-pituitary-adrenal axis dysfunction, sympathetic nervous system abnormalities, and involvement of specific areas in the brain such as the amygdala and hippocampus (Yehuda, 2002). As the development of law has been tied to scientific progress, our growing understanding of PTSD as a neuropsychiatric disorder has led courts to increasingly accept and apply the diagnosis of PTSD in both criminal and civil proceedings.

PTSD In Civil Proceedings

Tort Law: General Definitions

Posttraumatic stress disorder is brought to the civil courts as damages in tort claims. A tort is a civil (i.e., noncriminal) wrongful act that is not based on breach of contract and is executed by one person who has caused damage to another person.

An action in torts is a claim for compensation for damages that have occurred. The term derives from the Latin word *tortus* (twisted) and the French *torquere* (torture). The burden of proof for a civil plaintiff lies in a "fair preponderance of the evidence," a standard of evidence that is much lower than that required in criminal proceedings ("beyond a reasonable doubt"). Intentional infliction of emotional distress and negligent infliction of emotional distress are claims in torts that allow the recovery of damages due to mental harm.

Intentional Infliction of Emotional Distress

Courts originally denied claims that were based on mental harm (Partlett, 1997). Exceptions to this rigid rule initially developed with regard to intentional torts, a subcategory of tort law in which the wrongful act is performed with intent to cause harm. Examples are assault, battery, false imprisonment and, more specifically for PTSD, the intentional infliction of emotional distress. A pure psychiatric disorder has generally been sufficient to recover damages in cases of intentional infliction of emotional distress. In order to establish recovery under intentional infliction of emotional distress, one must demonstrate that: (1) the defendant's action amounted to extreme and outrageous conduct, (2) the defendant acted intentionally or recklessly in deliberate disregard, (3) the actions of the defendant caused the plaintiff's emotional distress, and (4) the emotional distress of the plaintiff was severe (Restatement (Second) of Torts§ 46).

Negligent Infliction of Emotional Distress

Another subcategory of torts is the group of negligent acts that includes malpractice cases and the negligent infliction of emotional distress in cases with PTSD. To establish *prima facie* case for negligence, there has to be: (1) a duty on the defendant's part to conform to a specific standard of conduct for protection of the plaintiff against an unreasonable risk of injury, (2) the defendant's breach of that duty is the actual (causation in fact) and proximate (legal causation) cause of the plaintiff's injury, and (3) the existence of damages. The general rule of proximate causation is that a duty of care in negligent acts is owed only to foreseeable plaintiffs (not all injuries that are "actually" caused by a defendant will be deemed to have been proximate by his acts). This doctrine deals with the liability of unforeseeable and/or unusual consequences of one's act.

In the 19th century there was no recovery for negligently inflicted mental harms, but here again, exceptions allowed recovery. One of the first individuals to observe the significance of mental distress as a possible cause of action was Judge Kennedy in England, who said, "I should not be surprised if the surgeon or the physiologist told us that nervous shock is or may be in itself an injurious affection of the physical organism" (*Dulieu v. White*, 1901). However, Judge Kennedy's opinion did not radically change the attitude of courts towards mental harm. Only after many years and significant progress in understanding mental illnesses did the courts finally allow recovery for psychic harm.

Recovery of mental harm caused by negligent acts became allowable over time under three rules (McQuade, 2001): (1) the physical contact rule, in which the mental harm was causally related to a physical injury, for example when amputation of a limb led to depression; (2) the physical consequences rule, when the mental distress led to physical symptoms or a medical condition, such as a perforated ulcer or back pain (*Consolidated Rail Corp. v. Gottshall*, 1994; *Sterling v. Velsicol Chem. Corp.*, 1988); and (3) the zone of danger rule, where recovery was permitted if the plaintiff had been threatened with physical harm but ended up escaping it. Some jurisdictions extended this rule to the bystander rule in cases in which a close relative suffered mental distress as a result of witnessing a child or spouse dying in an automobile accident (*Dillon v. Legg*, 1968). In *Dillon*, the court allowed a mother to recover damages for physically manifested severe mental distress endured after witnessing her daughter being struck by a negligently operated automobile.

These are restrictive rules intended to prevent fraudulent claims of mental harm and to limit the liability of defendants. Recently, some jurisdictions have abandoned the bodily contact, physical consequences, and zone of danger rules and have opted to treat mental harms on par with physical harms (McQuade, 2001; Bagdasarian, 2000).

The "Eggshell Skull" Rule and Its Application to PTSD

In order for a plaintiff to recover damages under negligent inflic-tion of emotional distress he or she needs to be a foreseeable plaintiff, i.e., the defendant should have expected/foreseen that his/her negligent act would cause the plaintiff to suffer from PTSD. Many plaintiffs with PTSD will not be able to meet this requirement (McQuade, 2001) as PTSD is not the natural con-sequence resulting from every traumatic event. PTSD is more likely to develop due to the concurrence of trauma and an under-lying condition or vulnerability such as a preexisting mental illness or long standing history of trauma. This may lead to the unjust and unwanted result of some plaintiffs' inability to recover damages. In order to avoid this consequence, courts have applied the "eggshell skull rule," stating that the defendant takes his plaintiff as he finds him. Thus, when a defendant's negligence causes an aggravation or a relapse of the plaintiff's mental or physical condition, the defendant would be liable for the damages caused by the aggravation.

The Importance of PTSD in Civil Claims and Specific Causes of Action Involving Minors

Because PTSD is a psychiatric condition linked to a specific trau-matic event "plaintiffs can argue that all of their psychological problems issue from the alleged traumatic event and not from myriad other sources encountered in life" (Slovenko, 1994). The trauma leading to PTSD thus meets the requirement of the causation tests (actual and proximate) that are required when a claim is brought under the rules of torts. The establishment of this diagnosis is often key to negligence or malpractice cases. Courts have accepted PTSD as a physical injury allowing the plaintiff to be awarded an increased amount of damages (Bagdasarian, 2000). Such is the case in airline disasters, medical malpractice, and workers' compensation claims, among others (Bagdasarian, 2000; *Ben-Shimol v. TWA*, 1996; *Edgar & Erica*, 2001; *Weaver v. Delta*, 1999). There are several circumstances in which a cause of action may accrue to initiate a civil claim regarding PTSD in children. One of the most common in both intentional and negligent infliction of emotional distress is child abuse. Another area is motor vehicle accidents. Every year, thousands of children are involved in serious car accidents. The risk of PTSD in children involved in motor vehicle accidents may be similar to those exposed to violent crimes. One study found that 25% of children and adolescents physically injured in traffic incidents met criteria for PTSD (de Vries et al., 1999). Iatrogenic trauma caused by invasive and painful medical treatments has also become a significant cause for action.

PTSD In Criminal Proceedings

Criminal Law: General Definitions

For an act to become a criminal offense, it generally needs to have the following elements: (1) *actus reus* (guilty act), a physical act (or unlawful omission) by the defendant; (2) *mens rea* (guilty mind), an intent of the defendant at the time of the act; (3) concurrence of the guilty act and mind; and (4) a harmful result caused factually and proximately by the defendant's act.

Defenses can be established if one of these elements does not exist. PTSD has been brought into criminal proceedings mainly for defensive purposes to mitigate criminal *mens rea*.

PTSD and the Battered Child Syndrome

Posttraumatic stress disorder has been commonly introduced to criminal courts in cases involving minors coupled with the "battered child syndrome" (while in cases involving adults, PTSD is often joined by the "battered woman syndrome"). Kempe and associates first coined the term "battered child syndrome" as: "a clinical condition in young children who have received serious physical abuse, generally from a parent or foster parent" (Kempe et al., 1962). Although Kempe and colleagues used battered child syndrome to describe physical injuries to bones, soft tissue, and the head, the scientific and legal arenas soon appreciated the psychiatric sequelae in children with the syndrome, particularly PTSD. Courts have accepted both the physical and psychiatric elements of battered child syndrome and applied it for both defensive (to mitigate criminal intent) and offensive purposes (to prove criminal intent). When battered child syndrome has been used to prove the required criminal intent, courts have focused on the physical consequences of the syndrome, which is beyond the topic of this chapter. Of greater relevance to us is the use of battered child syndrome for defensive purposes, as courts will examine the psychiatric effects of the abuse, specifically PTSD (Baldwin, 2001).

PTSD in Minors as a Defense in Criminal Court

Focusing on the psychiatric consequences of battered child syndrome, courts have used PTSD as a defense to mitigate criminal responsibility. In these cases mental health experts will be required to evaluate the extent of the psychiatric disorder that resulted from the abuse. An example of this is the case of *State v. Janes* (1993). Andrew Janes, a 17-year-old boy, was prosecuted for the murder of his mother's paramour, whom he shot after awaiting him in a doorway. Janes claimed that he had been physically abused, constantly beaten, attacked, and threatened for 10 years by the deceased. He argued that he believed that he could stop the abuse only by killing him. Janes was found guilty of murder as the trial court refused to give the jury a self-defense instruction. However, the appellate court reversed the decision, and the Washington Supreme Court granted review to evaluate the merits of battered child syndrome as a defense.

The court in *State v. Janes* acknowledged PTSD as a psychiatric consequence in battered children, causing such children to be hypervigilant and overly cautious. The court further drew the analogy between battered child syndrome and battered woman syndrome, a recognized defense: "if anything for battered children, the effects of PTSD are amplified. Children are entirely dependant on the parents for financial and emotional support. They are extremely vulnerable and tend to place great trust in their parents It is not as easy for a child as it is for an adult to leave a troubled home. Moreover, unlike the battered adult, a child has no outside context with which to compare the abusive reality." The court thus sanctioned the use of PTSD in cases of battered child syndrome as a defense (Baldwin, 2001). However, most courts have been reluctant to allow the introduction of such evidence as a defense (Baldwin, 2001). For example, in *Jahnke v. State* (1984) a 16-year-old boy shot his abusive father as he approached the garage door of their home. The court denied the introduction of the evidence of battered child syndrome, stating that expert testimony about abuse was neither relevant nor necessary to assist the jury in determining self-defense. Additionally, in *State v. Crabtree* (1991) the Kansas Supreme Court acknowledged extensive abuse suffered by the child defendant, but did not allow the introduction of battered child syndrome evidence due to the lack of physical confrontation on the part of the child prior to the criminal act (Baldwin, 2001).

Nevertheless, some states have followed the court opinion in *State v. Janes*. Texas, for instance, codified a provision to allow introduction of the psychiatric effects of the abuse: "(b) In a prosecution for murder, if a defendant raises as a defense a justi-fication . . . in order to establish the defendant's reasonable belief . . . {the defendant} shall be permitted to offer: (2) relevant expert testimony regarding the condition of the mind of the defendant at the time of the offense, including those relevant facts and circumstances relating to family violence that are the basis of the expert's opinion" (Tex Crim Proc Code Ann. 38. 36).

The Texas statute was first used defending a 17-year-old girl charged with the murder of her abusive father (Hegadorn, 1999). Wisconsin passed legislation in 1993 defining battered child syn-drome as a: "psychological condition of a victim of repeated physical and psychological abuse as a child" and that "in any criminal action, evidence that the defendant was suffering from . . . battered child syndrome is admissible on the issue of the exer-cise of the privilege of self-defense or defense of others" (Wis Laws 169). A Louisiana statute also allowed the introduction of an expert opinion discussing the psychiatric effects of the abuse: "when the accused plead self-defense and there is a history of assaultive behavior between the victim and the accused . . . such as . . . the husband-wife, parent-child . . . and further provided that an expert's opinion as to the effects of the prior assaultive acts on the accused's state of mind is admissible" (La Code Evid Ann Art 404A(2)a).

The use of PTSD in criminal proceedings has been highly controversial, resulting in different rulings made by different courts in similar cases, often based on the state residence of the child defendant.

Procedural Litigation Rules Involving PTSD in Minors

Childhood PTSD claims may be initiated during and after the claimant's minority. In criminal cases in which the allegations are made while the claimant is still a minor, the government has the power to initiate a prosecution without the consent of the child or the parents (or legal guardians). A civil (damages) claim on behalf of the child during minority must be instituted only by the child's parent or legal guardian (children cannot file claims by themselves as they lack the legal capacity).

General Rules of Statute of Limitations

Allegations that are made after the claimant has reached majority will be filtered by the statute of limitations, which governs the time within which a claim can be brought after the alleged act occurred. These statutes provide that no legal action can be maintained unless brought within a specified period of time. Usually the statute of limitations on a claim starts to run at the time the cause of action accrues. If a cause of action accrues in favor of a minor, the statute is tolled (tolling means stopping the clock on the time allowed to file a suit) until the minor reaches majority (commonly at the age of 18 years) at which time it will start to run. Criminal statutes of limitation vary for each criminal act and from state to state. For example, South Carolina and Wyoming have no statute of limitations for any criminal offense. Hawaii, on the other hand, has a three-year statute of limitations for a rape of a child. Murder generally has no statute of limitations (LaFave, 1992). The statutes of limitations for civil claims also vary among states based upon specific causes of action. Usually a claimant has one to three years from the time the cause of action accrued to bring a civil personal injury damages claim.

Tolling the Statute in Civil Cases of PTSD— The Delayed Discovery Doctrine

In some cases, plaintiffs do not know when a wrong has occurred and may not discover their cause of action until after the statute of limitations has expired. In response to such cases, courts have fashioned the "delayed discovery doctrine" (Meyer & Lansberry, 2001). The delayed discovery doctrine states that: "the statute of limitations does not begin to run until the plaintiff has discovered, or in the exercise of reasonable diligence should have discovered, all of the facts which are essential to the cause of action" (*DeRose v. Carswell*, 1987). This doctrine first emerged in medical malpractice cases where the defendant's own wrongful conduct prevented the plaintiff from learning of the injury, such as in cases in which foreign surgical objects were left in the patient's body (*Gaddis v. Smith*, 1967). The first case to challenge the applicability of the discovery doctrine to an instance of childhood sexual abuse, allegedly repressed by the victim for 15 years, was a 1986 case (*Tyson v. Tyson*, 1986). The 26-year-old plaintiff alleged that her father had sexually abused her from the time she was 5 until she was 11, although she had no recollection of these events until she recovered these memories in psychotherapy. Although the claim was denied due to the lack of "objective verifiable evidence of the original wrongful act and the resultant physical injury," courts have since applied the discovery doctrine in civil cases involving childhood abuse (Spadaro, 1998; Frasca, 2000). In *L.C. v. A.K.D.* (1994) the doctrine was accepted as the plaintiff presented "corroborating evidence" of the allegations and of the repression of the memories. Other courts require the plaintiff to prove that, as a result of repression of the original memories, they were not aware of the abuse (*Mary D. v. John D.*, 1989). Some jurisdictions have opted to allow the discovery doctrine to toll the statute of limitations when "a victim of sexual abuse represses memories of the abuse until a later date," requiring no corroboration of the repression of the actual memories of the event (Frasca, 2000). The delayed discovery doctrine does not apply in criminal actions because of constitutionally mandated concerns regarding the rights of the criminal defendant and different evidence rules.

Repressed Memories Testimony and The False Memory Syndrome

The "Repressed /Recovered Memories Theory" is a highly controversial issue in both the legal and medical arenas (Brahams, 2000; Brandon, 1999). In 1993, the American Psychiatric Association warned in a position paper that repressed memories could be false, especially when therapists were involved in the recovery process. The Royal College of Psychiatrists (1997) issued a set of recommendations for appropriate practice when treating patients with "recovered memories" of childhood sexual abuse and advised against psychotherapeutic techniques that may possibly suggest the abuse. Although many states have applied the repressed memory theory in civil cases of child abuse to satisfy the statute of limitations, courts have been reluctant to allow the admission of repressed memories testimonies as evidence (*State v. Hungerford*, 1995; *State v. Morahan*, 1995), particularly when hypnosis was used to refresh repressed memories (*Borawick v. Shay*, 1995). The possibility of false repressed memories led to the establishment in 1992 of the False Memory Syndrome Foundation (FMSF) in Philadelphia, by parents whose adult children had accused them based on recovered memories of sexual abuse during their childhood. The FMSF initiated malpractice suits that were brought by alleged abusers (joined at times by the former patient) against their children's therapists claiming that the abuse never occurred and was suggested by their therapists. Litigation actions included suits against attorneys who filed lawsuits against alleged abusers on behalf of former patients, who based their claim on recovered memories. One of the best known cases is that of *Ramona v. Isabella* (1994), in which a father sued his daughter's therapist alleging negligent and intentional infliction of emotional distress. He alleged that the therapist had suggested the memories of sexual abuse using an amobarbital sodium interview and had suggested that her eating disorder (bulimia) was the result of the abuse. The jury found in favor of the father and awarded him $500,000. In another recent case (Belluck, 1997), a woman diagnosed with multiple personality disorder recovered memories of having been a high priestess in a satanic cult and of having engaged in cannibalism, bestiality, and numerous bizarre sexual acts. After years of treatment, she retracted all of her memories and sued the therapists and hospital for malpractice. The case was settled for $10.6 million.

The Forensic Evaluation of PTSD in Children

Very often a child psychiatrist will testify in court as an expert witness in both criminal and civil cases involving PTSD. In this section we will present some of the topics related to the forensic evaluation of PTSD in children.

The Legal Tests Regarding Admissibility of Expert Testimony

A forensic evaluation must first pass the gatekeeping standards set out by the Supreme Court of the United States in three revolutionary cases: *Daubert v. Merrell Dow Pharmaceuticals, Inc.* (1993), *General Electric Co. v. Joiner* (1997), and *Kumho Tire Co. v. Carmichael* (1999). *Daubert* (1993) requires that the judge examine the proffered scientific testimony for falsifiability, error rate and the existence of protocols, peer review and publication, and general acceptance. *Joiner* (1997) added that the expert testimony should fit the facts of the case. Shortly after the court decided *Daubert*, experts in many disciplines that assist the law realized that they did not have the requisite data to support the opinions they routinely offered in court. Many of these disciplines claimed that the tough new gatekeeping standards did not apply to them, arguing that *Daubert* involved only "scientific" evidence. In *Kumho Tire Co. v. Carmichael* (1999), the Supreme Court held that all expert testimony, including that of mental health practitioners, be subject to the requirement.

Forensic Evaluation of PTSD in Children: General Aspects

The forensic evaluation is a psychiatric evaluation done for purposes of litigation. The evaluator may have to testify in court and defend his or her assessment, thus convincing the court that his or her opinion is the correct, objective truth. The forensic evaluator is required to be familiar with the legal setting and to prepare an evaluation based on the requirements of the court. As previously described, the professional scrutiny of methods, scientific data, and parameters used during the evaluation process need to meet the requirements held in *Daubert*.

The forensic assessment of children with PTSD is not limited to the presenting symptoms as told by the child or parents but expands to the difficult task of assessing the possibility of malingering, probability of the abuse, and the child's credibility. Therefore, forensic evaluators should avoid using leading questions that may suggest a symptom. Moreover, due to the important differences between clinical and forensic evaluations (Appelbaum, 1997; Greenberg & Shuman, 1997; Strasburger et al., 1997), the practical parameters and structured interview assessment tools that are used to evaluate children with PTSD for therapeutic purposes (American Academy of Child and Adolescent Psychiatry, 1998), should not be used in forensic settings, as they may suggest symptoms of PTSD and enhance the risk of malingering (Lubit et al., 2002). Due to the nature of legal proceedings the forensic assessment of PTSD should include the etiology of PTSD in the assessed case and its link to a specific event as well as long term sequelae due to PTSD (Lubit et al., 2002).

The latter is especially important in civil cases in which the claim is a request for compensation for damages. It is important to emphasize that forensic evaluators, as well as clinical therapists, must comply with state reporting requirements with regard to child abuse allegations (American Academy of Child and Adolescent Psychiatry, 1997).

Therapeutic/Forensic Conflicts

Although there is a compelling consensus that the roles of forensic evaluator and treating clinician should remain separate (American Academy of Child and Adolescent Psychiatry, 1997), many jurisdictions allow the therapist to act as a forensic evaluator as well as the treating therapist (Shuman & Madden, 1999). This may result in conflict of interest due to the significant difference of these two roles (Greenberg et al., 1996). The forensic examiner's role is to reach an objective truth with regard to the validity of the mental harm that is the subject matter of a claim. In order to successfully meet this goal, the expert's opinion must be based as much as possible on objective assessment, collateral sources, and a neutral stance in formulating his or her opinion. These requirements cannot exist in a therapeutic setting in which the subjective truth, or client's perspective, is usually the foundation for treatment (Wesson, 1985).

A therapist who accepts both roles may subject the client to unfavorable therapeutic and legal consequences. As an expert, this professional's evaluation may be viewed by the court as biased and raise questions of validity and judgment. As a therapist, the professional risks include jeopardizing the therapist-client alliance (Shuman & Madden, 1999).

Forensic Evaluation of Children as Witnesses

Courts often use the forensic evaluation of children with PTSD in the determination of a child's competence and credibility.

There are two levels of scrutiny that the court applies to testimony. First, in order to be allowed to testify, a witness must pass basic reliability tests to establish his or her competence. Every witness must have four testimonial attributes, or capacities: to observe, to recollect, to communicate, and to appreciate the obligation to speak truthfully. There is no precise age at which an child is deemed competent or incompetent to testify under oath. The competence of an infant depends on the capacity and intelligence of the particular child and is determined solely by the trial judge. The legal system focuses particularly on the child's ability to relay information accurately, to appreciate the difference between telling the truth and a lie, and to understand the need of being truthful in court (Committee on Psychosocial Aspects of Child and Family Health, 1999; Weissman, 1991).

If the child is found competent to testify, his or her credibility (truthfulness and accuracy) will be questioned and determined by the fact finder (jury or judge). The evidentiary rules concerning the impeachment process (attacking the credibility of a witness) by attorneys are complex and beyond the scope of this chapter. In brief, the child's credibility can be impeached either by cross-examination or by extrinsic evidence, such as testimony of an expert or lay person, which will introduce facts discrediting the child's testimony. Credibility can later be bolstered using re-direct testimony and the same methods of extrinsic evidence. The forensic psychiatrist is often called to participate in such proceedings. The medical literature, based on clinical experience and limited preliminary research, suggests that some factors may assist the evaluator in reaching an opinion on the child's credibility in cases of sexual abuse. These factors include the presence of sexual themes in play therapy and drawing, seductive or regressive behavior, the level of details recalled, the vocabulary that is used by the child, and appropriateness of affect when describing the trauma (Benedek & Schetky, 1987). Other testimonial characteristics such as increasingly inconsistent statements over time, dramatic and implausible descriptions of the sexual abuse, and statements that present initially as innocuous behavior and progress to intrusive and aggressive activities were suggested to invalidate the testimony of the child in cases of sexual abuse (Rogers, 1990).

Minors in Court

Another important topic related to legal proceedings involving PTSD in children is the effect of litigation on minors with PTSD.

The Effect of Litigation on Minors Involved in PTSD Claims

Litigation might affect the clinical course of children with PTSD in various ways. The term *nomogenic disorders*, coined by Tyndel (1974), aims to: "characterize [PTSD] as a psychopathological condition that was created, enhanced, and perpetuated by the law and its application and to denote the psychological and social consequences of the law in the way it affects the course of the disease" (Tyndel, 1999). This notion has been disputed (Mendelson, 1985). It is sometimes believed that patients in litigation with PTSD will hold on to their symptoms in order to increase the amount awarded. Although there is a dearth of data regarding this matter in children, it is possible that the same phenomenon may occur in them as well. Another possible consequence of litigation reported in the literature happens in cases when parents initiate a claim on behalf of their child (Schetky & Guyer, 2002). Some parents chose not to seek psychiatric treatment for their children throughout the litigation period (which may typically last several years) in order to maintain their children's symptoms and enhance the chances of symptom recovery in court (Schetky & Guyer, 2002). This may affect the long-term outcome of PTSD as these children need to cope not only with the emotional consequences of the traumatizing event but also with the potentially traumatizing effects of legal involvement, both of which therapy could provide support for. Of note, when a civil claim is made based on a medical condition, the plaintiff thereby waives his therapist-client privilege of confidentiality, thereby risking that therapeutic alliance.

Child Testimony in PTSD Claims

The dilemma as to whether children who were exposed to a trauma should testify has concerned both the legal and medical systems (Ash & Derdeyn, 1997). Testifying includes the risk of retraumatization of the child during testimony (which may include cross-examination and redirect testimonies) and the rights of the alleged abuser to confront the accuser. There is controversy in the medical literature regarding the effect that testifying has on a child. One opinion is that children benefit from facing their abusers (Runyan, 1988), suggesting that seeing the abusers being punished in the courtroom and taking responsibility for their acts improves children's sense of personal safety. On the other hand, a study that followed 218 children involved in sexual abuse cases suggested that children's greatest fear about testifying was facing the defendant (Goodman et al., 1997). Moreover, children who testified showed more disturbances compared with children who did not testify, and lack of improvement was associated with multiple testimonies, inferior maternal support, and less corroborating evidence. The court has tried to balance the constitutional rights of the defendant with the best interests of the child who may be retraumatized by the testifying process. Cross-examination and face-to-face confrontation is a matter of right in every trial of a disputed issue in fact and the principal basis for excluding hearsay testimony. Nevertheless, the court allowed allegedly abused children to testify in a separate room and have their testimony televised for the judge, jury, and defendant (*Maryland v. Craig*, 1990). In 1990 the court ruled as inadmissible hearsay the testimony of a physician who evaluated a child for sexual abuse using leading questions (*Idaho v. Wright*, 1990). However, in *White v. Illinois* (1992) the court unanimously allowed the admission as evidence of a spontaneous statement by an allegedly abused child that was made outside of a court room while receiving medical treatment following the trauma, as a *spontaneous utterance* exception to the general bar of the hearsay rule, allowing the child not to testify at all.

References

American Academy of Child and Adolescent Psychiatry. (1997). AACAP official action: practice parameters for the forensic evaluation of children and adolescents who may have been physically or sexually abused. *J Am Acad Child Adolesc Psychiatry*. 36(suppl):37S–56S.

American Academy of Child and Adolescent Psychiatry. (1998). AACAP official action: practice parameters for the assessment and treatment of children and adolescents with posttraumatic stress disorder. *J Am Acad Child Adolesc Psychiatry*. 37(10S):4S–26S.

American Psychiatric Association. (1993). APA issues statements on memories of sexual abuse, gun control, television violence (News Release No. 93-58). Washington, DC: American Psychiatric Association.

American Psychiatric Association. (1994). *Diagnostic and Statistical Manual of Mental Disorders* (4th ed.). Washington, DC: American Psychiatric Association.

Appelbaum PS. (1997). Ethics in evolution: the incompatibility of clinical and forensic functions. *Am J Psychiatry*. 154:445–446

Ash P, Derdeyn AP. (1997). Forensic child and adolescent psychiatry: a review of the past 10 years. *J Am Acad Child Adolesc Psychiatry*. 36(11):1493–1502.

Ault v. Jasko, 637 N.E.2d 870 (Ohio 1994).

Bagdasarian N. (2000). A prescription for mental distress: the principles of psychosomatic medicine with the physical manifestation requirement in NIED. *Am J L and Med*. 26:401.

Baldwin K. (2001). Battered child syndrome as a sword and a shield. *Am J Crim L.* 29:59.

Belluck P. (1997). "Memory" therapy leads to a lawsuit and big settlement. *New York Times.* November 6:A1.

Benedek EP, Schetky DH. (1987). Problems in validating allegations of sexual abuse. Part II. Clinical evaluation. *J Am Acad Child Adolesc Psychiatry.* 26:916–921.

Ben-Shimol v. TWA, No. C-93-1586 MHP WL 724782 (1996).

Borawick v. Shay, 68 F.2d 597 (2nd Cir 1995).

Bowman CG, Mertz E. (1998). Attorneys as gatekeepers to the court: the potential liability of attorneys bringing suits based on recovered memories of childhood sexual abuse. *Hofstra L Rev.* 27:223.

Brahams D. (2000). "Repressed memories" and the law. *Lancet.* 356(9227):358.

Brandon S. (1999). Recovered memories: some aspects of the controversy. *Med-Leg J.* 67:25–34.

Committee on Psychosocial Aspects of Child and Family Health. (1999). The child in court: a subject review. *Pediatrics.* 104(5) Part 1 of 2:1145–1148.

Consolidated Rail Corp. v. Gottshall, 512 US 532, 544 (1994).

Daubert v. Merrell Dow Pharmaceuticals, Inc. 509 US 579 (1993).

DeRose v. Carswell, 196 Cal. App. 3d 1011, 1017 (Cal 1987).

de Vries AP, Kassam AN, Cnaan A, Sherman SE, Gallagher PR, Winston FK. (1999). Looking beyond the physical injury: posttraumatic stress disorder in children and parents after pediatric traffic injury. *Pediatrics.* 104(6):1293–1299.

Dillon v. Legg, 441 P.2d 912, 915 (Calif 1968).

Dulieu v. White, 2 K.B. 669, 677 (1901).

Edgar GR, Erica BM. (2001). Gatekeeping Stress: The Science and Admissibility of Posttraumatic Stress Disorder. *University of Arkansas Little Rock L Rev.* 24:9.

Estelle v. McGuire, 502 US 62 (1991).

Frasca M. (2000). Tolling the statute of limitations in childhood sexual abuse civil cases. *J Contemp Legal Issues.* 11:45.

Gaddis v. Smith, 417 S. W.2d 557 (Tex 1967).

General Electric v. Joiner, 522 US 136 (1997).

Goodman GS, Taub EP, Jones DP, England P, Port LK, Rudy L, Prado L. (1997). Testifying in criminal court: emotional effects on child sexual assault victims. *Monogr Soc Res Child Dev.* 57(5):1–161.

Greenberg SA, Shuman DW. (1997). Irreconcilable conflict between therapeutic and forensic roles. *Prof Psychol Res Pract.* 28:50-57.

Hegadorn RC. (1999). Clemency: doing justice to incarcerated battered children. *J Mo Bar.* 55(2):70.

Horner TM, Guyer MJ, Kalter NM. (1993). The biases of child sexual abuse experts: believing is seeing. *Bull Am Acad Psychiatry Law.* 21:281–292.

Idaho v. Wright, 497 US 805 (1990).

Jahnke v. State, 682 P.2d 991 (Wyo 1984).

Kempe CH, Silverman FN, Steele BF, Droegmueller W, Silver H. (1962). The battered child syndrome. *JAMA.* 181:17–24.

Kumho Tire Co. v. Carmichael, 526 US 137 (1999).

LaFave WR, Israel JH. (1992). *Criminal Procedure.* St. Paul, Minn: West.

Large M, Nielssen O. (2001). An audit of medico-legal reports prepared for claims of psychiatric injury following motor vehicle accidents. *Australian & New Zealand J of Psychiatry.* 35(4):535–540.

L.C. v. A.K.D., No. 05-92-02867-CV, 1994 WL 59968 (Tex 1994).

Louise BH. (1999). Nervous shock, nervous courts: the Anns/Kamloops Test to the rescue. *Alberta L Rev.* 37:553.

Lubit R, Hartwell N, van Gorp WG, Eth S. (2002). Forensic evaluation of trauma syndromes in children. *Child Adolesc Psychiatr Clin N Am.* 11(4):823–857.

Martineau v. Angelone, 25 F 3d 734 742-43 (9th Cir 1994).

Mary D. v. John D., 264 Cal Rptr 633 (Cal App. 1989).

Maryland v. Craig, 497 US 836, 110 S Ct 3157 (1990).

McQuade SJ. (2001). The eggshell skull rule and related problems in recovery for mental harm in the law of torts. *Campbell L Rev.* 24:1

Mendelson G. (1985). Compensation neurosis. *Med J Aust.* 142:561–564.

Meyer TJ, Lansberry KA. (2001). Tort law: recent development in Indiana tort law. *Ind. L Rev.* 34:1075.

Modlin HC. (1983). Traumatic neurosis and other injuries. *Psychiatric Clinics N Am.* 6:661–662.

Partlett DF. (1997). Tort liability and the American way: reflections on liability for emotional distress. *Am J Comp. L.* 45:171.

Quinn K. (1995). Guidelines for the psychiatric examination of posttraumatic stress disorder in children and adolescents. In: Simon R, ed. *Posttraumatic Stress Disorder in Litigation.* Washington, DC: American Psychiatric Press; 85–98.

Ramona v. Isabella, No. 61898 (Cal. Super. Ct., May 13, 1994).

Rodrigues v. State, 472 P2d 509, 520 (Haw 1970).

Rogers ML. (1990). Coping with alleged false sexual molestation: examination and statement analysis procedures. *Issues Child Abuse Accusations*. 2:57–68.

Royal College of Psychiatrists. (1997). Reported recovered memories of child sexual abuse: recommendations for good practice and implications for training, continuing professional development and research. *Psychiatric Bull.* 21:663–665.

Runyan DK, Everson MD, Edelsohn GA, Hunter WM, Coulter ML. (1998). Impact of legal intervention on sexually abused children. *J Pediatr.* 113(4):647–653.

Schetky DH, Guyer MJ. (2002). Psychic trauma and civil litigation. In: Schetky DH, Benedek EP, eds. *Child and Adolescent Foresic Psychiatry.* American Psychiatric Publishing, Inc.; 355–364.

Shuman DW. (1998). The role of ethical norms in the admissibility of expert testimony. *Am Bar Assoc Judge J.* 37: 4–43.

Shuman DW, Madden DJ. (1999). Legal issues in the forensic assessment of traumatized youth. In: Saigh PA, Bremner JD, eds. *Posttraumatic Stress Disorder: A Comprehensive Text.* Needham Heights, Mass.: Allyn & Bacon.

Slovenko R. (1994). Legal aspects of post-traumatic stress disorder. *Psychiatr Clin North Am.*17(2):439–46.

Spadaro JA. (1998). An elusive search for the truth: the admissibility of repressed and recovered memories in light of *Daubert v. Merrell Dow Pharmaceuticals, Inc.* Conn. L. Rev. 30:1147.

State v. Crabtree, 805 P.2d 1 9 (Kan 1991).

State v. Hungerford, WL 378571 (NH Super 1995).

State v. Hunter. 695 NE2d 653, 657 (Mass 1998).

State v. Janes, 850 P2d 491 501 (Wash 1993).

State v. Morahan, WL 378571 (NH Super 1995).

Sterling v. Velsicol Chem. Corp, 855 F.2d 1188, 1205 (6th Cir 1988).

Stone AA. (1993). Posttraumatic stress disorder and the law: critical review of the new frontier. *Bulletin of the Am Academy of Psychiatry and the Law.* 21:23–36.

Strasburger LH, Gutheil TG, Brodsky A. (1997). On wearing two hats: role conflict in serving as both psychotherapist and expert witness. *Am J Psychiatry.* 154:448–456.

Taylor R, Buchanan A. (1998). Ethical problems in forensic psychiatry. *Current Opinion in Psychiatry.* 11(6):695–670.

Tyndel M. (1974). Offenders without victims? In: Drapkin I, Viano E, eds. *Victimology: A New Focus* (vol 1., pp 55–62) Lexington, Mass: Lexington Books.

Tyndel M. (1999). Posttraumatic stress disorder and outcomes for functioning and quality of life. *Am J of Psychiatry*. 156(5):804–805.

Tyson v. Tyson, 727 P2d 226 227 (Wash 1986).

Weaver v. Delta Airlines, 56 F Supp 2d 1190 (D Mont 1999).

Weissman HN. (1991). Forensic psychological examination of the child witness in cases of alleged sexual abuse. *Am J Orthopsychiatry*. 61:48–58.

Wesson M. (1995). Historic truth, narrative truth, and expert testimony. *Wash L Rev*. 60: 331–354.

White v. Illinois. (1992). 502 US 346 (1992).

World Health Organization. (2003). *International Classification of Diseases. Mental and Behavioral Disorders (Including Disorders of Psychological Development), Clinical Descriptions and Diagnostic Guidelines,* Tenth Revision. Geneva: WHO.

Yehuda R. (2002). Current concepts: post-traumatic stress disorder. *N Engl J of Med*. 346(2):108–114.

5
■

Neurobiology of PTSD in Children and Adolescents

Sharon Christina Kowalik

Current knowledge of the neurobiology of posttraumatic stress disorder (PTSD) is interesting albeit complicated when studied in adults. However, among children and adolescents, while equally fascinating, its complexity seems to be exponentially greater. One of the reasons for this is the inherent differences between children and adolescents and adults.

Comparing Children and Adults

It has been suggested that the phenomenon of stress or trauma has the potential to damage the brain (Heim et al., 2000). Such damage in adults, depending on its location in the brain and the severity of the traumatic event, can result in changes with a variety of consequences. The outcome of trauma or stress on the immature brain, however, can be much more complex, because the trauma may occur during a critical period in the brain's development. This may, in addition to damaging the existing brain pathways or structure, interfere with the development of subsequent pathways or structures.

It has been relatively well established that myelination, including that of the corpus callosum, increases significantly during the period of 6 months to 3 years of age and continues well into the 20s in human subjects (Jernigan & Sowell, 1997). The subcortical gray matter and septal area, hippocampus, amygdala, or the limbic system structures also increase in volume until the 20s (also Jernigan). The prefrontal cortex develops last and its development continues into the 20s (Goldman, 1971). It is known that differentiation in the brain can be affected by stimulation from the environment, and that the processes of myelination, neurogenesis, and synaptic pruning are sensitive to changes such as stress and may be time dependent (Cicchetti & Tucker, 1994). Therefore, abuse in young children could cause the development of the immature brain to be altered. Such alterations might not only include damage to specific structures, as in the mature brain, but may also lead to the faulty development or the failure to develop of other important structures or pathways in the brain. This, in turn, may make the damage caused by trauma much more catastrophic, as it may interfere with the foundation of the structure of the brain with the potential development of other deficits, such as problems with cognition, attention, executive functioning, and affect regulation.

Difficulties with Research Studies in Children and Adolescents

Research regarding the neurobiology of PTSD in adults is often difficult to interpret. Part of the reason for this has to do with the discrepancies in findings, which in turn are attributed to confounding factors in the research (e.g., type of trauma, duration of trauma, acute versus chronic trauma). Research in children and adolescents share many of these confounding factors, and have a few additional ones of their own. The maturational stage at the time of the study and whether the child is still exposed to the perpetrator or trauma source or in a supportive environment at the time of the study can make it difficult to interpret and compare results of these studies. Suffice it to say, not only is it difficult to compare studies within a population (e.g., child studies to child studies), but there are also problems comparing different populations, such as between children and adults. Some reasons for these problems include the following.

THE TYPE, FREQUENCY, AND TIMING OF ABUSE
Whether comparing one child study to another study, or to a study involving adult subjects, one wonders if all forms of abuse have similar physiological effects. For instance, is emotional abuse or neglect in a child comparable to sexual abuse, or is living in a war zone comparable to physical abuse? Similarly, can chronic abuse in a child be considered similar to one-time events such as a solitary rape or car accident? And how does one approach studies of adult women who were sexually abused as young girls? Into which pool of literature do their results go, that of children or that of adults?

EXPOSURE TO TRAUMA VERSUS PTSD
Many PTSD studies use children or adolescents who have been "maltreated," "abused," or "traumatized" but it is not often clear if they meet full criteria for PTSD (e.g., DeBellis, Charousos et al., 1994; Cichetti & Rogosch, 2001a). In some of these studies, the authors do not say that their subjects meet criteria for PTSD, but neither do they say that they do not meet the criteria. Thus these studies may consist of a varied psychiatric population, as some subjects may meet criteria for PTSD, some partially meet PTSD criteria, and some not at all. This does not mean that these studies are without merit, as they may represent naturalistic conditions. However, this point needs to be taken into consideration when interpreting the findings of a given study.

COMORBID DIAGNOSES
Children who are maltreated or exposed to trauma are at high risk for comorbid diagnoses, with perhaps the most common

being depressive or anxiety disorders, although disruptive disorders are also seen. Such comorbid diagnoses can not only confound the results of an individual research, but can make it difficult to compare different studies. This is particularly true in the studies of cortisol in children with PTSD and comorbid depression.

CONTROL GROUPS

When evaluating studies of PTSD in children, it is important to assure that the appropriate control groups have been used. Inappropriate control groups can be troublesome, such as in studies in which the subjects with PTSD are compared to controls with no diagnosis of PTSD but also no history of trauma. Obviously, an important control group is one that has subjects with a history of trauma but who do not have PTSD. Unfortunately, this is a group often lacking in studies in children and adolescents. When reading these studies, it is important to look at the type of control group used in the study.

The bottom line is that one must be careful when comparing studies and attempting to draw generalized conclusions.

The Neurobiology of PTSD in Children and Adolescents

Despite the limitations noted above, there are good reasons to examine the neurobiology of children and adolescents with PTSD. One reason is that children appear to develop problems more easily after a trauma when compared to adults. In a meta-analysis by Fletcher (1996), children and adolescents were shown to be 1.5 times more likely to be diagnosed with PTSD after exposure to a trauma when compared to adults. In addition, and perhaps more importantly, if stress can in fact damage the brain and cause problems with memory, learning, and cognition, the potential for further consequences on academic and social development makes it important to understand this in order to help the affected children develop optimally.

Neurotransmitters

Given the symptom profile of increased arousal, as demonstrated by the increased startle response and hypervigilance seen in PTSD, neurotransmitters, in particular but not limited to the catecholamines have been targeted for study in the attempt to better understand the neurobiology of this disorder.

Brief Description of the Studies in Adults

NOREPINEPHRINE (NE)

Symptoms of heightened arousal, anxiety, and sympathetic hyperactivity have suggested that the noradrenergic system is overstimulated in PTSD. Most of the data comes from indirect studies, such as exaggerated central nervous system (CNS) responses with antagonism of the presynaptic alpha two auto receptor (Bremner et al., 1997). Compounds such as yohimbine, a presynaptic alpha two auto-receptor agonist, have been shown to increase these symptoms in PTSD patients, cause panic attacks in combat victims affected with PTSD, and enhance the startle response in PTSD victims when compared to controls (Morgan, 1993; Southwick et al., 1997). When urinary and plasma norepinephrine (or its metabolites) has been measured in subjects with PTSD, however, the results have been equivocal (Mason et al., 1988; Murburg et al., 1995); such inconsistencies have been attributed to differences under which the samples were obtained. Recently, more direct studies involving cerebrospinal fluid (CSF) have demonstrated higher levels of NE in subjects with PTSD (Geracioti et al., 2001).

DOPAMINE (DA) AND SEROTONIN (5-HT)

Increased dopamine in urine has suggested the involvement of dopamine in PTSD (Antelman & Yehuda, 1994). M-chlorophenyl-piperazine (m-CPP), a serotonin agonist, has been also shown to cause panic attacks in PTSD victims (Southwick, 1997). Interestingly, the subjects who underwent m-CPP-induced panic attacks did not necessarily also have panic attacks stimulated by yohimbine. These results suggest that there may be at least two subtypes of PTSD and may be important in determining the type of treatment. Serotonin has been also implicated because SSRIs have been shown to be effective in the treatment of PTSD (Stein et al., 2000; Davidson et al., 2002).

Studies in Children

Studies in children have generally involved the measurement of catecholamines (CA) and their metabolites. Most studies have used the 24-hour urine test, as this method is less invasive and better tolerated by children. The 24-hour urine test is also desirable as it obviates the stress-induced rise in CA secondary to venipuncture. It also avoids diurnal variations of the CA and is thought to be an adequate reflection of daily baseline CA functioning. (See Table 1 for a summary of these studies.)

One of the first studies was that of Rogeness (1991). This group found elevated levels of catecholamines in maltreated children not formally diagnosed with PTSD. Soon after, DeBellis, Keshavan, and colleagues (1994) measured 24-hour urinary catecholamines in sexually abused girls. Although 58% of the girls had histories of severe depression with suicidal behavior, only one had a diagnosis of PTSD. Regardless, these girls had significantly higher 24-hour urinary "total catecholamine synthesis" (the sum of epinephrine, NE, dopamine and their respective metabolites) compared to non-abused girls who were similar demographically. This group also found significantly higher levels of urinary metanephrine, vanilmandelic acid (VMA), and homovanillic acid (HVA) in the abused group. Of note, when co-varied for height only HVA was significantly higher. Twenty-four-hour urinary NE was also found to be elevated in boys with severe depression and a history of parental neglect, but the authors of this study did not find a similar significant increase in girls with similar histories (Queiroz et al., 1991). DeBellis, Baum, and colleagues (1999) measured catecholamines obtained from 24-hour urine tests in 18 children with PTSD secondary to past maltreatment, 10 nontraumatized children with overanxious disorder (OAD), and 24 healthy age-matched controls. They found that the subjects with PTSD had significantly greater concentrations of urinary NE and DA in this 24-hour period compared to those with OAD and normal controls. Urinary catecholamines were also found to be positively correlated with the duration of the PTSD trauma and with the severity of the PTSD symptoms in this study.

Given the possible association between the PTSD symptoms of hyperarousal and increased sympathetic activity in the CNS, Perry (1994) used a different approach to assess NE activity. As a result, these authors found a decreased number of platelet adrenergic receptors and increased heart rate after an orthostatic challenge in children with PTSD secondary to physical or sexual abuse. These results represent an overall increase in adrenergic activity and are consistent with the findings of the 24-hour urine studies.

Conclusions

The results of these studies suggest that there is increased catecholaminergic activity in children who have been abused. This appears to be true regardless of whether the child has a formal diagnosis of PTSD. These findings are similar to those found in adults and are further supported by the fact that adrenergic medications such as clonidine and propranolol have been found to be effective in children with PTSD (Harmon & Riggs, 1996; Famularo et al., 1988). The only exception to these results is the work of Rogeness (1991). However, this study cautioned that it had

TABLE 1.
Catecholamine Studies of Children Who Have PTSD or Have Been Abused

Study	Population/ Comorbid Diagnosis	PTSD Diagnosed	Method	Control Group	Brief Summary of Results
Rogeness, 1991	Neglected children	No	Measured catecholamine levels	Non-neglected children	The 24-hour norepinephrine/m2 was lower in the neglected group, but theres was a large difference between group number and variance.
DeBellis, 1994	Sexually abused girls (58% with depression)	One subject had PTSD	Measured 24-hour urine catecholamines	Matched normal non-abused girls	Abused girls had higher levels of "total catecholamine synthesis" and metanephrine, vanillylmandelic acid, and homovanillic acid.
Queiroz, 1991	Children with parental neglect and depression	No	Measured 24-hour urine catecholamines	Depressed versus nondepressed, and/or emotionally neglected children	Depressed boys with history of parental neglect had higher urinary norepinephrine compared to girls.

TABLE 1. *continued*

DeBellis, 1999	Abused children with PTSD	Yes	Measured 24-hour urine catecholamines	Non-abused children with overanxious disorder and non-abused normal children	Children with PTSD had higher norepinephrine and DA compared to both groups. Children with PTSD had more epinephrine compared to overanxious disorder group.
Perry, 1994	Abused children with PTSD	Yes	measured platelet adrenergic receptors and heart rate	Age matched normal children	Platelet adrenergic receptors were decreased and heart rate increased after orthostatic challenge in abused children

several limitations, such as a small number of neglected children compared to non-neglected children and large variances in the results for each group. In addition, the control groups were not normal but rather had psychiatric symptoms.

Neuroendocrine Abnormalities

Given the proposed relationships between hormones and stress, it is of no surprise that considerable research has been done studying the role of hormones in PTSD. In particular, the focus of these investigations has involved the association between the neuroendocrine system and PTSD.

Hypothalamic-Pituitary-Adrenal Axis (HPA Axis) and Stress

The response of the HPA axis in the face of stress or a traumatic event has been long established. Stress results in the release of corticotropin releasing factor (CRF) from the hypothalamus, which then stimulates the release of corticotropin from the pituitary. The secretion of corticotropin in turn stimulates the adrenal glands to secrete cortisol. In time, in the healthy individual this circulating cortisol acts via negative feedback to decrease the amount of ACTH being secreted. Corticotropin itself can also trigger fear-related behaviors. One way it may do this is by stimulating the locus ceruleus and thus noradrenergic activity (Bremner and Vermetten, 2001). Responses triggered by corticotrophin-releasing hormone (CRH) in the locus ceruleus and the limbic system include symptoms of anxiety, hyperarousal and hypervigilence, all designed to help the individual to deal with the stressful situation (Bremner, 1999). Cicchetti and Rogosch (2001b) described the importance of an intact HPA axis for survival in the face of trauma. This is particularly true of the ability to increase the levels of circulating cortisol during these times.

Cortisol secretion follows a circadian rhythm, with levels highest upon awakening and lowest levels at the onset of sleep. Although high levels of cortisol aid the ability to deal with a stressful situation, when cortisol is chronically elevated there is the risk of damage to the brain. This is because high levels of cortisol have been associated in animal studies with neuronal loss in the hippocampus, as well as decreases in dendritic branching neuronal regeneration (Uno et al., 1990; Wooley et al., 1990; Gould et al., 1998). This neuronal loss may in turn lead to deficits in cognition (in particular the process of memory) as well as affective functioning. Thus it is possible that an individual experiencing ongoing traumatic stress may first develop hypercortisolemia, which may in turn cause damage to the hippocampus (site of memory and learning). This can in turn make it more difficult for the subject to deal with the ongoing stress. In addition, chronic hypersecretion of cortisol can induce negative feedback, which may result in hypocortisolemia, which can also decrease the ability of the individual to deal with the stressor.

Brief Description of the Studies in Adults

Although both increased and decreased cortisol levels have been found in adult PTSD subjects, PTSD generally has the distinction of being associated with normal to low cortisol levels despite the hypersecretion of corticotrophin-releasing factor (CRF) (Maes et al., 1998; Newport & Nemeroff, 2000). Decreased basal plasma cortisol levels have been reported in combat veterans with PTSD when compared to veterans without PTSD, and low urinary cortisol was seen in Holocaust survivors with PTSD compared to those without PTSD (Yehuda et al., 1993, 1995). Mason and colleagues (1986) suggested that people who are under marked stress with significant denial may also have low plasma cortisol levels. In addition, glucocorticoid receptors on lymphocytes in those subjects with PTSD have been found to be increased (Yehuda, Boisoneau et al., 1995a) which could be interpreted as further support of decreased basal cortisol in PTSD. When all of these results are considered together, it has been hypothesized that the HPA axis may have increased sensitivity to suppression (the negative feedback) in adults with PTSD. Further support of this has been the fact that enhanced dexamethasone depression of cortisol has been reported in sexually abused women and combat victims with PTSD (Stein, 1997; Yehuda et al., 1995).

PTSD AND DEPRESSION

Some researchers feel that the neurobiology of PTSD may be similar to that of the neurobiology of major depression. However, there are some significant differences. It is clear that both have been associated with a dysregulation of the HPA axis and the catecholamine systems (and by default, the sympathetic nervous system). However, whereas in major depression the levels of cortisol tend to be elevated, in PTSD cortisol levels are low to normal, despite hypersecretion of CRF in both cases (Yehuda, 2001).

This becomes an important point to consider when interpreting the results of PTSD studies, given the frequent comorbidity of depression and PTSD, and is particularly of concern since many of the children in the PTSD studies published to date have comorbid depression or depressive symptomotology. As discussed previously, such comorbidity has the ability to confound the findings in pediatric studies and to make it difficult to compare studies both within the pediatric population and between children and adults.

Further confounding the results is the fact that although in adults with depression, one often finds hypercortisolemia, dexamethasone non-suppression, and blunting of corticotropin secretion after CRH infusion, similar phenomena have not been reported in children (Dahl et al., 1989; Kaufman et al., 1997). However, some researchers feel that the reason for this may be due to environmental factors, such as abuse itself. This is further supported by the fact that when a group of abused, depressed children was studied, they had blunted ACTH secretion post-CRF infusion (Kaufman, 1993). Thus it is important to consider this comorbidity when reviewing the PTSD literature in children and adolescents.

Studies in Children

Techniques used to study PTSD in children and adolescents have included the determination of salivary cortisol, 24-hour urinary cortisol or plasma corticotropin and cortisol levels in response to CRF challenge. Among the key problems encountered in these studies have been the inclusion of comorbid diagnoses, in particular depression; the use of children who have a history of abuse, but who may not meet full criteria for PTSD; or the failure to include control groups of traumatized children without PTSD. Such factors may explain discrepant results. (The results are summarized in Table 2.)

SALIVARY CORTISOL LEVELS

Kaufman (1991) measured salivary cortisol levels in the morning and again in the late afternoon in a group of maltreated children attending a winter day camp. Posttraumatic stress disorder was not formally diagnosed in these children; in addition many had comorbid depressive symptomatology. This study had no control group. However, the children were grouped as those with major depressive disorder (MDD) or those who met diagnostic criteria for dysthymic disorder (DD); when this was done those in the MDD or DD group were more likely to not have the expected decrease in afternoon cortisol. The authors interpreted this to suggest that abused children with depression may have hypercortisolemia.

Hart and colleagues (1995) examined salivary cortisol levels in a group of maltreated preschool children and compared them to nonmaltreated, healthy preschoolers who came from a similar socioeconomic background. These authors found decreased cortisol activity and social competence in the maltreated group.

Hart and colleagues (1996) measured morning and afternoon salivary cortisol in a group of maltreated children attending a summer camp for children from backgrounds with low socioeconomic status (SES). As in Kaufman's study, although it did not seem that these children met criteria for PTSD, they did have comorbid depression. Comparing maltreated children with and without depression, they found that the depressed maltreated children had lower morning cortisol levels compared to the nondepressed, maltreated children. In addition, the depressed, maltreated children were more likely to show a rise rather than the expected decrease in the afternoon. Further comparison with a group of depressed, nonmaltreated children did not show a similar pattern. The authors concluded that HPA axis dysfunction may be present in maltreated children with depression.

Cicchetti and Rogosch (2001a, 2001b) examined morning and afternoon salivary cortisol levels in 175 maltreated children comparing them to 209 low-income nonmaltreated children. Although these authors found no difference in morning and afternoon cortisol levels in abused children compared to the controls, they did note that there was wide variability in the results. Further examination of their findings suggested that there were differences when the type of maltreatment that the child had experienced was taken into consideration. Specifically, children who suffered from multiple abuse tended to have elevated morning and afternoon cortisol levels compared to the comparison group. On the other hand, those children who were only physically abused had lower levels of morning cortisol, and a smaller decrease in the afternoon cortisol compared to the control population.

Carrion and colleagues (2002) studied children with a history of exposure to trauma and with PTSD symptoms. This group measured salivary cortisol levels collected four times per day over a period of up to three days. Compared to nontrauma exposed healthy controls, these authors found increased cortisol through the day in the PTSD group; this did not appear to be related to depressive symptoms. Girls in the PTSD group were more likely to have this increase compared to girls in the control group. The authors were careful to point out that only 12 of 51 subjects met diagnostic criteria for PTSD and that the control group was noted to have average income that was three times that of the PTSD group.

Cicchetti and Rogosch (2001b) examined 371 children from an urban setting who attended a day camp research program. This camp served maltreated and nonmaltreated children from a low SES. The object of this study was to look for differences in salivary cortisol in maltreated children with primarily externalizing symptoms compared to those with primarily internalizing symptoms. Salivary cortisol levels were obtained at 9 a.m. and 4 p.m. Using the Teacher Report Form of the Child Behavior Checklist and Child Depression Inventory, the children were classified as internalizers, externalizers, or both. Among the findings of this study were the fact that "clinic level problems" were more prevalent in the maltreated children compared to the nonmaltreated children. Physiologically, maltreated children with internalizing symptoms had increased morning and across-the-day average levels of cortisol compared to all other groups. This is consistent with increases seen in children with depressed mood and is suggestive of hypercortisolemia. In those maltreated children with primarily externalizing symptoms, the nonmaltreated males had the lowest morning cortisol and also overall daily cortisol levels, which was suggestive of hypocortisolemia. In support of this finding, low cortisol has been associated with early onset aggressive conduct disorder (McBurnett et al., 2000). Maltreated children with both internalizing and externalizing symptoms did not show the expected diurnal decrease in the afternoon cortisol.

The overall impression of the authors was that the differences in HPA axis regulation might be related to whether the child's symptom profile was primarily internalizing, externalizing, or both.

24-HOUR URINARY CORTISOL

DeBellis, Baum, and colleagues (1999) examined cortisol levels in maltreated children with PTSD compared to children who had overanxious disorder (OAD) but no maltreatment as well as normal controls. These authors found that the children with a diagnosis of PTSD had higher 24-hour urinary cortisol levels compared to the other groups. They concluded that since hypersecretion of cortisol did not appear to be associated with depression in children (Dahl & Ryan, 1996), the maltreatment (and or PTSD) might be the cause of the increase in cortisol.

CRH CHALLENGE

DeBellis, Charousos, and colleagues (1994) investigated a group of sexually abused girls, the majority of whom had severe depression with suicidality. Only one, however, had a diagnosis of PTSD. After a challenge of ovine CRH, the authors found that the sexually abused girls had an attenuated ACTH response, though their basal and post-CRF cortisol levels were not different compared to controls. The authors concluded that these sexually abused girls exhibited a dysregulation of the HPA axis as demonstrated by a blunted response to CRH and normal basal and post-CRF cortisol levels.

On the other hand, in a similar study, Kaufman and colleagues (1997) challenged depressed abused, nonabused, and normal control children aged 7 to 13 years with CRF. These authors found that the depressed abused children had significantly greater peak, total, and net corticotropin secretion. However, these findings appeared to be specific to those who were currently undergoing chronic adversity, such as poverty or domestic violence. Since these authors did not include a control group that was abused but not depressed for comparison, it was difficult to separate the effects of depression from the effects of abuse in this study.

CONCLUSIONS

The overall results of these studies are best summarized by the fact that maltreated children, whether they formally meet criteria for PTSD, whether they have comorbid depression, or whether they demonstrate internalizing or externalizing symptoms, tend to exhibit some form of HPA axis dysfunction. A trend may exist wherein traumatized children with comorbid depression experience higher levels of cortisol, whereas traumatized children without depressive symptoms, or traumatized children with externalizing symptoms, may experience hypocortisolemia. However, many more studies with more stringent control groups are needed in order to determine this unequivocally.

Changes in Brain Morphology

It has been hypothesized that continued exposure to stress or traumatic events may result in subsequent changes in the brain. Such changes may be reflected by alterations in brain chemistry or hormone activity, as described in the previous sections. However, other ways these variations may manifest themselves include changes in the size and/or symmetry of the structures of the brain. The subsequent examination of this hypothesis has evoked a number of imaging studies (in particular magnetic resonance imaging [MRI]) in subjects with exposure to trauma and/or PTSD.

Brief Description of Studies in Adults

Those disorders associated with elevated levels of glucocorticoids, such as PTSD and Cushing's syndrome, have also been associated

TABLE 2.
Cortisol Studies

Study	Population/ Comorbidity	PTSD Diagnosed	Method	Control Group	Brief Summary of Results
Kaufman, 1991	Maltreated children with PTSD, many with depression	No	Measured salivary cortisol	No control group	Abused children with major depressive disorder or dysthymic disorder more likely to have expected decrease in afternoon cortisol levels
Hart, 1995	Maltreated preschoolers	No	Measured salivary cortisol	Non-maltreated, age, socioeconomic status matched	Less cortisol reactivity and lower social competence in maltreated subjects
Hart, 1996	Maltreated children from low socioeconomic status with and without depression	No	Measured morning and afternoon salivary cortisol	Depressed, nondepressed, maltreated children	Hypothalamic-pituitary-adrenal axis dysfunction in depressed abused population: lower morning and rise in the afternoon salivary cortisol levels.

TABLE 2. *continued*

Cicchetti, 2001a	Maltreated children	No	Measured morning and afternoon salivary cortisol	Non-maltreated children from similar low-income, disadvantaged backgrounds	Children with multiple abuse had higher morning and afternoon salivary cortisol levels. Physically abused children had lower morning and afternoon cortisol levels.
Carrion, 2002	Children with trauma	12/51 fulfilled DSM-IV criteria for PTSD	Measured plasma cortisol	Age and gender matched healthy controls	Increased cortisol through the day, not related to depression and more in females
Cicchetti, 2001b	Maltreated children	No	Measured morning and afternoon salivary cortisol	Non-maltreated children from similar low income, disadvantaged backgrounds	Abused children with internalizing symptoms had increased salivary cortisol throughout the day. Abused children with externalizing symptoms had lower salivary cortisol throughout the day.

(continued)

TABLE 2. continued

Study	Population/Comorbidity	PTSD Diagnosed	Method	Control Group	Brief Summary of Results
DeBellis, 1999	Maltreated children with PTSD	Yes	Measured 24-hour urinary free cortisol	Overanxious disorder, non-abused, non-trauma	Maltreated children with PTSD and depression had increased cortisol secretion. Not found in depression
DeBellis, 1994a	Sexually abused girls with depression (did not meet criteria for major depressive disorder)	No	Corticotrophin releasing hormone challenge	Non-abused girls matched for age, Tanner stage, socioeconomic status, height, Child Depression Inventory score	Attenuated ACTH response and normal cortisol secretion
Kaufman, 1997	Abused children, depressed	No	Corticotrophin releasing hormone challenge	Not abused, not depressed	Depressed abused had greater peak, total and net ACTH secretion

in some studies with decreased hippocampal volumes. In fact, the hippocampus volume has been found to be decreased in adults who have been exposed to trauma such as that found in combat veterans with PTSD (Bremner et al., 1995; Gurvits et al., 1996), adult PTSD survivors of child abuse (Bremner, 1997), or sexual abuse as children (Stein et al., 1997). Elevated levels of glucocorticoids seem to destroy hippocampal neurons as well as disrupt the connections between other brain structures; hence they have been described as neurotoxic to the hippocampus (Bremner, 1999). This may be in part due to the subsequent glucocorticoid induced elevation in excitatory amino acids such as glutamate (Moghaddam et al., 1994). In some studies, the left hippocampus volume has been reported to be decreased, in some the right, and in some there are bilateral decreases. Such decreases even seem to occur in the face of nonelevated cortisol levels. Because many of the current studies do not include trauma-exposed individuals without PTSD, it has been difficult to determine if PTSD is associated with the changes in the hippocampal volume, or the changes in the hippocampal volume result in PTSD.

Studies in Children

Given the reported effects of glucocorticoids on the hippocampus, one would wonder what the effect of alterations of the HPA axis would have on the developing brain in the trauma-exposed child. Of course, many things can impede brain growth, including genetics, hormones, and malnutrition. Smaller intracranial and cerebral volumes may also be due to living in a chronically stressful or environment lacking in mental stimulation or suffering from chronic mental illness (DeBellis, Keshavan et al., 1999).

In the healthy developing child, the process of myelination in the brain, including that of the corpus callosum, increases significantly during the period of 6 months to 3 years of age and continues well into the 20s. Although gray matter in general decreases after age 4, the subcortical gray matter and septal area, hippocampus, amygdala, or the limbic system structures increase in volume until the 20s (Jernigan & Sowell, 1997). The prefrontal cortex is the last to develop, and its development continues into the 20s (Goldman, 1971). Of note, elevated levels of catecholamines and cortisol may result in deficits in myelination (Dunlop et al., 1997) or neuronal death (Sapolsky et al., 1990). Thus it follows that if trauma occurs at those critical periods when the brain is developing, this may be reflected by changes in the brain itself, in particular that of changes in the size of brain structures.

DeBellis, Keshavan, and colleagues (1999) examined brain magnetic resonance images (MRIs) of 44 children and adolescents with PTSD and 61 healthy controls with no history of abuse. The authors chose a control group of 2:1 because of the known variability of brain structures in children. Thirty-eight of the 44 PTSD subjects also had at least one comorbid diagnosis, including MDD (20), dysthymia (29), oppositional defiant disorder (ODD) (23) or attention deficit hyperactivity disorder (ADHD) (14). The birth weights and histories of full-term pregnancies did not differ between the two groups, but the PTSD subjects had a lower SES compared to the control group. Many of the PTSD subjects had suffered sexual abuse (34 of 44), although most also had experienced multiple forms of trauma.

Maltreated children and adolescents had smaller cerebral and prefrontal cortex volumes when controlled for age, height, weight, and gender. They also had smaller cerebral, prefrontal, and right and left amygdala gray matter. Both the right and left amygdala total volumes were decreased. The left and right temporal lobes and the corpus callosum (CC) (in particular regions, 4, 5, 6, and 7) in this group were smaller as well. When these results were co-varied with SES, the intracranial and cerebral volume remained significantly smaller. The total lateral ventricles and cortical and prefrontal cortical CSF were larger than controls and the CC was smaller, including regions 4, 5, 6, and 7. However, there was no decrease in hippocampal volume.

The authors found the changes in the PTSD subjects were independent of comorbid MDD, ADHD, ODD, use of psychotropic medication, substance use, or prenatal substance abuse. They also found that intracranial volume, CC total area, and CC regions 4, 5, and 7 correlated negatively with the duration of maltreatment leading to the PTSD diagnosis, suggesting that the longer the abuse, the larger the effect on brain development, on volume in particular. In addition, intracranial volume correlated positively with the age of onset of maltreatment, corrected for age, which suggested that the younger the age that the abuse started, the greater the decrease on total brain development. Other correlations found in this study included the finding that total CC and specific regions correlated negatively with PTSD symptoms as well as symptoms of dissociation, and the volume of lateral ventricles correlated positively with duration of maltreatment and PTSD symptoms. Of particular importance, IQ showed strong negative correlations with duration of the maltreatment in years that led to the PTSD.

Despite the fact that abused children with PTSD had higher urinary free cortisol concentrations compared to healthy control children (DeBellis, Baum et al., 1999), hippocampus volumes were not decreased as has been seen in adult studies. One hypothesis proposed by DeBellis and colleagues was that the hippocampus was still in the process of developing, and that if one examined a child with PTSD later in his or her development the examiner might find a retardation of hippocampal growth. As a result, DeBellis and colleagues (2001) did a pilot longitudinal study of nine prepubertal maltreated subjects with PTSD compared to yoked age and sex matched controls in which he measured hippocampus volumes at baseline and two years later. No differences were found in hippocampal volume between the two groups. These authors suggested that it may take longer for changes in the hippocampus to become evident. They also wondered if the adult studies were confounded by the tendency of adults with PTSD to use alcohol (which may also be associated with decreased hippocampus volume).

Carrion and associates (2001) examined brain MRIs of 24 children between the ages of 7 and 14 who were at high risk for chronic PTSD. All of them had suffered a trauma and had posttraumatic symptoms. Of these, 50% met criteria for PTSD and 16.7% had comorbid depression. The researchers were also careful to exclude children with clinically significant head trauma, epilepsy, or neurological disorders. The control group consisted of age and gender matched controls with no psychiatric problems and no history of trauma or abuse. The results showed that the PTSD group had significantly smaller volumes of gray matter as well as total brain volume. Further analysis showed that the frontal lobe asymmetry usually seen in normal children was not seen in the PTSD group.

Of note, this study also found elevated salivary cortisol in the children with PTSD, so the researchers then examined the hippocampus in this group of children. Their findings demonstrated decreased hippocampal volumes, similar to Bremner and associates' 1995 study of combat veterans with PTSD. However, after controlling for total brain volume, this was not a significant decrease

Since the total brain volume was in fact less in these traumatized children, the authors proposed that the neurotoxic effects of glucocorticoids may be more generalized in the developing brain of a child compared to their effects on the mature adult brain.

DeBellis and colleagues (2002) proposed that the superior temporal gyrus (STG) is a structure involved in receptive and nonverbal auditory and language processing. Deficits in nonverbal auditory and language processing have been proposed to exist in PTSD. Event related potentials (ERP) abnormalities have also been reported in PTSD (Kimble et al., 2000). As the STG and the temporal lobes in general contribute to the generation of the

ERP P300 component (O'Donnell et al., 1999) there may be morphological changes in this region in the brain in subjects with PTSD. This in turn, may result in language difficulties, in addition to the PTSD, if the STG is involved. In fact, Cahill and colleagues (1999) have reported deficits in language development with children who had suffered abuse. Using a previous sample of maltreated children (DeBellis, Baum et al., 1999; DeBellis, Keshavan et al., 1999), this same group of researchers examined the STG in brain MRIs of subjects.

Briefly, their results showed that the STG gray matter volume was larger in the PTSD population. This was unexpected given the fact that other brain regions, including total brain volumes, had been found in previous studies to be smaller (DeBellis, Baum et al., 1999; DeBellis, Keshavan et al., 1999). When this group looked more closely at the data, this increase appeared to be more specific to the right-sided STG.

In addition, this study found that there was a more pronounced right greater than left asymmetry in the total and posterior STG volumes in the children with PTSD compared to the control group. It also found that STG gray matter volumes were larger in the PTSD group, thus resulting in a loss of the left greater than right asymmetry usually seen in total, anterior, and posterior STG gray matter volumes.

The authors suggested that possible clinical correlations include studies showing that healthy adults with high trait anxiety had greater right-left cerebral metabolism (Stapleton et al., 1997) and adults with social phobia showed an increased right-sided electroencephalographic (EEG) activation of the anterior temporal region (Davidson, 2000). The authors also hypothesized that these changes may be related to decreased synaptic pruning due to the timing of the trauma in regard to brain development. Because the study did not include a comparison group of abused children with no PTSD, it is not clear if these changes are related to anxiety or depressive symptoms or the trauma itself.

Conclusions

Traumatized children and adolescents did seem to share the decrease in hippocampal volume seen in adult studies. This may be related to: differences in type, severity, or duration of abuse; severity and duration of PTSD symptoms; the presence of comorbid diagnoses; less likely exposure to alcohol or drugs of abuse; duration of exposure to elevated levels of cortisol; and differences in plasticity of the immature brain. Complicating the findings in many of these studies are many confounding factors, including comorbid diagnoses, different types of abuse, as well as different times of onset and duration. In addition, the number of subjects in these studies is often small. However, one finding that appears to be relatively consistent is the fact that abused children with PTSD appear to have smaller total brain volumes, and this might suggest that glucocorticoid toxicity is less specific in the immature brain. In these studies the role of SES is an important variable that needs to be controlled. Regardless, more studies are needed to further substantiate these findings.

Dynamic Studies: Event Related Potentials, Functional Magnetic Resonance Imaging, and Neuropsychological Testing

Because PTSD has the distinction of existing in symptomatic interspersed with nonsymptomatic periods, there has been interest in the use of "dynamic" methods to measure changes in brain activity during the symptomatic state. As a result, studies involving the use of functional magnetic resonance imaging (fMRI), regional cerebral blood flow, and neuropsychological testing in individuals with PTSD have become an important part of the PTSD literature.

Event Related Potentials: Sensory Processing in PTSD

Disturbances in arousal, attention, and sensory processing are established problems in PTSD. Event related potentials (ERPs) are one way in which sensory processing is studied, and ERPs have provided some of the best information on sensory processing in PTSD. ERPs measure the neurophysiological response to a stimulus, for instance, a sound or a flashing light. This is depicted graphically by a series of positive (P) and negative (N) peaks, the number referring to the time of the peak. The P50, N1, P2, and N2 peaks are considered to be a reflection of the physical characteristics of the stimulus, whereas the P300 is in response to the stimulus itself. Auditory evoked potentials involving an "oddball" paradigm present "odd" or different sounds; the amplitude of the P300 is a reflection of the subject's response to this stimulus. The P300 has been shown to represent attention-dependent processing of events.

Brief Descriptions of Studies in Adults

Changes in the P300 are thought to reflect changes in concentration, leading researchers to hypothesize that decreases in the P300 found in subjects with PTSD (Charles et al., 1995; McFarlane et al., 1993) suggest a decreased ability to concentrate among these subjects. Event related potentials can be divided into earlier sensory components than the P300; one of these is the mismatch negativity (MMN). The MMN reflects a specific stage of sensory information processing; it does not represent an attention dependent process, but rather reflects a stage in which new stimuli are processed that is not under the direct control of the subject, but is instead "preconscious." Morgan and Grillon (1999) looked at the mismatch negativity in women with PTSD secondary to sexual assault. These authors were able to demonstrate that peaks of the mismatch negativity were increased in the assaulted individuals compared to controls, thus suggesting there was an exaggerated physiological response to a sensory stimulus that occurred before the subject was conscious of the stimulus.

TABLE 3.
Changes in Brain Structures

Study	Population/ Comorbidity	PTSD Diagnosed	Method	Control Group	Brief Summary of Results
DeBellis, 1999	Children with abuse and PTSD; comorbid major depressive disorder, dysthymia or oppositional defiant disorder	Yes	MRI	No abuse Normal	Overall decreases in total cortex, white and gray matter; when covaried with socioeconomic status, the intracranial and cerebral volume remained significantly smaller. The total lateral ventricles and cortical and prefrontal corticol cerebrospinal fluid were larger than controls, and the corpus callosum was smaller, including regions 4, 5, 6, and 7. There was no decrease in hippocampal volume.

TABLE 3. *continued*

DeBellis, 2001	Abused children with PTSD	Yes	Longitudinal MRI over 2 years	No abuse Normal	No differences in hippocampus
Carrion, 2001	Abused children at high risk for PTSD	50% met criteria for PTSD	MRI	Age and gender matched healthy subjects	PTSD group had smaller volume of gray matter and total brain volume. PTSD group did not have the expected frontal lobe asymmetry
DeBellis, 2002	Abused children with PTSD	Yes, also other comorbid diagnoses	MRI	No abuse Normal	STG gray matter volume, particularly right sided, was larger in PTSD. More pronounced right greater than left assymetry in the total and posterior STG volumes in PTSD, and a loss of the left greater than right assymetry usually seen in the total, anterior and posterior STG gray matter volumes.

Studies in Children

McPherson and colleagues (1997) performed ERPs on 174 children with a history of physical abuse, sexual abuse, or both. This study had a design similar to a study done by Paige and colleagues (1990), which focused on the P2 component of the ERP. The P2 is an early component that is still within conscious realm. Using a paradigm of four tones of increasing intensity, Paigne's group found that combat veterans of the Vietnam War with PTSD reduced the amplitude of the P2 whereas Vietnam veterans without PTSD increased the amplitude of the P2. The authors suggested that the decreased P2 with increasing stimulus intensity was a way to attenuate or dull the response; perhaps an explanation for the numbing symptoms often seen in PTSD. McPherson's study looked at the P2-N2 and the N1-P2 gradients, which are a reflection of the amplitude of the P2 peak. They found that the P2-N2 gradient increased as the intensity of the stimulus increased in abused children with PTSD compared to abused children. However, this was not seen in children without PTSD. These results are opposite to those found in adult PTSD studies. The authors suggested that one possible reason for this difference had to do with the child's perception of the trauma. That is, whereas the combat veterans perceived their situation as "life or death," a child may have not viewed the abuse as equally threatening, citing the less advanced cognitive ability of the child affecting perceptions. However, this study did find that children with the largest number of arousal symptoms tended to have a reduction in the N1-P2 component, which is similar to adults. This study was limited by a very small control group, but did suggest that there might be a subset of PTSD in children who demonstrate excessive arousal, in which these patients try to dampen this excessive stimulation. The authors advocate for more work in this area.

Functional Magnetic Resonance Imaging (fMRI), Regional Cerebral Blood Flow (rCBF), and Neuropsychological Testing

One of the problems found in studying the neurobiology of PTSD is the fact that PTSD can exist in two different states. Symptomatic periods are interspersed with nonsymptomatic periods. Techniques that measure one point in time may therefore miss significant findings, particularly if they are done during the nonsymptomatic state. One way researchers have attempted to get around this problem has been to "evoke" periods of symptoms by using techniques such as trauma stimulus exposure (e.g., sounds of combat are played for the subject to hear). Another is using guided mental imagery (a script is read describing both neutral [e.g., lying on a beach] or traumatic events [either actual or similar to that of the person being evaluated]). Then he or she is asked to "imagine" what is occurring. Then techniques such as positron emission topography (PET) scans, fMRI, regional cerebral blood flow (rCBF) studies, and even certain neuropsychological tests can be administered in order to determine any differences in these measures in the trauma stimulus state compared to the neutral state (Fullerton & Ursano, 1997).

One of the goals of these studies has been to study the patterns of brain activation associated with the recollection of traumatic memories. The areas of interest in these studies have included the amygdala, anterior cingulate gyrus, anterior temporal pole, insular cortex, and orbit frontal cortex. This has been because these areas are associated with the processing of emotional stimuli as well as the modulation of heart rate and respiration through projections to the autonomic centers of the brain stem (Shin et al., 1999).

Brief Description of Studies in Adults

There are a number of studies using these procedures to study PTSD in adult subjects. Briefly, Lanius and colleagues (2001) showed lower levels of brain activation in adult subjects with PTSD compared to control subjects in the medial frontal cortex, anterior cingulated gyrus, and the thalamus using fMRI and script-driven traumatic imagery. Although the medial frontal cortex and the anterior cingulate gyrus have been shown to be altered in other studies, thalamic changes had not been reported in previous studies. These authors hypothesized that the high levels of arousal during trauma leads to altered sensory processing in the thalamus, which can subsequently lead to a disruption of transmission of sensory information to the frontal cortex, cingulate gyrus, amygdala, and hippocampus, and further suggested that such phenomena may underlie dissociative symptoms and play a role in the development of flashbacks. In individuals with PTSD, exposure to the trauma results in increases in rCBF in the amygdala, orbital frontal cortex, anterior temporal poles, insular cortex, and posterior cingulated cortex (Shin et al., 1999). Of note, and in support of these findings, Pardo and colleagues (1993) found that increases of rCBF in orbital frontal cortex in healthy people when they recalled sad events, and Lane and colleagues (1997) reported increases of rCBF in anterior temporal lobes when they recalled emotional events and viewed emotional video clips.

Studies in Children

At the time of this writing, there were no script-driven studies using PET scans, fMRI, or rCBF in children or adolescents with PTSD. However, somewhat similar studies have been done in children by using neutral and emotionally laden words during psychodiagnostic tests. One such study involved the use of the Stroop color test.

The Stroop test is used to determine the emotion bias or "preoccupation" of certain words. The tester presents a series of cards with the names of colors. The subject must name the ink color on the card, which may be different than the word (the word *blue* may be written in red ink). When performing this task, there is latency associated with the task as the subject attempts to separate the semantic component. In these modified studies, the Stroop test is revised to include emotionally laden words. If a word is threatening to a person, reportedly the latency of the response will be longer (Williams et al., 1996). When the Stroop was used in children with a spider phobia, selective Stroop interference with threatening words was found (Martin, 1992).

Moradi and colleagues (1999) administered the Stroop test in 23 children and adolescents aged 9 to 13 years who met criteria for PTSD. The study included a control group with the same number of age and gender matched subjects. These authors used a repertoire of 60 words from five different categories: happy, neutral, depression, general threat, and trauma related. Each word was presented two times in each of two colors from red, blue, green, and yellow. The PTSD group had slower overall responses, which was significantly different for trauma-related words in the PTSD group compared to the control group. The authors referred to this phenomenon as a processing bias.

These existing results appear to be similar to those in adults. Clearly much more research is needed in order to have greater understanding of these results.

CONCLUSIONS

It can be hypothesized that exposure of an individual to a traumatic event could result in increased hypothalamic CRF mRNA, with a resulting increase in glucocorticoids (Bremner & Vermetten, 2001). An increase in glucocorticoids could then exert a toxic effect on the brain, particularly the hippocampus, which could be significant if the traumatic event was ongoing.

Any damage caused by stress or the resulting glucocorticoids could clearly cause deficits in adults who are exposed to a traumatic event. However, as alluded to earlier, the potential effect in a younger individual may be far greater. In support of this, whereas studies in traumatized children do not appear to find decreases in hippocampal volume as is seen in adults, these studies instead have demonstrated decreases in different brain structures, such as the frontal cortex and sections of the corpus callosum. One finding that appears to be relatively consistent is the fact that abused children with a history of trauma appear to have smaller total brain volumes, and this might suggest that glucocorticoid toxicity is less specific in the immature brain.

Regardless, it seems clear that exposure to trauma in childhood has the potential to have a large negative effect on cognitive functioning. Decreased frontal volumes can potentially result in deficits of attention and executive functioning. Beers and DeBellis (2002) have reported deficits in measures of attention and abstract reasoning/executive functioning on the Wisconsin Card Sorting Test and the Controlled Oral Word Association Test in children with PTSD. Thus children may be at risk to not only develop PTSD from a traumatic event, but other psychiatric disorders as well, such as ADHD.

Evidence that glucocorticoid exposure can result in decreased dentrictic branching or alterations in the structure of the synaptic terminal (Wooley et al., 1990; Margarinos et al., 1997; Bremner, 1999) in the developing brain also puts the child at high risk for deficits in cognitive and affective functioning. Thus, a child who experiences a traumatic event may not only be at risk for developing PTSD, but also other psychiatric disorders and difficulties in learning, with the resulting deficits in cognitive functioning. Perry (1994) has suggested that those children who are abused (and in particular those who develop PTSD) are at increased risk to suffer from developmental delays.

In short, exposure to traumatic events in children has the potential to result in a greater constellation of problems and deficits, many of which may be permanent. Such potential makes the prevention of exposure to trauma, such as child abuse, even more important. It also makes it important to screen for such exposure in at-risk populations, and to initiate early and intensive treatment in affected children and adolescents.

References

Antelman SM, Yehuda R. (1994). Time-dependent change following acute stress: relevance to the chronic and delayed aspects of PTSD. In: Murburg, MM ed. *Catecholamine Function in Post-traumatic Stress Disorders*. Washington, DC: American Psychiatric Press; 87–98.

Beers SR, DeBellis MD. (2002). Neuropyschological function in children with maltreatment-related posttraumatic stress disorder. *Am J Psychiatry*. 159(3):483–486.

Bonne O, Brandes D, Gilboa A, et al. (2001). Longitudinal MRI study of hippocampal volume in trauma survivors with PTSD. *AM J Psych*. 158(8):1248–1251.

Bremner JD. (1999). Does stress damage the brain? *Biol Psychiat*. 45(7):797–805.

Bremner JD, Randall P, Capelli, S, Scott T, McCarthy, G., Charney, DS. (1995). Deficits in short-term memory in adult survivors of childhood abuse. *Am J Psychiatry*. 152:973–981.

Bremner JD, Randall P, Vermetten F, et al. (1997). Magnetic resonance imaging-based measurement of hippocampal volume in posttraumatic stress disorder related to childhood physical and sexual abuse: a preliminary report. *Biol Psychiatry*. 41:23–32.

Carrion VG, Weems CF, Eliez S, et al. (2001). Attenuation of frontal asymmetry in pediatric posttraumatic stress disorder. *Biol Psychiatry*. 50:943–951.

Carrion VG, Weems CF, Ray RD, Glaser B, Hessl Dand Reiss AL. (2002). Diurnal salivary cortisol in pediatric posttraumatic stress disorder. *Biol Psychiatry*. 51(7):575–582

Charles G, Hansenne M, Ansseau M, Pitchot R, Machowski, Schittecatte M. (1995). P300 in post traumatic stress disorder. *Neuropsychobiology*. 32:72–74.

Cicchetti D, Rogosch FA. (2001a). Diverse patterns of neuroendocrine activity in maltreated children. *Develop Psychopathol*. 13:677–693.

Cicchetti D, Rogosch FA. (2001b). The impact of child maltreatment and psychopathology on neuroendocrine functioning. *Develop Psychopathol*. 13:783–804.

Cicchetti D, Tucker D. (1994). Development and self-regulatory structures of the mind. *Develop Psychopathol.* 6:533–549.

Dahl R, Puig-Antich J, Ryan N, et al. (1989). Cortisol secretion in adolescents with major depressive disorder. *Acta Psychiatr Scand.* 80(1): 18–26.

Dahl R, Ryan N. (1996). The psychobiology of adolescent depression. In: Cicchetti D, Toth SL, eds. *Rochester Symposium on Developmental Psychopathology: Vol. 7. Adolescence: Opportunities and Challenges.* Rochester, NY: University of Rochester Press; 197–232.

Davidson JR, Landerman LR, Farfel GM, Clary, CM. (2002). Characterizing the effects of sertraline in post-traumatic stress disorder. *Psychol Med.* 32(4):661–670.

Davidson RJ, Marshall JR, Tomarken AJ, Henriques JB. (2000). While a phobic waits: regional brain electrical and autonomic activity in social phobics during anticipation of public speaking. *Biol Psychiatry.* 47:85–95

DeBellis MD, Baum AS, Birmaher B, et al. (1999). Developmental traumatology, Part I: Biological stress symptoms. *Biol. Psychiatry.* 45(10):1259–1270.

DeBellis MD, Charousos GP, Dorn LD, et al. (1994). Hypothalamic pituitary adrenal dysregulation in sexually abused girls. *J Clin Endocrinol Metab.* 78:249–255.

DeBellis MD, Hall J, Boring AM, Frustaci K, Moritz G. (2001). A pilot longitudinal study of hippocampal volumes in pediatric maltreatment-related posttraumatic stress disorder. *Biol. Psych.* 50:305–309.

DeBellis MD, Keshavan MS, Clark DB, et al. (1999). Developmental traumatology, Part II: Brain development. *Biol. Psychiatry.* 45(10):1271–1284.

DeBellis MD, Keshavan MS, Frustaci K, et al. (2002). Superior temporal gyrus volumes in maltreated children and adolescents with PTSD. *Biol Psychiatry.* 51(7):544–552.

DeBellis MD, Lefter L, Trickett PK, Putnam FW. (1994). Urinary catecholamine excretion in sexually abused girls. *J Am Acad of Child Adol Psych.* 33:320–327.

Dunlop SA, Archer MA, Quinlivan JR, Beazley, LD, Newham JP. (1997). Repeated prenatal corticosteroids delay myelination in the ovine central nervous system. *J Matern Fetal Med.* 6(6):309–313.

Femularo R, Kinscherff R, Fenton T. (1988). Propranolol treatment of childhood posttraumatic stress disorders, acute type. A pilot study. *Am J Dis Child.* 142(11):1244–1247.

Fletcher KE. (1996). Childhood posttraumatic stress disorder. In: Mash EJ, Barkley RA, eds. *Child Psychopathology.* New York: Guilford Press; 242–276.

Fullerton, CS, Ursano RJ (Eds.). (1997). *Post-Traumatic Stess Disorder: Acute and long-term responses to trauma and disaster.* Washington, D.C.: American Psychiatric Press.

Geracioti TD, Bsaker DG, Ekhator NN. (2001). CSF norepinephrine concentrations in posttraumatic stress disorder. *Amer J Psychiatry.* 158(8):1227–1230.

Goldman, PS. (1971). Functional development of the prefrontal cortex in early life and the problem of neuroplasticity. *Exp Neurel.* 32(3):366–387.

Gould, E, Tanapat, P, McEwen, BS, Flugg G, Fuchs. (1998). Proliferation of granule cell precursors in the dentate gyrus of adult monkeys is diminished by stress. PNAS 95 USA (6):3168–3171.

Gurvits TV, Shenton ME, Hokama H, et al. (1996). Magnetic resonance imaging study of hippocampal volume in chronic, combat-related posttraumatic stress disorder. *Biol Psychiatry.* 40:1091–1099.

Harmon RJ, Riggs PD. (1996). Clonidine for posttraumatic stress disorder in preschool children. *J Am Acad Child Adolesc Psychiatry.* 35(9):1247–1249.

Hart J, Gunnar M, Cicchetti D. (1995). Salivary cortisol in maltreated children: evidence of relations between neuroendocrine activity and social competence. *Development and Psychopathology.* 7:11–26.

Hart J, Gunnar M, Cicchetti D. (1996). Altered neuroendocrine activity in maltreated children related to depression. *Develop Psychopathol.* 8:201–214.

Heim C, Elert U, Hellhammer DH. (2000). The potential role of hypocortisolism in the pathophysiology of stress-related bodily disorders. *Psychoneuroendocrinology.* 25:1–35.

Jernigan TL, Sowell ER. (1997). Magnetic resonance imaging studies of the developing brain. In: Keshaven MS, Murray RM, eds. *Neurodevelopment and Adult Psychopathology.* Cambridge, UK: Cambridge University Press; 63–70.

Kaufman J. (1991). Depressive disorders in maltreated children. *Journal of Am Acad Child Adolesc Psychiatry.* 156:505–524.

Kaufman J, Birmaher B, Perel J, et al. (1997). The corticotropin-releasing hormone challenge in depressed abused, depressed nonabused, and normal control children. *Biol Psychiatry.* 42:669–679.

Kaufman J, Brent D, Birmaher B, et al. (1993). *Measures of family adversity, clinical symptomatology, and cortisol secretion in a sample of preadolescent depressed children.* Presented at Annual Meeting of the Society of Research in Child and Adolescent Psychopathology. Santa Fe, NM.

Kimble M, Kaloupek D, Kaufman M, Deldin P. (2000) Stimulus novelty differentially affects attentional allocation in PTSD. *Biol Psychiatry.* 47:880–890.

Lane RD, Reiman EM, Ahern, GL, Schwartz GE, Davidson RJ. (1997). Neuroanatomical correlates of happiness, sadness, and disgust. *Am J Psychiatry.* 154:926–933.

Lanius, RA, Williamson PC, Densmore MB, et al. (2001). Neural correlates of traumatic memories in posttraumatic stress disorder: a functional MRI investigation. *Am J Psych.* 158(11):1920–1922.

Maes M, Lin A, Bonaccorso S, et al. (1998). Increased 24-hour urinary cortisol excretion in patients with posttraumtic stress disorder and patients with major depression, but not in patients with fibromyalgia. *Acta Psychiatr Scand.* 98:32–335.

Magarinos AM, Verdugo JM, McEwen BS. (1997). Chronic stress alters synaptic terminal structure in hippocampus. *PNAS* 94:14002–14008.

Martin M, Hordeer P, Jones GV. (1992). Integral bias in naming of phobia-related words. *Cognition and Emotion.* 6:479–486.

Mason JW, Giller EL, Kosten TR, Harkness L. (1988). Elevation of urinary norepinephrine/cortisol ratio in posttraumatic disorder. *J Nerv Ment Dis.* 176:498–502.

Mason JW, Giller EL, Kosten TR, Ostroff RB, Podd L. (1986). Urinary free-cortisol levels in posttraumtic stress disorder poteients. *J Nerv Ment Dis.* 174(3):145.

McBurnett K, Lahey BB, Rathouz PJ, Loeber R. (2000). Low salivary cortisol and persistent aggression in boys referred for disruptive behavior. *Arch Gen Psych.* 57:38–43.

McFarlane AC, Weber DL, Clark CR. (1993). Abnormal stimulus processing in post-traumatic stress disorder. *Biol Psychiatry.* 34:311–320.

McPherson VB, Newton JE, Ackerman P, Oglesby DM, Dykman RA. (1997). An event-related brain potential investigation of PTSD and PTSD symptoms in abused children. *Integr Physiol Behav Sci.* 32(1):31–42.

Moghaddam B, Bolinao ML, Stein-Behrens B, Aspolsky R. (1994). Glucocorticoids mediate the stress-induced extracellular accumulation of glutamate. *Brain Res.* 655:251–254.

Moradi AR, Taghavi MR, Doost HT, Yule W, Dalgleish T. (1999). Performance of children and adolescents with PTSD on the Stroop colour-naming task. *Psychol Med.* 29(3):412–419.

Morgan III CA. (1993). Yohimbine-facilitated acoustic startle reflex in humans. *Psychopharmacology.* 110:342–346.

Morgan III CA, Grillon C. (1999). Abnormal mismatch negativity in women with sexual assault-related posttraumatic stress disorder. *Biol. Psychiatry.* 45(7):827–832.

Murburg MM, McFall ME, Lewis N, Veith RC. (1995). Plasma norepinephrine kinetics in patients with posttraumatic stress disorder. *Biol Psychiatry.* 38:819–825.

Newport DJ, Nemeroff CB. (2000). Neurobiology of posttraumatic stress disorder [Current Opinion]. *Neurobiology.* 10:211–218.

O'Donnell BF, McCarley RW, Potts GF, et al. (1999). Identification of neural circuits underlying P300 abnormalities in schizophrenia. *Psychophysiology.* 36:388–398.

Paige SR, Reid GM, Allen MG, Newton JE. (1990). Psychophysiological correlates of posttraumatic stress disorder in Vietnam veterans. *Biol Psychiatry.* 27(4):419–430.

Pardo JV, Pardo PJ, Raichle ME. (1993). Neural correlates of self-induced dysphoria. *Am J Psych.* 150:713–719.

Perry BD. (1994). Neurobiological sequelae of trauma: posttraumatic stress disorders in children. In: Murberg MM, ed. *Catecholamine function in posttraumatic stress disorder: emerging concepts.* Washington, DC: American Psychiatric Press; 253–276.

Prange AJ. (1999). Thyroid axis sustaining hypothesis of posttraumatic stress disorder. *Psychosomatic Medicine.* 61(2):139–140.

Queiroz EA, Lombardi AB, Santos Furtado CRH, et al. (1991). Biochemical correlate of depression in children [in Portuguese]. *Arq Neuro Psiquiat.* 49:418–425.

Rauch SL, Van der Kolk BA, Fisler RE, et al. (1996). A symptom provocation study of posttraumatic stress disorder using positron emission tomography and script-driven imagery. *Arch Gen Psych.* 53:380–7.

Reiss AL, Abrams MT, Singer HS, Ross JL, Dencla MB. (1996). Brain development, gender and IQ in children: a volumetric imaging study. *Brain.* 119:1763–1774.

Rogeness GA. (1991). Psychosocial factors and amine systems. *Psychiatry Res.* 39:215–217.

Saplsky RM, Uno H, Rebert CS, Finch, CE. (1990). Hippocampal damage associated with prolonged corticoid exposure in primates. *J Neurosci.* 10(5):2893–2902.

Shin LM, McNally RJ, Kosslyn SM, et al. (1999). Regional cerebral blood flow during script-driven imagery in childhood sexual abuse-related PTSD: a PET investigation. *Am J Psych.* 156(4):575–584.

Shin LM, Whalen PJ, Pitman RK, et al. (2001). An fMRI study of anterior cingulate function in posttraumatic stress disorder. *Biol Psych.* 50:932–942.

Southwick SM, Krystal JH, Bremner D, et al. (1997). Noradrenergic and serotonergic function in posttraumatic stress disorder. *Arch Gen Psychiatry.* 54:749–758.

Stapleton SR, Kiriakopoulos E, Mikulis D, et al. (1997). Combined utility of functional MRI, cortical mapping, and frameless sterotaxy in the resection of lesions in eloquent areas of brain in children. *Pediatr Neurosurg.* 26(2): 68–82

Stein MB, Koverola C, Hanna C, Torchia MG, McLlarty B. (1997). Hippocampal volume in women victimized by childhood sexual abuse. *Psycho Med.* 27: 951–959.

Stein DJ, Seedal S, van der Linden GJ, Zungu-Dirwayi, N. (2000). SSRIs in the treatment of PTSD: a meta analysis of randomized controlled studies. *Int Clin Psychopharm.* Aug 15 Suppl 2: S31–S39.

Uno H, Lohmiloler L, Thieme C, et al. (1990). Brain damage induced by prenatal exposure to dexamethasone in fetal rhesus monkeys. I. Hippocampus. *Dev Brain Res.* 52:157–167.

Wang S, Mason J. (1999). Elevations of serum T3 levels and their association with symptoms in World War II veterans with combat-related posttraumatic stress disorder: replication of findings in Vietnam combat veterans. *Psychosom Med.* 61:131–138.

Williams, JM, Mathews A, MacLeod C. (1996). The emotional Stroop Test and psychopathology. *Psychological Bulletin.* 120:3–24.

Wooley CS, Gould E, McEwen BS. (1990). Exposure to excess glucocorticoids alters dendritic morphology of adult hippocampal pyramidal neurons. *Brain Res.* 53:225–231.

Yehuda, R. (2001). Biology of posttraumatic stress disorder. *J Clin Psychiatry.* 62(suppl.):41–46.

Yehuda R, Boisoneau D, Lowy MT, Giller ER Jr. (1995). Dose-response changes in plasma cortisol and lymphocyte glucocorticoid receptors following dexamethasone administration in combat veterans with and without posttraumatic stress disorder. *Arch Gen Psychiatry.* 52:583–593.

Yehuda R, Giller Jr E, Mason JW. (1993). Psychoneuroendocrine assessment of posttraumatic stress disorder: current progress and new directions. *Prog Neuropsychopharmacol Biol Psychiatry.* 17:541–550.

Yehuda R, Kahana B, Binder-Brynes K, Southwick SM, Mason JW, Giller EL. (1995). Low urinary cortisol excretion in Holocaust survivors with posttraumatic stress disorder. *Am J Psychiatry.* 152:982–986.

6

◼

Etiology and Pathogenesis of PTSD in Children and Adolescents

Barbara Farkas

The factors that contribute to posttraumatic stress disorder (PTSD) in children and adolescents are multi-fold. Although a paucity of research exists in this area regarding children, and there are important differences in symptomotology between posttraumatic stress reactions in children and adults (Yule, 2001), we can still glean much from studies involving adults.

Neurochemical Aspects of PTSD

Consider the psychobiological aspects of PTSD. Once a traumatic event occurs, the neurobiologic system in a child goes to work. The major systems seen to play a role are the neurotransmitter and neuroendocrine systems. Evidence shows that a severe or intense psychological shock will traumatize a child (Pynoos et al., 1987) and that this trauma may chronically alter his or her biological response (Bremner et al., 1993; Charney et al., 1993).

There are a number of neurotransmitters involved, including norepinephrine, dopamine, serotonin, the internal opiods, glutamate and γ-aminobutyrate (GABA).

Catecholamines

Catecholamines exhibit peripheral nervous system excitatory and inhibitory effects as well as actions in the central nervous system (CNS) such as respiratory stimulation and an increase in psy-

chomotor activity. The principal catecholamines are norepinephrine, epinephrine, and dopamine, and are formed from phenylala-
nine and tyrosine. The catecholamines bind to two different
classes of receptors, termed the α- and β-adrenergic receptors, and
are therefore also known as adrenergic neurotransmitters. Neurons
that secrete them are adrenergic neurons; norepinephrine-secret-
ing neurons are noradrenergic. Some of the norepinephrine
released from presynaptic noradrenergic neurons is recycled in the
presynaptic neuron by a reuptake mechanism.

NOREPINEPHRINE

Norepinephrine has been implicated in both acute and long-
term response to acute trauma. There is research demonstrating
the role of norepinephrine in the acute stress response and emotionally influenced memory (Cahill, 1997). In addition, there
are indications for the role of norepinephrine hyperresponsive-
ness of the CNS in PTSD (Charney et al., 1993; Southwick et
al., 1999). This, along with the fact that β-adrenergic blockers
have been shown to be effective in the blockade of emotional
arousal, may indicate that the intensity of catecholamine
response at the time of the trauma may be important in determining the type of traumatic memory that is laid down for the
long term (McFarlane, 1999).

Alpha-adrenergic postsynaptic receptors are distributed in
the prefrontal cortex, hippocampus, and amygdala (Gross-
Isseroff et al., 1990). Activation of the α receptors has been associated with fear response behaviors and is important in the
modulation of the sleep and startle responses (Stevens et al.,
1994; Pickworth et al., 1977). Activation of the α receptors is
associated with quiet concentration (Arnsten, 1993). This has
been thought to suggest that the activation of the α receptor may
be beneficial for PTSD symptoms by down-regulating the noradrenergic outflow (as cited in Taylor & Raskind, 2002, per personal communication with Southwick).

DOPAMINE

Drugs that increase dopamine turnover can cause symptoms similar to those seen in PTSD, such as an acute increase in anxiety or agitation, an exaggerated startle response, and hypervigilence. An acute stress increases dopamine release in the prefrontal cortex, which therefore may be related to these specific posttraumatic stress disorder symptoms in an individual (Antelman, 1988).

Serotonin

Serotonin (5-hydroxytryptamine, 5HT) is formed by the hydroxylation and decarboxylation of tryptophan. Neurons that secrete 5HT are termed *serotonergic*. Following the release of 5HT, a portion is taken back up by the presynaptic serotonergic neuron in a manner similar to that of the reuptake of norepinephrine. The function of serotonin is exerted upon its interaction with specific receptors. Some serotonin receptors are presynaptic and others postsynaptic. The $5HT_6$ and $5HT_7$ receptors are distributed throughout the limbic system of the brain and the $5HT_6$ receptors have high affinity for antidepressant drugs.

Studies looking at paroxetine platelet binding and m-chlorophenylpiperazine (mCPP, a serotonin agonist) challenge tests in trauma victims found that mCPP was shown to induce panic attacks, flashbacks, and dissociative episodes. In addition, it has been found that conditioned fear stimuli activate serotonergic neurons in the dorsal raphe nucleus, which project to the amygdala and forebrain. These conclusions suggest a role for serotonin in PTSD (Arora et al., 1993; Southwick et al., 1997).

Impairment in serotonin synthesis secondary to a genetic abnormality may be related to proneness to violence (Kagan et al., 1988). The likelihood of exposure to high-risk situations and the consequent development of PTSD increases in these individuals.

GABA

The amino acid derivative, γ-aminobutyrate, also called 4-aminobutyrate (GABA), is a well known inhibitor of presynaptic transmission in the CNS. The formation of GABA occurs by the decarboxylation of glutamate catalyzed by glutamate decarboxylase (GAD), which is present in many nerve endings of the brain. Neurons that secrete GABA are termed *GABAergic*. Glutamate and GABA are involved in encoding memory. These may therefore play a role in remembering the traumatic event (Nutt, 2000).

Along with the propensity for dopamine to play a role in the exaggerated startle seen with PTSD, a proneness to startle can be related to a defect in the regulation of GABA, which is normally an inhibitory neurotransmitter (Dubowitz et al., 1992). Further research in this area is required.

Opiates

The brain releases β-endorphins when the pituitary releases adrenocorticotropic hormone (ACTH) (Dent et al., 1981). These endorphins may stimulate the trauma-seeking behaviors seen in some adult trauma victims (Kosten & Krystal, 1988). For example, plane crash survivors have described getting a new found "rush" from subsequently putting themselves in risky situations such as skydiving or extreme sports. Charney and colleagues (1993) found that opiates introduced into the body can either decrease or attenuate the stress-induced increases in norepinephrine release.

Hypothalamic-Pituitary-Adrenal Axis

The hypothalamic-pituitary-adrenal (HPA) axis has been shown to be affected in the short term (McFarlane et al., 1997) as well as in the long term (DeBellis et al., 1994; Heim et al., 2000) in victims of PTSD.

Trauma victims have shown a highly sensitized HPA axis with decreased basal cortisol levels and increased negative feedback regulation (Yehuda & McFarlane, 1995; Yehuda, 1997). This is the opposite of what is seen with the normal stress response, as illustrated below.

What has yet to be determined is whether the cortisol levels measured after acute trauma reflect a biological vulnerability to develop PTSD, perhaps secondary to prior trauma (Resnick et al., 1995) or are indicative of an HPA response to the acute traumatic event (McFarlane et al., 1997).

Cortisol levels in the urine of traumatized veterans were measured and found to be low (Mason et al., 1986; Yehuda et al., 1991; Yehuda et al., 1995). These values were calculated as a ratio to their serum norepinephrine. A difference was found between the norepinephrine/cortisol ratio of schizophrenic or bipolar veterans and those of traumatized veterans. This has suggested to some that the stress altered norepinephrine/cortisol ratios may produce slow and relatively long lasting brain changes through the action of genomes, in contrast to the quick actions of catecholamines alone (McEwen et al., 1987). These findings have not been replicated in all studies though. Elevated urinary cortisol levels were found in 24-hour urines of people with combat-related PTSD (Pitman & Orr, 1990); in women with childhood sexual abuse-related PTSD (Lemieux & Coe, 1995) and in children with abuse-related PTSD (DeBellis, Baum et al., 1999).

The interrelationship between the noradrenergic system and the HPA axis has been postulated by some to account for the symptom patterns seen with trauma (Yehuda et al., 1990). They suggested that the inhibitory responses, such as numbing and avoiding, come from the effect of corticosteroids on the genetic activities of the brain; while the excitatory responses of PTSD, such as repetitions and startle responses, may come from the stimulating effect of corticosteroids on the noradrenergic functions of the brain cells.

As of yet there is no data addressing the functioning of the HPA axis during the acute trauma in patients who subsequently develop PTSD. This may, in fact, initially look like a normal stress response in regards to increased cortisol levels, which subsequently decrease below normal with time.

Brain Morphology

Neuroimaging techniques such as positron emission tomography (PET) and magnetic resonance imaging (MRI) have become an interesting way of looking at the pathogenesis of posttraumatic stress disorder. Structural abnormalities in PTSD seen with an MRI include nonspecific white matter lesions (Canive et al., 1997; Myslobodsky et al., 1995) and decreased hippocampal volume (Bremner et al., 1995). However, a study by DeBellis, Keshavan, and colleagues (1999) in children with PTSD did not find a reduction in hippocampal volume. This suggests that long-term exposure to either stress or PTSD may be necessary to bring about a noticeable change. Bremner (2002) postulated that the chronic stress of PTSD may inhibit the capacity for neurogenesis, which would prevent the ability of the hippocampus to regenerate neurons in patients with a history of prior exposure to stress. This, Bremer goes on to write, would explain the aforementioned findings of DeBellis, Keshavan, and colleagues (1999) in children who have had PTSD for a relatively short time.

Positron emission tomography (PET) scans of regional cerebral blood flow reveal greater activation of the amygdala and anterior paralimbic structures (involved in the processing of negative emotions), greater deactivation of Broca's region, and failure of activation of the cingulate cortex (Rauch et al., 1996; Shin et al., 1999; Bremner, Narayan et al., 1999; Bremner, Staib et al., 1999)

Pitman and colleagues (2001) reviewed these studies and were unable to determine whether these abnormalities were secondary to the trauma itself, secondary to the posttraumatic stress disorder, or were preexisting brain abnormalities, which may have increased the individual's risk of exposure to the traumatic event or increased the individual's vulnerability to developing posttraumatic stress disorder. Prospective studies evaluating victims prior to and following a traumatic event would be needed to elucidate this.

Genetics

When discussing the etiology of mental illness, genetics is an area that cannot be overlooked. Genes have already been found to play a significant role in an individual's propensity towards certain illnesses. For example, in psychiatry, evidence for a genetic basis for schizophrenia has been found. Schwab and associates (1998) found that in families with schizophrenia there is evidence for a susceptibility locus on chromosome 10p14-p11. Gill and associates (1996) found that in affected sibling pairs there is evidence of a susceptible locus for schizophrenia at chromosome 22q12.

Another more recent example, involving a history of trauma as abuse and a possible predisposition towards the formation of PTSD symptoms, was shown by Terrie Moffitt heading up a study that postulates an X-linked gene that produces lower than normal level monoamine oxidase-A (MAO-A). In the case of abused boys, these lower levels of MAO-A may lead to an increased rate of violence when they become adults (Begley, 2002). This implies a genetic vulnerability for certain behaviors, which is kindled by certain environmental influences.

We need to consider whether a person is susceptible to PTSD, as it is quite possible that some people develop PTSD following very severe traumas without any significant contribution from genetic factors. Orcutt and associates (2002) postulated that the PTSD symptoms themselves might mediate a link between trauma exposure and later traumatic events. They found that with Persian Gulf War veterans, PTSD symptomotology did partially mediate the link between combat exposure and later trauma. Taking this a step further, Yehuda and colleagues (2002) suggested that stress-induced changes in gene expression (Duman et al., 1994; McEwen & Magarinos, 1997) might lay the groundwork for an intergenerational effect of traumatic stress, thereby implying a genetic basis for individual differences in stress reactivity.

If in fact susceptibility to PTSD exists, other factors need to be considered as well. Is there a history of mental illness in the patient or the family? If so, would this make the person more likely to partake in dangerous behaviors, thereby leading to a trauma and subsequent PTSD? Or perhaps the individual has a genetic predisposition towards developing PTSD, which makes the person more likely to react to a given trauma.

Some studies have suggested a role for genetics in the etiology of PTSD. However, we need to take into account the many complicating factors, including the high frequency of comorbid psychiatric illness, different types of environmental exposure, a poor control base, and the heterogeneity of the genes themselves (Radant et al., 2001).

As for a family history of mental illness, studies have found connections between this and an individual developing PTSD. Bromet and colleagues (1998) and Deykin and Buka (1997) found that a family history of psychotic, anxiety, mood, and substance abuse disorders increased an individual's risk of exposure to trauma by upwards of 50%.

Breslau and associates (1991) found that the risk of developing PTSD was almost four times as high in patients with a family history of psychosis and about twice as high with a family history of depression versus controls.

Sack and colleagues (1995) found that parental PTSD was associated with a fivefold increased risk of PTSD in offspring

Breslau and associates (1995), Reich and colleagues (1996), and Skre and colleagues (1993) found that the risk of developing PTSD was up to three times higher in patients with a family history of psychiatric disorders. Breslau goes on to state that vulnerability factors, such as a family history of psychiatric illness, do not only exert their influence by increasing the likelihood of an individual developing the disorder, but also by increasing the likelihood of their exposure to adverse experiences.

Several studies looked at war-exposed patients with PTSD. Koenen and colleagues (2002) examined the individual and familial risk factors with exposure to trauma and PTSD in male twins (n = 6744) from the Vietnam Era Twin Registry. Using the independent reports of familial psychopathology from co-twins, they found that the risk of exposure to traumatic events was increased by a family history of mood disorders. In addition, they found that the risk of developing PTSD following exposure was increased by paternal depression.

Connor and Davidson (1997) reviewed studies of PTSD patients from World Wars I and II. Of the studies that included a control group, a greater incidence of psychiatric problems was found in the family members of the soldiers with PTSD symptoms.

When considering an individual with mental illness, some studies suggest either a link between this and the propensity towards risky behavior leading to PTSD or a direct link to developing PTSD itself. Bromet and colleagues (1998) found that a past or present history of a substance abuse disorder increased the individual's risk of exposure to trauma by 50%, while Kessler and colleagues (1995) showed that patients with PTSD have rates of comorbid psychiatric disorders approaching 100%.

Koenen and associates (2002) also found that preexisting conduct disorder and preexisting substance dependence increased the risk of exposure to traumatic events. The risk of developing PTSD following exposure was increased by preexisting conduct disorder, panic disorder, generalized anxiety disorder, and major depressive disorder. Interestingly, they found that pre-existing mood disorders in the individual were associated with decreased odds of traumatic exposure.

Chantarujikapong and associates (2001) conducted a twin study of GAD symptoms, panic disorder symptoms, and PTSD in men from the Vietnam Era Twin Registry of mono- and dizygotic male-male twin pairs aged 33 to 53. They looked at the lifetime co-occurence of generalized anxiety disorder symptoms, panic disorder symptoms, and PTSD and found additive genetic contributions from all three disorders. In fact, they found that the additive genetic contributions specific to PTSD accounted for 13.6% of the genetic variance in PTSD.

Xian and colleagues (2001) conducted a twin study of the overlap symptoms of PTSD, alcohol dependence and drug dependence in men from the Vietnam Era Twin Registry of mono- and dizygotic male-male twin pairs. In the end, they found that the liability for PTSD was partially due to a 15.3% genetic contribution common to alcohol dependence and drug dependence and a 20% genetic contribution specific to PTSD.

As for the heritability of PTSD in and of itself, King and colleagues (2001) used an animal model of congenital learned help-lessness to study the effects of genetic predisposition as a risk factor for the development of PTSD-like behaviors. Exposure to intermittent stress in the presence and absence of situational cues resulted in an increase in pain tolerance and a decrease in performance on spatial memory tests. These animals also had a blunted post-stress corticosterone response and exhibited physi-ologic symptoms of analgesia, cognitive deficits, and hypore-sponsivity of the HPA axis similar to those observed in human subjects with PTSD.

True and associates (1993) looked at Vietnam War veterans and Skre and colleagues (1993) looked at Scandinavian anxiety disorder patients. Both were twin studies that supported the her-itability of most PTSD symptoms.

In 1999, True and Lyons conducted twin studies of PTSD symptoms and the contributions of genetic and environmental factors using the Vietnam Era Twin Registry. They found that genetic predisposition, as opposed to environmental factors, accounted for approximately 30% of the predilection toward developing PTSD symptoms (intrusive unpleasant memories, only 10%).

There have been very few molecular studies involving PTSD. Comings and colleagues in 1996 reported that the A1 allele of the dopamine-2 receptor was significantly more common among PTSD patients than controls. This could not be replicated by Gelernter and associates (1999).

When studying the genetics of PTSD, we may fare better by considering the use of disease-associated traits to designate affected status in genetic studies of diseases. This approach has been useful towards studying the genetics of other diseases such as schizophrenia, seizure disorders, and diabetes. For example, Ryan and colleagues (1992) found that proneness to startle may be related to alterations on chromosome 5. This in turn may be related to a defect in the regulation of GABA (Dubowitz et al., 1992). As previously mentioned, proneness to violence may be a component of some PTSD cases or may lead to PTSD. Kagan and associates (1988) hypothesized that this may be related to impairment in serotonin synthesis secondary to a genetic abnormality. Or, as quoted above from Terrie Moffit's group, secondary to an X-linked gene that produces lower than normal level MAO-A, which in turn may lead to higher levels of adult male violence in the presence of a history of childhood maltreatment (Begley, 2002).

The variety of symptoms that constitute the PTSD phenotype, a high frequency of comorbid conditions, and a wide range of psychopathology present among family members of patients with PTSD all suggest a more complex mode of inheritance. In addition, it is likely that more than one gene collaborates to produce the phenotype and that different sets of genes can cause the PTSD phenotype (Radant et al., 2001).

In conclusion, what must be kept in mind while assessing children with suspected PTSD is that it is important to conduct thorough interviews with the parents and the child. These interviews should include the family history, the child's developmental history prior to the traumatic event, a detailed description of the event, a subjective opinion from the child of how the traumatic event affected him or her, and the parents' perception of how the child has changed after the traumatic event (Yule, 2001).

References

Antelman SM. (1988). The dependent sensitization as the cornerstone for a new approach to pharmacotherapy: drugs as foreign or stressful stimuli. *Drug Dev Res.* 14:1–30

Arnsten AFT. (1993). The biology of being frazzled. *Science.* 280:1711–1712.

Arora FC, Fichtner CG, O'Connor F, et al. (1993). Paroxetine binding in the blood platelets of posttraumatic stress disorder patients. *Life Sci.* 53:919–928.

Begley, S. (2002). Genes may determine which abused kids will 'grow up bad.' *Wall Street Journal.* September 20:B1.

Bremner JD. (2002). Effects of stress on memory and the brain. In: *Does Stress Damage the Brain?* New York: Norton; 100–135.

Bremner JD, Davis M, Southwick SM, et al. (1993). Neurobiology of posttraumatic stress disorder. In: *Review of Psychiatry*, Vol. 12, JM Oldham, MB Riba, A Tasman, eds. Washington, DC: American Psychiatric Press; 183–205.

Bremner JD, Narayan M, Staib LH, et al. (1999). Neural correlates of memories of childhood sexual abuse in women with and without posttraumatic stress disorder. *Am J Psychiatry.* 156:1787–1795.

Bremner JD, Randall P, Scott TM, et al. (1995). MRI-based measure of hippocampal volume in patients with PTSD. *Am J Psychiatry.* 152:973–981.

Bremner JD, Staib LH, Kaloupek D. (1999). Neural correlates of exposure to traumatic pictures and sound in Vietnam combat veterans with and without posttraumatic stress disorder: a positron emission tomography study. *Biol Psychiatry*. 45:806–816.

Breslau N, David GC, Andreski P. (1995). Risk factors for PTSD-related traumatic event: a prospective analysis. *Am J Psychiatry*. 152:529–535.

Breslau N, David GC, Andreski P, Peterson E. (1991). Traumatic events and posttraumatic stress disorder in an urban population of young adults. *Arch Gen Psychiatry*. 48:216–222.

Breslau N, Kessler RC, Chilcoat HD, Schultz LR, David GC, Andreski P. (1998). Trauma and posttraumatic stress disorder in the community: the 1996 Detroit area survey of trauma. *Arch Gen Psychiatry*. 55:626–632.

Bromet, Sonnega A, Kessler RC. (1998). Risk Factors for DSM-III-R posttraumatic stress disorder: finding from the National Comorbidity Survey. *Am J Epidemiol*. 147:353–361.

Cahill L. (1997). The neurobiology of emotionally influenced memory: implications for understanding traumatic memory. *Ann NY Acad Sci*. 821:238–246.

Canive JM, Lewine JD, Orrison WW Jr. (1997). MRI reveals gross structural abnormalities in PTSD. *Ann NY Acad Sci*. 821:512–515.

Chantarujikapong SI, Scherrer JF, Xian H, et al. (2001). A twin study of generalized anxiety disorder symptoms, panic disorder symptoms and post-traumatic stress disorder in men. *Psychiatry Res*.103:133–146.

Charney DS, Deutsch AY, Krystal JH, et al. (1993). Psychobiological mechanisms of posttraumatic stress disorder. *Arch Gen Psychiatry*. 50:294–305.

Comings DE, Mehleman D, Gysin R. (1996). Dopamine D2 receptor (DRD2) gene and susceptibility to posttraumatic stress disorder: a study and replication. *Biol Psychiatry*. 40:368–372.

Connor KM, Davidson JR. (1997). Familial risk factors in posttraumatic stress disorder. *Ann NY Acad Sci*. 821:35–51.

DeBellis MD, Baum AS, Birmaher B, et al. (1999). A.E. Bennett Research Award: Developmental traumatology: Part I: Biological Stress Systems. *Biol Psychiatry*. 45:1259–1270.

DeBellis MD, Chrousos GP, Dorn LD, et al. (1994). HPA axis dysregulation in sexually abused girls. *J Clin Endocrinol Metab*. 78:249–255.

DeBellis MD, Keshavan MS, Clark DB, et al. (1999). A.E. Bennett Research Award: Developmental traumatology: Part II: Brain Development. *Biol Psychiatry*. 45:1271–1284.

Dent RRM, Guilleminault G, Albert LH, et al. (1981). Diurnal rhythm of plasma immunoreactive beta-endorphin and its relationship to sleep stage and plasma rhythms of cortisol and prolactin. *J Clin Endocrinol Metab*. 52:942–947.

Deykin EY, Buka SL. (1997). Prevalence and risk factors for posttraumatic stress disorder among chemically dependent adolescents. *Amer J Psychiatry*. 154:752–757.

Dubowitz LM, Bouz AH, Hird MF, et al. (1992). Low cerebrospinal fluid concentration of free gamma-aminobutyric acid in startle disease. *Lancet*. 340:80–81.

Duman RS, Heninger GR, Nestler EJ. (1994). Molecular psychiatry: adaptations of receptor-coupled signal transduction pathways underlying stress- and drug-induced neural plasticity. *J Nerv Ment Dis*. 182:692–700.

Gelernter J, Southwick S, Goodson S, Morgan A, Nagy L, Charney DS. (1999). No association between D2 dopamine receptor (DRD2) 'A' system alleles, or (DRD2) haplotypes, and posttraumatic stress disorder. *Biol Psychiatry*. 45:620–625.

Gill M, Vallada H, Collier D, et al. (1996). A combined analysis of D22S278 marker alleles in affected sib-pairs: support for a susceptibility locus for schizophrenia at chromosome 22q 12. Schizophrenia Collaborative Linkage Group (Chromosome 22). *Am J Med Genetics*. 67:40–45.

Gross-Isseroff R, Dillon KA, Fieldust SJ, et al. (1990). Autoradiographic analysis of alpha-2 noradrenergic receptors in the human brain. *Arch Gen Psychiatry*. 47:1049–1053.

Heim C, Newport J, Heit S, et al. (2000). Pituitary-adrenal autonomic responses to stress in women after sexual and physical abuse in childhood. *JAMA*. 284:592–597.

Kagan J, Reznick JS, Snidman N. (1988). Biological basis of childhood shyness. *Science*. 240:167–171.

Kessler C, Sonnega A, Bromet E, Hughes M, Nelson CB. (1995). Posttraumatic stress disorder in the National Comorbidity Survey. *Arch Gen Psychiatry*. 52:1048–1060.

King JA, Abend S, Edwards E. (2001). Genetic predisposition and the development of posttraumatic stress disorder in an animal model. *Biol Psychiatry.* 50:231–237.

Koenen HC, Harley R, Lyons MJ, et al. (2002). A twin registry study of familial and individual risk factors for trauma exposure and posttraumatic stress disorder. *J Nerv Ment Dis.* 190:209–218.

Kosten TR, Krystal J. (1988). Biological mechanisms in posttraumatic stress disorder: Relevance for substance abuse. In: Galanter M, ed. *Recent Developments in Alcoholism.* New York: Plenum; 49–68.

Lemieux AM, Coe CL. (1995). Abuse related posttraumatic stress disorder: evidence for chronic neuroendocrine activation in women. *Psychosomatic Medicine.* 57:105–115.

Mason JW, Giller EL, Kosten TR, et al. (1986). Urinary free-cortisol levels in posttraumatic stress disorder patients. *J Nerv Ment Dis.* 174:145–149.

McEwen BS, Brinton R, Harrelson A, et al. (1987). Modulatory interactions between steroid hormones, neurotransmitters and neuropeptides in hippocampus. In: Nerozzi D, Goodwin G, Costa E, eds. *Hypothalamic Dysfunction in Neuropsychiatric Disorders.* New York: Raven Press; 87–102.

McEwen BS, Magarinos AM. (1997). Stress effects of morphology and function of the hippocampus. *Ann NY Acad Sci.* 821:271–284.

McFarlane AC. (1997). The prevalence and longitudinal course of PTSD: implications for the neurobiological models of PTSD. *Ann NY Acad Sci.* 821:10–23.

McFarlane AC. (1999). Risk Factors for the acute biological and psychological response to trauma. In Yehuda R, ed. *Risk Factors for Posttraumatic Stress Disorder.* Washington, DC: American Psychiatric Press; 163–190.

McFarlane AC, Atchison M, Yehuda R. (1997). The acute stress response following motor vehicle accidents and its relation to PTSD. *Ann NY Acad Sci.* 821:437–441.

Myslobodsky MS, Glickson J, Singer J, et al. (1995). Changes of brain anatomy in patients with posttraumatic stress disorder: a pilot magnetic resonance imagine study. *Psychiatry Res.* 58:259–264.

Nutt DJ. (2000). The psychobiology of posttraumatic stress disorder. *J Clin Psychiatry.* 61 (suppl):24–29.

Orcutt HK, Erickson DJ, Wolfe J. (2002). A prospective analysis of trauma exposure: the mediating role of PTSD symptomotology. *J Trauma Stress.* 15:256–266.

Pickworth WB, Sharpe LG, Nozaki M, et al. (1977). Sleep suppression induced by intravenous and intraventricular infusions of methoxamine in the dog. *Exp Neurol.* 57:999–1011.

Pitman R, Orr S. (1990). Twenty-four hour urinary cortisol and catecholamine excretion in combat-related posttraumatic stress disorder. *Biol Psychiatry.* 27: 245–247.

Pitman RK, Shin LM, Rauch SL. (2001). Investigating the pathogenesis of posttraumatic stress disorder with neuroimaging. *J Clin Psychiatry.* 62 (suppl 17):47–45.

Pynoos R, Frederick C, Nader K, et al. (1987). Life threat and posttraumatic stress disorder in school age children. *Arch Gen Psychiatry.* 44:1057–1063.

Radant A, Tsuang D, Peskind E, McFall M, Raskind W. (2001). Biological markers and diagnostic accuracy in the genetics of posttraumatic stress disorder. *Psychiatry Res.* 102:203–215.

Rauch SL, van der Kolk BA, Fisler R, et al. (1996). A symptom provocation study using positron emission tomography and script driven military imagery. *Arch Gen Psychiatry.* 53:380–387.

Reich J, Lyons M, Cai B. (1996). Familial vulnerability factors to posttraumatic stress disorder in male military veterans. *Acta Psychiatrica Scandinavica.* 93:105–112.

Resnick HS, Yehuda R, Pitman RK, et al. (1995). Effect of previous trauma on acute plasma cortisol level following rape. *Am J Psychiatry.* 152:1675–1677.

Ryan SG, Sherman SL, Terry JC, et al. (1992). Startle disease of the gene (SHTE) to chromosome 5q linkage analysis. *Ann Neurol.* 31:663–668.

Sack WH, Clarke GN, Seeley J. (1995). Posttraumatic stress disorder across two generations of Cambodian refugees. *J Am Acad Child Adolesc Psychiatry.* 34:1160–1166.

Schwab G, Hallmayer J, Albus M, et al. (1998). Further evidence for a susceptibility locus on chromosome 10p14-p11 in 72 families with schizoprenia by nonparametric linkage analysis. *Am J Med Genetics.* 81:302–307.

Shin LM, McNally RJ, Kosslyn SM, et al. (1999). Regional cerebral blood flow during script-driven imagery in childhood sexual abuse-related posttraumatic stress disorder: a ET investigation. Am J Psychiatry. 156: 575–584.

Skre I, Onstad S, Torgersen S, Lygren S, Kringlen E. (1993). A twin study of DSM-III-R anxiety disorder. Acta Psychiatrica Scandinavica. 88:85–92.

Southwick SM, Bremner D, Rasmussen A, et al. (1999). Role of norepinephrine in the pathophysiology and treatment of posttraumatic stress disorder. Biol Psychiatry. 45:1192–1204.

Southwick SM, Krystal JH, Bremner J. (1997). Noradrenergic and serotenergic function in posttraumatic stress disorder. Arch Gen Psychiatry. 54:749–758.

Stevens DR, McCarley RW, Greene RW. (1994). The mechanisms of noradrenergic alpha-1 excitatory modulation of pontine reticular formation neurons. J Neuroscience. 14:6481–6487.

Taylor F, Raskind MA. (2002). The a1-adrenergic antagonist prazosin impoves sleep and nightmares in civilian trauma posttraumatic stress disorder. J Clin Psychopharmacology. 22:82–85.

True WR, Lyons MJ. (1999). Genetic risk factors for PTSD: a twin study. In: Yehuda R, ed. Risk Factors for Posttraumatic Stress Disorder. Washington DC: American Psychiatric Press; 68–71.

True WR, Rick J, Eisen SA, et al. (1993). A twin study of genetic and environmental contributions to liability for posttraumatic stress symptoms. Arch Gen Psychiatry. 50:257–264.

Xian H, Chantarujikapong SI, Scherrer JF, et al. (2001). Genetic and environmental influences on posttraumatic stress disorder, alcohol and drug dependence in twin pairs. Drug Alcohol Dependence. 61:95–102.

Yehuda R. (1997). Hypothalamic-pituitary-adrenal in PTSD. In: Yehuda R, Mc Farlane AC, eds. Psychobiology of Posttraumatic Stress Disorder. NY Acad Sci. 821:437–441.

Yehuda R. (2001). Biology of posttraumatic stress disorder. J Clin Psychiatry. 62 (suppl.)17:41–46.

Yehuda R, Bierer LM, Schmeidler J, et al. (2000). Low cortisol and the risk for PTSD in adult offspring of holcaust survivors. Am J Psychiatry. 157:1252–1259.

Yehuda R, Keefer RSE, Harvey PD, et al. (1995). Learning and memory in combat veterans with posttraumatic stress disorder. *Am J Psychiatry*. 152:137–139.

Yehuda R, McFarlane AC. (1995). Conflict between current knowledge about PTSD and its original conceptual basis. *Am J Psychiatry*. 152:1705–1713.

Yehuda R, Southwick SM, Nussbaum EL, Giller EL, Mason JW. (1991). Low urinary cortisol in PTSD. *J Nerv Ment Dis*. 178:366–369.

Yehuda R, Southwick SM, Perry BD, et al. (1990). Interactions of the hypothalamic-pituitary-adrenal axis and the catecholaminergic system in posttraumatic stress disorder. In: Giller EL, ed. *Biological Assessment and Treatment of Posttraumatic Stress Disorder*. Washington, DC: American Psychiatric Press; 115–134.

Yule W. (2001). Posttraumatic stress disorder in the general population and in children. *J Clin Psychiatry*. 62 (suppl.)17:23–28.

7

■

Clinical Findings Regarding PTSD in Children and Adolescents

Kenneth Spitalny

Since 1980, when the American Psychiatric Association formally recognized posttraumatic stress disorder (PTSD) as a mental disorder, our knowledge of PTSD in children has grown. Initially, there was controversy as to whether children could suffer from this disorder (Benedek, 1985). However, recent studies of children and life studies of adults have deepened our understanding of the extent and nature of PTSD in children. It has been found that, especially in younger children, the clinical presentation of PTSD can have a different presentation from that of the adult (Yule, 2001; Scheeringa et al., 1995).

This chapter will examine how children and adolescents with PTSD present in clinical practice. In order to do so, we must better understand the natural course of PTSD from the initial trauma to psychological processing to clinical presentation. In clinical practice, children and adolescents often present with difficulty functioning in settings in which they previously thrived. In these cases, the role of the clinician is to determine the presence, nature, and source of the problem, working backwards from clinical presentation to psychological processing to the initial trauma.

We will examine evidence-based information and will grapple with those questions that are harder to answer but are of utmost concern to the treating therapist. The chapter will examine the following questions: (1) defining PTSD; what the

141

DSM-IV criteria for PTSD are and what some issues that arise from that definition are; (2) the natural course of PTSD in children; what we know about the course of life-threatening trauma and the development of PTSD in children; (3) the epidemiology of trauma and PTSD in children; what we know about the circumstances that place children at risk for developing PTSD; (4) the clinical presentation; how children present with PTSD and which presentations are more difficult to diagnose; and (5) the future direction of state-of-the-art research in PTSD; from the clinician's point of view what the essential questions are that should be brought to the attention of those working in clinical research.

Defining Posttraumatic Stress Disorder

Posttraumatic stress disorder is categorized as an anxiety disorder. In order to meet the criteria for diagnosis, it requires features from three different symptom constellations: re-experiencing, avoidance, and hyperarousal. These symptom clusters represent a mixture of social, psychological, and biological processes (Shalev, 2001). Table 1 shows the *Diagnostic and Statistical Manual of Mental Disorders, Fourth Edition (DSM-IV)* criteria for the diagnosis of PTSD (American Psychiatric Association, 1994). The following are some issues that require attention regarding the *DSM-IV* diagnosis of posttraumatic stress disorder:

1. the overlap in criteria among PTSD and other psychiatric disorders, in particular depressive disorders,
2. the importance of the conditional criteria of significant distress or impairment of functioning, criteria F,
3. severity, because of its bearing on clinical presentation and its potential impact on prognosis and treatment decisions,
4. delayed onset PTSD, when symptom onset occurs more than 6 months after the traumatic event (the follow-up

period for children who have been exposed to life-threatening trauma needs to be carefully thought out),

5. and, the difficulties in identifying childhood PTSD by health care providers and clinicians.

There is much overlap in the diagnostic criteria for posttraumatic stress disorder in children and other psychiatric disorders, especially depressive disorders. This issue requires close attention because it may confound diagnoses and impact on treatment plans. The characteristics identified in Table 1 are jointly held in the diagnosis of PTSD and depressive disorders.

TABLE 1.

Comparison of DSM-IV Symptom Overlap between Posttraumatic Stress Disorder and Major Depressive Disorder

Posttraumatic Stress Disorder	Major Depressive Episode
1 C. (4) markedly diminished interest . . . in significant activities	A. (2) markedly diminished interest . . . in all, or almost all, activities . . .
2 C. (6) restricted range of affect	A. (1) depressed mood most of day. . .
3 D. (1) difficulty falling or staying asleep	A. (4) insomnia or hypersomnia nearly every day
4 D. (2) irritability or outburst of anger	A. (1) in children and adolescents, can be irritable mood [instead of depressed mood]
5 D. (3) difficulty concentrating	A. (8) diminished ability to think or concentrate. . .
6 E. Duration of the disturbance . . . is more than a month.	A. . . . symptoms have been present during the same 2-week period. . .
7 F. The disturbance causes clinically significant distress or impairment in social, occupational, or other important areas of functioning	C. The symptoms cause clinically significant distress or impairment in social, occupational, or other important areas of functioning.

This overlap means that a depressed patient who has experienced life-threatening trauma and has one of the five reexperiencing symptoms would most likely meet the criteria for PTSD. Conversely, PTSD patients who have broader symptoms not related to a specific trauma would meet criteria for depressive disorders. The overlapping criteria seem to be one of the reasons that these two disorders are frequently diagnosed concurrently. Overlaps can be found for other depressive and anxiety disorders. Furthermore, severe stress would tend to exacerbate the underlying condition.

Although the *DSM-IV* criteria define the diagnosis PTSD, it does not give any indication as to the severity of the disorder. The degree of impairment of functioning serves as one indicator of severity. In the *DSM-IV*, functional impairment is a bedrock concept. It is included as a part of multiaxial assessment and a necessary condition for diagnosis of most psychiatric disorders. "[It] is useful in planning treatment and measuring its impact, and in predicting outcome" (American Psychiatric Association, 1994). It is through functional impairment that the psychiatric disorder impinges on the ability of the person to meet basic goals. Although further study is necessary, the degree of impairment of function probably has prognostic implications for the course of posttraumatic stress disorder and the need for intervention. This is one reason why functioning is an integral and required component of the diagnostic statement. In fact, it is often the impairment that brings the child or adolescent to the attention of the family and requires a clinician's attention. Sometimes, the impairment in functioning is noted by the parents or caretakers; they observe that the child is withdrawing from participating in family activities, has become more defiant towards them, or more aggressive towards siblings or housemates. Frequently, those overseeing the child in other life activities, such as school, day care, and after-school programs, note changes. They observe deterioration in the child's schoolwork or the ability to reach goals of directed activities. In addition, relationships with peers and adults may have become either divisive or disengaged. The relationship of PTSD to functional impairment is beginning to be explored. In the section on the natural course of this disorder, the first steps in understanding this relationship will be described using longitudinal studies that examine single-event traumas.

The issue of severity requires further attention because of its importance to clinical presentation, duration of illness, and functioning. Research studies have had to deal with this issue by creating standardized scales to measure severity. One such instrument, which is the one most commonly used in research on children with PTSD, has been the PTSD Reaction Index (Frederick, 1985; Goenjian et al., 1995; Pynoos et al., 1987). It has undergone the most thorough examination for reliability and validity and has been shown to have a high correlation with clinical diagnosis (Cohen et al., 1998). Pynoos and colleagues (1993), in their study of PTSD in children after the 1988 Armenian earthquake, found severity to be related to degree of exposure. In addition, they found those children who had a high degree of severity by their instrument were those who were likely to be diagnosed as having PTSD by clinical interview.

A fourth issue in the discussion of the diagnosis of posttraumatic stress disorder is that of delayed onset PTSD. In adults, many of those initially thought to be presenting with delayed-onset PTSD have turned out to be delayed in seeking help or were patients with partial PTSD with exacerbation. Solomon and colleagues (1989) reviewed 150 Israeli soldiers seeking psychiatric help at 6 months to 5 years after the war with Lebanon and found 40% had delayed in seeking help, 33% had subclinical PTSD, 4% had another psychiatric disorder, 13% had reactivation of PTSD in remission, and only 10% were considered to have delayed-onset PTSD. In addition, over time, individuals are exposed to other traumatic events and the relationship between the original stressor and the disorder can become muddled. In a 17-year follow-up study of children exposed to a dam collapse, Green and colleagues (1994) found that there was no difference in PTSD symptoms in those exposed to the flooding in comparison to those who were not directly exposed. Scheeringa and colleagues (1995) have noted the difficulty of meeting the case definition in young children (less than 48 months of age) because of its dependence on verbal ability. He has challenged the applicability of the *DSM-IV* criteria in this age cohort. At a later age, when a child's cognitive abilities mature, they would be able to meet the case criteria. Furthermore, the initial diagnosis is often dependent on a caretaking adult who might not initially recognize the child's symptoms (Yule, 2001). For all of these reasons, one must be cautious in making a diagnosis of delayed-onset PTSD in children.

Frequently, caregivers, teachers, and clinicians miss the depth of a child's response to a traumatic event. Psychiatrists paralleled this situation in the 1980s when there was ongoing controversy as to whether children could develop PTSD. It was argued that children were not cognitively or emotionally capable of responding in such a way. In addition, parents often have difficulty identifying the profound impact of trauma on their children. Some reasons for this may be that often parents or caregivers are responding to the traumatic event themselves and deny its effects on both themselves and their children; sometimes the parents or caregivers are the source of the trauma and have difficulty acknowledging their complicity; and sometimes, it is difficult for parents or caregivers to have insight into their children's psyches. Therefore, although clinicians might be able to discern the depth of response and be able to diagnose an internalizing disorder (i.e., depression), without insight from the parent or disclosure from the patient, they may not be able to determine an exacerbating source.

The Natural Course of Posttraumatic Stress Disorder

Over the past two decades, a series of studies on life-threatening events affecting children has deepened our understanding of the natural course of posttraumatic stress disorder in children. These studies have a core set of features and design elements. The common features include: (1) a traumatic event that lasted for a discrete period, usually hours to days; (2) the events were beyond the control of the community or family; and (3) several children concomitantly experienced the events. In addition, the events were examined using a similar methodological frame in that they were longitudinal, a cohort of children similarly exposed were systematically examined in at least two periods; most of the exposed population or a representative sample were examined; a standardized format was used; an appropriate comparison group was also studied to determine the relative impact of the exposure on the affected population; and there was a good measurement of PTSD. This measurement was either based on clinical interview, an instrument based on *DSM III-R* or *IV* criteria, or was a measurement that was validated against a clinical interview (Pine & Cohen, 2002). Although we can learn more about how stressors are related to psychiatric disorders from discrete stressors, the more common phenomenon are ongoing stressors, frequently initiated by a person well known by the child. Terr (1991) referred to such traumas, including physical and sexual abuse, that result in psychiatric disorders that she called *Type II trauma disorders*. These have a different course and prognosis than the single event Type I trauma disorders.

In this section, we will review those studies that have met the preceding characteristics concerning the discrete event trauma and the methodological rigor of the study. In total, these studies have made a major contribution to our understanding of the effect of traumatic exposure on the psyche of the child. We will first give an overview of those studies, then discuss what was learned about the natural course of PTSD in children, including modifying factors, other psychopathologies, and the relationship of this disorder to the ability to function. Finally, those key points that bear on clinical presentation will be reviewed.

Table 2 compares the characteristics of seven of these studies, in terms of the type of exposure, number of children with most intense type of exposure, age of children, time periods at which the children were studied, and date of the traumatic event.

Seven Studies of the Effects of Life-Threatening Events on Children

1. On February 26, 1972, a dam in an Appalachian community collapsed, killing 125 people and leaving thousands homeless. Forty-eight percent (99/207) of the children of families involved in a lawsuit were followed at 2 and 17 years later (Green et al., 1991; Green, 1994; Green et al., 1994).

2. In February 1984, a sniper with a semi-automatic weapon and two 12-gauge shotguns opened fire on a crowded elementary playground, killing one child, wounding one staff member, and injuring more than 13 children. Nineteen of the playground children and comparison groups were examined at 1, 6, and 14 months after the event (Pynoos et al., 1987; Nader, 1990).

3. In June 1985, a train hit a bus with 3 adults and 33 children in it. The 3 adults and 19 children were killed. Survivors and a comparison group were examined at 1 week, 9 months, and 7 years after the collision (Milgram et al., 1988; Tyano et al., 1996).

4. In October 1988, about 400 school children from the United Kingdom were on board the cruise ship *Jupiter*, leaving Pireaus, Greece, when it was struck by another ship. The *Jupiter* sank within 45 minutes. One school child and a teacher remained unaccounted for, and 2 rescue workers were crushed to death during the rescue. The investigations took place at 5 months and 5 to 8 years afterwards (Yule et al., 2000; Udwin et al., 2000).

5. On December 7, 1988, an earthquake with a magnitude of 6.9 on the Richter scale struck Armenia, killing at least 25,000 people. The study included children from three sites, which were at varying distances from the epicenter. Forty-seven of the children were from the town of Spitak and had the highest exposure. Children from the three sites were examined at 18 months and 3 years after the event (Pynoos et al., 1993; Goenjian et al., 1995; Goenjian et al., 1997).

6. In January 1991, during the Persian Gulf War, the Israeli civilian population was attacked for 3 weeks by Iraqi SCUD missiles. The study compares people from one neighborhood in Tel Aviv who were displaced because their homes had been destroyed by the missiles with others whose homes remained intact. Children ages 3 to 5 years old at the onset of the study were examined at 5, 30, and 60 months after exposure (Laor et al., 1996, 1997, 2001).

7. On August 24, 1992, Hurricane Andrew devastated southern Florida. Winds of 164 miles per hour damaged approximately 100,000 homes, causing 35 deaths. Studies were done at 8 weeks, 32 weeks, and 21 months after the hurricane on 30 children who were in a high impact area exposed to the hurricane (Shaw et al., 1995, 1996).

TABLE 2.
Key Studies on the Relationship between Exposure to Trauma and PTSD

Key Study	Nature of Trauma	Time of Study After Exposure	Source of Example	Instrument	Comparison Group(s)	PTSD Measurement by Exposure
Green, et al., 1994	Dam collapse	17 years	Lawsuit registry	SCID	Similar community (HE, NE)	3% less cases (HE<NE)
Nader, et al., 1990	Sniper attack	14 months	School registry	CPTSDRI	Exposure level (HE, ME, LE, NE)	≈ 3.5% more symptoms* (HE>ME)
Tyano, et al., 1966	Train-Bus collision	7 years	Accident registry	PTSD Inventory	Exposure level (HE, ME, LE, NE)	2.9% more symptoms* (HE>ME)
Yule, et al., 2000	Ship disaster	5–8 year	Ship registry	CAPS	Community control (HE NE)	48.3% more cases* (HE, NE)
Pynoos, et al., 1993	Earthquake	1.5 years	School survey	CPTSDRI	Exposure level (HE, ME, LE)	23.1% more were classified as having severe symptomatology* (HE>ME)

TABLE 2. *continued*

| Laor, et al., 1997 | SCUD missile attack | 30 months | Victim registry | PTSD Inventory | Exposure level (HE, ME) | 4.3% more were classified as having severe symptomatology (HE>ME) |
| Shaw, et al., 1995 | Hurricane | 8 weeks | School survey | CPTSDRI | Exposure level (HE, ME) | 17.8% more were classified as having severe symptomatology (HE>ME) |

* P<.05

CAPS, Clinician Administered PTSD Scale; CPTSDRI, Children's Posttraumatic Stress Disorder Reaction Index; HE, high exposure; LE, lower exposure; ME, medium exposure; NE, no exposure; PTSD Inventory, Posttraumatic Stress Disorder Inventory; SCID, Structured Clinical Interview for DSM-III-R.

All seven studies showed a relationship between intensity of exposure and proportion of the population or sample affected. In fact, in comparing the studies, there tended to be a relationship between the magnitude of life threat and the proportion of the population being diagnosed with PTSD, the duration, and the severity of symptoms. Of the seven events, there were two patterns of exposure. The first was a limited-duration type of exposure in which the trauma was short lived and directed at the affected children themselves. In the other type of exposure, the trauma was directed at the community and affected families as well as the children, and the impact on families included their livelihood and displacement from their homes. The two different patterns of exposure cannot be compared to each other, as the first was an acute, severe threat to the children themselves, while the other was more complex in that it also affected the families and communities of the children, making them less available to support the children afterwards.

In those three events whose major impact was on the children, the exposure was profound but short lived. In the sniper attack on children, at 1 month, 94% of the children on the playground were noted to have PTSD symptoms, and at 14 months, 74% of those children had PTSD symptoms (Pynoos et al., 1987; Nader et al., 1990). Tyano and colleagues (1996) reported that after 7 years, the individuals involved in the train collision had more PTSD symptoms (4.38 symptoms) than those individuals who witnessed the collision (1.45 symptoms). In the other study of British children followed for PTSD after their boat sank, 34% were suffering from the disorder at 5 to 8 years later (Yule et al., 2000).

In the four studies involving the family, the traumatic event had profound effects on the community. In those children exposed to a dam collapse, 37% were given a probable diagnosis of PTSD at 2 years after the event. Fifteen years later, only 4% were noted probably to have PTSD (Green et al., 1991, 1994). In those children exposed to the earthquake in Spitak, the city closest to the epicenter, 92% had severe symptoms 18 months after the event (Pynoos et al., 1993). In young children exposed to SCUD missiles, 8% had severe symptoms 3 years after the event, and those numbers did not change at 5 years (Laor et al., 1997, 2001). It is unclear whether the low rate is due to the nature of the threat or the younger age of the children. In children exposed to Hurricane Andrew, severe PTSD symptoms were found in 55% of the children studied at 2 months, 48% at 8 months, and 33% at 21 months (Shaw et al., 1995, 1996). Three studies undertook a more thorough examination using a multivariate model to determine the likelihood of developing PTSD. In order to determine that this relationship is due to a putative factor and not the result of a confounding factor, one needs to look at multiple factors related to the outcome variable. In the most comprehensive study, that of the British school children by Udwin and colleagues (2000), preliminary information was obtained at 5 months, but further information was sought on children 5 to 8 years after the ship accident. Multiple factors were examined including demographic variables, predisaster risk factors, disaster-related factors, and postdisaster factors. In addition, data from a screening battery of queries using the Impact of Events Scale, the Revised Children's Manifest Anxiety Scale, and the Birleson Depression Inventory were used. They found that the factors related to developing PTSD were degree of exposure and appraisal of threat to life and ratings of anxiety obtained 5 months postdisaster. For those survivors who developed PTSD, the duration and severity, determined by the number of symptoms, was best predicted by: (1) vulnerability factors of social, physical, and psychological difficulties in childhood; (2) ratings of depression obtained 5 months postdisaster, and (3) whether survivors received postdisaster support at school.

Laor and colleagues (1997) looked at the relationship of developing PTSD symptoms in children exposed to SCUD missiles and found only one variable related to symptoms, which was the mother's avoidant symptoms based on the Impact of Events Scale. However, it should be noted that the model could explain only 8% of the variability in PTSD symptoms. Green and colleagues (1991) also looked at the PTSD symptoms in children affected by the collapse of the dam. The multivariate analysis model and showed that the magnitude of threat, gender, parental psychopathology, and an irritable and/or depressed family atmosphere were associated with the children's symptoms.

Several of the studies have looked at the relationship between PTSD symptoms and other psychopathology. The most comprehensive seems to be the one examining the Armenian earthquake. Goenjian and colleagues (1995) looked at psychiatric comorbidity after the earthquake, testing school age children on the Child Posttraumatic Stress Disorder Reaction Index, the Depression Self-Rating Scale (DSRS; Asarrow & Carlson, 1985) and a section on separation anxiety disorder from the Diagnostic Interview Schedule for Children and Adolescents. They found that there was a strong correlation between PTSD and depressive symptoms, $r = .55$. In this sample, 66% were diagnosed with PTSD, 51% with major depression, and 43% with both. In addition, they found that the strongest predictor of depression severity was the severity of PTSD symptoms. Shaw and colleagues (1996) in the study on children affected by Hurricane Andrew found a relationship between PTSD symptoms and anxiety/depression using the Achenbach's Teachers Report Form. It was the only psychiatric scale that was found to be significantly abnormal in both genders. Udwin and colleagues (2000) in the study examining the ship disaster found that the score on the Revised Children's Manifest Anxiety Scale taken at 5 months after the event was an independent predictor of developing PTSD and the score on the Birleson Depression Inventory at 5 months after the event to be predictor of duration and severity of PTSD.

The degree of functional impairment has been less rigorously investigated. In the study of the effects of the SCUD missile attacks on young children, Laor and colleagues (1997) found no relationship between adaptive behavior using the Vineland Adaptive Behavior Scales and PTSD symptoms. Due to the young age of the children, this finding may not be generalized to older children.

The Epidemiology of Trauma and Posttraumatic Stress Disorder in Children and Adolescents

The previous studies highlight the psychological sequelae from life threatening trauma. However, most trauma does not occur as result of a community disaster. What can we learn from studies examining trauma that has affected individuals?

In a retrospective study examining a community sample whose ages ranged from 18 to 45 from the Detroit area, Breslau and colleagues (1998) looked at four types of trauma: (1) assault, (2) other types of trauma resulting in injury, (3) learning about trauma experienced by a loved one, and (4) the unexpected death of a loved one. The peak age for each type of trauma, except for the death of a loved one, occurred between 16 and 20 years old. In addition, Breslau's group described the risk of developing PTSD as extremely high at 36% in women sustaining trauma by assault, which included being mugged, badly beaten, raped, and sexually assaulted. Other studies in adults have found higher PTSD prevalence in women than in men (Breslau, 2001).

Giaconia and colleagues (1995) and Silverman and colleagues (1996) followed 384 children in an ongoing longitudinal survey in a northeastern American city. They found that 43% experienced trauma and of those 14.5% developed PTSD symptoms. Those who were raped (2%) had the highest incidence of PTSD (50%). When comparing the groups who sustained

trauma and developed PTSD, sustained trauma without developing PTSD, and those without trauma, they found those with
PTSD had poorer psychological functioning. This included
much higher rates of suicide attempts, 17% compared to 6% in
the trauma group, and 2% in the nontrauma group. In addition,
they found that those with PTSD had the highest prevalence of
major depression at 42%, compared to 9% and 6% respectively
in the three groups. Other disorders found to be significantly different in the three groups were simple phobias, social phobia,
and alcohol as well as drug dependence.

Fergusson and colleagues (1996) and Lynskey and Ferguson
(1997) studied sexual abuse of children and child psychiatric disorders by following a birth cohort of more than 1,000 New
Zealand children. They found that children who were sexually
abused had higher rates of major depression, anxiety disorder,
conduct disorder, substance use disorder, and suicidal behaviors
than children not reported to being abused. (Of note, PTSD was
not examined.) In addition, they found those who were reported
to have had sexual intercourse were at higher risk for the disorders. However, this relationship did not persist after the multivariate analysis was conducted incorporating other childhood
and family variables.

Horowitz and colleagues (1995) assessed past trauma and
PTSD symptoms in a cohort of teenage girls receiving care at an
adolescent clinic. Of 82 girls registered for an appointment at the
Yale-New Haven Hospital Clinic, 79 agreed to participate. Of
that group, 81% were African-American, 15% were Hispanic,
and 3% were white. The adolescents were queried on types of
community and domestic violence they experienced and
whether they met PTSD criteria based on reexperiencing, avoidance, and hyperarousal symptoms. Of the adolescent girls
studied, 67% met PTSD criteria and experienced a mean number
of 28 different types of community and domestic violence. Of

note, 30% saw violence between family members, 28% had been beaten up, 12% had been stabbed, at least 12% had been forced to have unwanted sexual contact, and 10% had been shot at.

In another study undertaken with inner-city children, Silva and colleagues (2000) followed 100 consecutive referrals to an inner-city child and adolescent psychiatric clinic to determine the type of trauma experienced and the proportion meeting PTSD criteria. They found that 59 children sustained trauma, and 13 (22% of the 59) met criteria for PTSD. Of note, antecedent anxiety correlated with meeting PTSD criteria and those with oppositional and defiant disorder and conduct disorder tended not to develop PTSD.

Galea and colleagues (2002) published one of the first of many studies on the psychological sequelae of the terrorist attacks on the World Trade Center in New York City on September 11, 2001. The researchers used random-digit dialing to obtain a representative sample of 1,008 adults living in a section of Manhattan. They found that 7.5% of the sample had PTSD related to the attack. In a multivariate model, they identified the following predictors for PTSD: Hispanic ethnicity, two or more prior stressors, a panic attack associated with the event, residence close to the World Trade Center, and loss of possessions. Studies on children have been undertaken to help us better understand the relationship of prior illness and PTSD, the impact of care provider response on children, the impact of media on PTSD, and the difference of predictive factors between children and adults.

In summary, adolescents living in cities have a high likelihood of being exposed to trauma and the development of PTSD. Previous anxiety and depressive symptoms place the adolescent at additional risk for developing PTSD. In those adolescents with PTSD, there is a high association with depressive disorder and higher likelihood of having anxiety disorder and alcohol and drug dependence. We will have a better understanding of PTSD in children living in cities when studies of the terrorist attacks on the World Trade Center are completed.

Confounds in Clinical Presentation of Posttraumatic Stress Disorder in Children

It is not uncommon for children and adolescents to present to a therapist with a change in mood or behavior after a traumatic event or having reexperiencing and hyperarousal symptoms that diminish their ability to function in school or other settings. In this section, we will address other presentations of PTSD that are more difficult to diagnose. Parents frequently are affected concurrently by traumatic events and life circumstances, and may not recognize that their children are also affected. In children, it is often more difficult to identify internalizing than externalizing disorders. The key to understanding difficult presentations is placing the psychological response in a developmental framework. With this in mind, we will discuss these presentations in terms of age cohorts: preschool children, school-aged children, and adolescents.

Because of limited cognitive and expressive language development, young children may present differently than older children. Scheeringa and colleagues (1995) had noted that 8 of the 18 clinical criteria of PTSD require verbal expression. In their review, they found young children more likely to present with anxiety symptoms: separation, stranger, and new fears. The young children might have avoidance symptoms that are not related to the original trauma. Scheeringa and associates suggested that the following symptoms might be indicative of PTSD in younger children: posttraumatic play, play reenactment, nightmares, constriction of play, social withdrawal, restricted range of affect, new fears, change towards aggressive behavior, and regression of developmental skills.

In school-aged children, Terr (1991) noted that these children tend to have less avoiding and numbing symptoms. They tend to reenact the trauma through their different modalities of communication, including play. Terr noted an increase in omen formation, believing that certain signs were warnings of the traumatic event that occurred and will reoccur. This is connected to the magical thinking of younger school-aged children.

Finally, with adolescents, as discussed in the epidemiological section, one should consider PTSD with a depressed youth, perhaps with drug and alcohol dependence. In these cases, it is often difficult to ascertain the nature of the trauma due to the youth's reluctance to disclose because of a perceived threat to his or her physical well-being, self-esteem, or regard held by others.

References

American Psychiatric Association (1994). *Diagnostic and Statistical Manual of Mental Disorders*, 4th ed. Washington, DC: American Psychiatric Association.

Asarrow JR, Carlson GA. (1995). Depression Self Rating Scale: utility with child psychiatric patients. *J Consult Clin Psychol.* 53:491–499.

Benedek E. (1985). Children and psychic trauma: A brief review of contemporary thinking. In: Eth S, Pynoos RS, eds. *Posttraumatic Stress Disorder in Children*. Washington, DC: American Psychiatric Press; 1–16.

Breslau N. (2001). The epidemiology of posttraumatic stress disorder: what is the extent of the problem? *J Clin Psychiatry.* 62 (suppl 17):16–22.

Breslau N, Kessler RC, Chilcoat HD, et al. (1998). Trauma and posttraumatic stress disorder in the community: the 1996 Detroit area survey of trauma. *Arch Gen Psychiatry.* 55:626–632.

Cohen JA, Work Group on Quality Issues (1998). Practice parameters for the assessment and treatment of children and adolescents with posttraumatic stress disorder. *J Am Acad Child Adolesc Psychiatry.* 37 (Suppl 10):4S–26S.

Fergusson DM, Horwood LJ, Lynskey MT. (1996). Childhood sexual abuse and psychiatric disorders in young adulthood: Part II: Psychiatric outcomes of childhood sexual abuse. *J Am Acad Child Adolesc Psychiatry.* 35:1365–1374.

Frederick CJ. (1985). Children traumatized by catastrophobic situations. In: Eth S, Pynoos RS, eds. *Posttraumatic Stress Disorder in Children.* Washington, DC: American Psychiatric Press; 71–100.

Galea S, Ahern J, Resnick H, et al. (2002). Psychological sequelae of the September 11 terrorist attacks in New York City. *N Engl J Med.* 346:982–987.

Giaconia RM, Reinherz HZ, Silverman AB, et al. (1995). Traumas and posttraumatic stress disorder in a community population of older adolescents. *J Am Acad Child Adolesc Psychiatry.* 34:1369–1380.

Goenjian AK, Karayan I, Pynoos RS, et al. (1997). Outcome of psychotherapy among early adolescents after trauma. *Am J Psychiatry.* 154:536–542.

Goenjian AK, Pynoos RS, Steinberg AM, et al. (1995). Psychiatry comorbidity in children after the 1988 earthquake in Armenia. *J Am Acad Child Adolesc Psychiatry.* 34:1174–1184.

Green B. (1994). Psychosocial research in traumatic stress: an update. *J Trauma Stress.* 7:341–362.

Green BL, Grace MC, Vary MG, et al. (1994). Children of disaster in the second decade: a 17-year follow-up of Buffalo Creek survivors. *J Am Acad Child Adolesc Psychiatry.* 33:71–79.

Green BL, Korol M, Grace M, et al. (1991). Children and disaster: age, gender, and parental effects on PTSD symptoms. *J Am Acad Child Adolesc Psychiatry.* 30:945–951.

Horowitz K, Weine S, Jekel J. (1995). PTSD symptoms in urban adolescent girls: compounded community trauma. *J Am Acad Child Adolesc Psychiatry.* 34:1353–1361.

Laor N, Wolmer L, Cohen D. (2001). Mothers' functioning and children's symptoms 5 years after a SCUD missile attack. *Am J Psychiatry.* 158:1020-1026.

Laor N, Wolmer L, Mayes L, et al. (1996). Israeli, preschool children under SCUDs missile attacks. *Arch Gen Psychiatry.* 53:416–423.

Laor N, Wolmer L, Mayes L, et al. (1997). Israeli preschool children under SCUDS: a 30-month follow-up. *J Am Acad Child Adolesc Psychiatry.* 36:349–356.

Lynskey MT, Fergusson DM. (1997). Factors protecting against the development of adjustment difficulties in young adults exposed to childhood sexual abuse. *Child Abuse Neglect.* 12:1177–1190.

Milgram NA, Toubiana Y, Klingman A, et al. (1988). Situational exposure and personal loss in children's acute and chronic reactions to a school disaster. *J Trauma Stress.* 1:339–352.

Nader K, Pynoos R, Fairbanks L, et al. (1990). Children's PTSD reactions one year after a sniper attack at their school. *Am J Psychiatry.* 147:1526–1530.

Pine DS, Cohen JA. (2002). Trauma in children and adolescents: risk and treatment of psychiatric sequelae. *Biol Psychiatry.* 51:519–531.

Pynoos RS, Frederick KC, Nader K, et al. (1987). Life threat and posttraumatic stress in school-age children. *Arch Gen Psychiatry.* 44:1057–1063.

Pynoos RS, Goenjian A, Tashjian M, et al. (1993). Posttraumatic stress reactions in children after the 1988 Armenian earthquake. *Br J Psychiatry.* 163:239–247.

Scheeringa MS, Zeanah CH, Drell MJ, et al. (1995). Two approaches to the diagnosis of posttraumatic stress disorder in infancy and early childhood. *J Am Acad Child Adolesc Psychiatry.* 34:191–200.

Shalev AY. (2001). What is posttraumatic stress disorder? *J Clin Psychiatry.* 62 (suppl 17): 4–10.

Shaw JA, Applegate B, Schorr C. (1996). Twenty-one-month follow-up study of school-age children exposed to Hurricane Andrew. *J Am Acad Child Adolesc Psychiatry.* 35:359–364.

Shaw JA, Applegate B, Tanner S, et al. (1995). Psychological effects of Hurricane Andrew on an elementary school population. *J Am Acad Child Adolesc Psychiatry.* 34:1185–1192.

Silva RR, Alpert M, Munoz D, et al. (2000). Stress and vulnerability to posttraumatic stress disorder in children and adolescents. *Am J Psychiatry.* 157:1229–1235.

Silverman AB, Reinherz HZ, Giaconia RM. (1996). The long-term sequelae of child and adolescent abuse: a longitudinal community study. *Child Abuse Neglect.* 20:709–723.

Solomon Z, Kotler M, Shalev A, et al. (1989). Delayed onset PTSD among Israeli veterans of the 1982 Lebanon War. *Psychiatry.* 52:428–436.

Terr LC. (1991). Childhood traumas: an outline and overview. *Am J Psychiatry.* 148:10–20.

Tyano S, Iancu I, Solomon Z, et al. (1996). Seven-year follow-up of child survivors of bus-train collision. *J Am Acad Child Adolesc Psychiatry*. 35:365–373.

Udwin O, Boyle S, Yule W, et al. (2000). Risk factors for long-term psychological effects of a disaster experienced in adolescence: predictors of posttraumatic stress disorder. *J Child Psychol Psychiatry*. 41:969–979.

Yule W. (1992). Posttraumatic stress disorder in child survivors of shipping disasters: the sinking of the *Jupiter*. *Psychother Psychosom*. 57:200–205

Yule W. (2001). Posttraumatic stress disorder in the general population and in children. *J Clin Psychiatry*. 62 (suppl 17):23–28.

Yule W, Bolton D, Udwin O, et al. (2000). The long-term psychological effects of a disaster experiences in adolescence: I: The incidence and course of PTSD. *J Child Psychol Psychiatry*. 41:503–511.

8

∎

Gender Differences in Childhood PTSD

Patricia Karen Abanilla

There is much to be learned about the role of gender in the development of posttraumatic stress disorder (PTSD). This role in childhood and adolescent PTSD also needs further study.* Warnes, in his 1972 paper on *traumatic syndrome*, a diagnostic precursor to posttraumatic stress disorder, makes no mention of gender as a factor. Progressively, gender-related studies have begun to consider prevalence rates of PTSD in men as compared to women (Breslau et al., 1997). Currently, investigators of PTSD use gender as one variable in their data set, though rarely as the primary focus. More recently, interactions between gender and etiology, presentation, natural history, treatment, and outcome are being examined in the literature. For the most part, these studies have used adult populations and employed uniform diagnostic criteria. The same standards have not been applied as rigorously in the child and adolescent PTSD literature. That literature shows marked variability in methodology, illustrated by the evolving criteria set used to establish the diagnosis in children. In addition, description of symptomatology and more importantly, age of study subject, are often not comparable from one study to the next. Subjects range in age from childhood to early adulthood, yet findings often do not address the developmental relationship to gender, despite the axiom of child psychiatry that a child's developmental stage affects both psychopathology and symptom presentation (Lewis & King, 2002).

---

* References to children in this chapter include adolescents unless otherwise indicated.

163

The combination of inconsistent diagnostic criteria, small sample sizes, and variability of subject age raises questions about the ability to generalize findings and makes comparisons between studies difficult. It is important to keep these limitations in mind when interpreting implications of available data.

Nature of the Trauma

In studies involving both children and adolescents, the nature of trauma exposure differed on the basis of gender. Boys were significantly more likely to have experienced physical assault, while girls had greater exposure to sexual assault (Lipschitz, Grilo, et al., 2000; Schwab-Stone, et al., 1999). Kaminer and colleagues (2000), in their review of violent trauma among girls, reported disturbingly high rates of sexual abuse. Their examination identified a United States community study with a 34% rate, a German study with a 25% rate, and a New Zealand study showing a 10% rate by age 16. Additionally, at a South African clinic, sexual trauma emerged as the most common trauma among adolescent girls being treated for PTSD.

Rate of Exposure to Trauma

Consensus as to whether there is a gender difference in rates of exposure to trauma has yet to be achieved. According to Schwab-Stone and colleagues (1995, 1999), boys have greater rates of exposure to trauma than girls, mirroring the adult literature (Breslau et al., 1998, 1999). Other researchers have found the opposite. Cuffe and associates' (1998) study of the prevalence of PTSD in a community sample of older adolescents, ages 16 to 22 years, found that females reported more traumatic events than males and satisfied criteria for PTSD three times as often as males. On the other hand, Giaconia and colleagues (1995) reported equal rates of trauma exposure between sexes.

Probable Mediating Factors on Gender Effects in PTSD Development

The most consistent finding is that girls are more likely to develop PTSD after trauma exposure than boys are (Flannery et al., 2001; Yule et al., 2000; Kaminer et al., 2000; Korol et al., 1999; Cuffe et al., 1998; March et al., 1997; Berton & Stabb, 1996; Vernberg et al., 1996; Giaconia et al., 1995). This finding remains true in both children with preexisting psychiatric diagnoses as well as those carrying no psychiatric diagnosis other than PTSD. Regarding the former, Lipschitz and colleagues (1999) looked at the incidence of PTSD in a sample of adolescents hospitalized with psychiatric disorders other than PTSD. They found that 93% of subjects reported exposure to at least one type of traumatic event. Of those, 32.4% met criteria for PTSD with a 2:1 female to male ratio (43.6% versus 20%).

While studies listed in Table 1 consistently show a higher absolute rate of PTSD development for females, the actual risk ratio within each sex varies from study to study. The table presents the variables, which might explain these differences.

Exposure Level

March and colleagues (1997) looked at posttraumatic symptomatology in 1,019 children, ages 10 to 16 years, following an industrial fire. They found that females were more likely to exhibit posttraumatic symptoms than males. However, of the subjects that met criteria for PTSD (9.7%), exposure level interacted with gender. Specifically, the difference in prevalence rates between genders became significant only in the children that had the highest exposure levels. The girls with the greatest exposure were at a higher risk for developing PTSD than boys exposed to similar levels of trauma, whereas at lower levels of exposure, the incidence of PTSD development was similar.

TABLE 1.

Study	Sample Size	Age	N Sex Ratio (M:F) (%)	Incidence (%)	Scale Used	Exposure to Trauma	PTSD Prevalence (Sex ratio)
Flannery et al. (2001)	484	14–19y	72/28	25	TSC-C	NA	F>M (2:1)
Yule et al. (2000)	217	11–17y	26/74	51.5	CAPS	M = F	F>M (2:1)
Lipschitz et al. (2000)	95	13.2–18.5y	40/60	23	Child PTSD checklist	NA (F-sexual; M-physical)	NA
Korol et al. (1999)	120	7–15y	50/50	88	CPTS-RI	NA	F>M
Schwab-Stone et al. (1999)	5,348	6th–10th grade	48/52			M>F	NA
Lipschitz et al. (1999)	74	11.1–18.3y	47.3/52.7	32	CPTS-RI	F>M	F>M (2:1)
Cuffe et al. (1998)	490	16–22y	43/57	2	K-SADS (PTSD)	F>M	F>M (3:1)

TABLE 1. *continued*

	N	Age	%		Measure		
March et al. (1997)	1,019	7–15y	50/50	9.7	SRPTS	NA	M>F
Berton and Stabb (1996)	97	15–19y	76/22	25	CM PTSD	NA	F>M
Vernberg et al. (1996)	568	3rd–5th grade	45/55	86	CPTS-RI		F>M
Giaconia et al. (1995)	384	17.9y (mean)	51/49	6.3	DIS-III-R	NS	F>M (6:1)
Schwab-Stone et al. (1995)	2,248	6th–10th grade	45/55			M>F	

CAPS, Clinician Administered PTSD Scale CM PTSD, Civilian Mississippi Scale for PTSD; CPTS-RI, Child PTSD Reaction Index; DIS III-R, NIMH Diagnostic Interview Schedule, Version III-R; F, female; K-SADS, Schedule for Affective Disorders and Schizophrenia for School Aged Children; M, Male; NA, not available; SRPTS, Self-Reported Post-Traumatic Symptomalogy Scale for PTSD; TSC-C, Trauma Symptom Checklist for Children; y, year.

Age

Looking at the interaction between age and gender in the development of PTSD, Korol and associates (1999) investigated the responses of 120 children (ages 7 to 15 years) to a nuclear waste disaster. The study divided the sample according to specific age groups—7 to 9, 10 to 12, and 13 to 15—and asked the question of whether there were differences in the children's responses based on their age. They found that as girls became older, they showed an increase in PTSD symptoms while boys showed an almost linear decrease. The researchers speculated that the older girls may have had a greater understanding of the severity of the stressor, resulting in an increase in PTSD symptoms.

Violent Trauma and Cognitive Attributions

Berton and Stabb (1996) studied exposure to violence and PTSD in 97 urban adolescents. The authors found that at the school with the highest rates of violence (e.g., murder, assault, robbery), girls manifested significantly higher PTSD scores than boys. However, Weaver and Clum (1995), considered subjective aspects of trauma (perceived life threat, self-blame) to be a greater determinant of distress than objective factors such as those cited above by Berton and Stabb. To the extent that trauma is considered a crucial variable, females may tend to feel more vulnerable and may perceive the traumatic event as posing a serious threat to life and, therefore, are predisposed to develop PTSD. It is also tempting to consider the hypothesis put forward by March and associates (1997) that the more internalized the locus of control prior to trauma exposure, the greater the sense of personal efficacy and the lower the level of posttraumatic symptoms. Since in March's study, females had higher external locus of control scores, he reasoned that this might have contributed to their higher incidence of PTSD.

Trauma Types

Giaconia and colleagues (1995), looked at trauma and posttraumatic stress disorder in 384 older adolescents with an average age of 17.9. Females were more likely to report either rape or having received news of the sudden death or injury of someone close as the traumatic event, while males more often recounted that they had received threats. Adolescents who reported being raped were 8 times more likely to show symptoms of avoidance or numbing, 12 times more likely to report that the symptoms persisted for over 1 month, and 7 times more likely to meet all *DSM III-R* criteria for PTSD. In this particular study, males and females were equally likely to experience serious traumas, but females were 6 times as likely to develop PTSD. However, despite the implication that both genders were equally likely to experience certain types of serious trauma, rape seems to have a special impact on the development of PTSD.

Race

March and associates (1997) and Schwab-Stone and colleagues (1999), have examined the interaction between race and gender in the development of PTSD. Among whites, females were at greater risk for developing posttraumatic symptoms than males'. These studies also looked at the relationship between race and symptom clusters. The authors found that younger adolescent white females were less likely to exhibit externalizing behavior than the rest of the sample. Females irrespective of race, and both males and females of Hispanic background were more likely to report internalizing symptoms than either their African American counterparts or white males. Additionally, Cuffe and colleagues (1998) found that symptom profiles between African American and white subjects varied as a function of gender.

Other Trauma-Related Symptomatology

Not all children respond to stress—even severe trauma—with significant symptomatology. Exposure to trauma may result in a spectrum of responses, ranging from resiliency to development of full-blown PTSD. Gender has been implicated in determining emerging symptoms or presentation in response to trauma. A number of studies (Kaminer et al., 2000; Lipschitz, Grilo, et al., 2000; March et al., 1997; Schwab-Stone et al., 1995, 1999; Giaconia et al., 1995) point out that trauma can elicit internalizing or externalizing symptoms, both of which may be mediated by gender.

Kaminer and colleagues (2000) examined the relationship between exposure to violence and other psychopathology. They found that girls were more likely to report internalizing symptoms (depression, anxiety), while boys reported more externalizing symptoms (aggression, conduct disorders). For those youths who experienced traumas without developing PTSD, Giaconia and associates (1995) noted that males did not differ significantly from females in terms of overall behavioral-emotional problems, clinical levels of externalizing problems, or suicidal behavior.

March and colleagues (1997), examining the relationship between trauma exposures and externalizing symptoms, found that, at greater exposure levels, gender had an effect on externalizing symptomatology. They observed that trauma had a tendency to elicit externally directed behavior in both genders; this was most evident in females who had the highest levels of exposure.

Schwab-Stone and associates (1995, 1999), in examining the levels of violence exposure and their effects in 2,248 and 5,348 students, respectively, found that males in general, and older adolescents irrespective of gender, tended to exhibit more externalizing behavior (aggression, antisocial behavior), while females and younger adolescents tended to exhibit more internalizing symptoms. Males reported more willingness to use aggression, a diminished perception of risk during high-risk activities, and lower expectations for the future, as compared to females. All three variables appeared to be related to the degree of exposure to violence, which was greater among males. In terms of adaptation, females were more likely to report symptoms of depression and anxiety as compared to males. Males had more involvement in aggressive and antisocial activities coupled with lower levels of school achievement.

Lipschitz, Grilo, and colleagues (2000) reported that girls with PTSD had significantly higher rates of problematic drug and alcohol use than girls without PTSD. The differential effect of PTSD on substance abuse was not noted in the male cohort. This study also revealed that for girls, problematic drug use was significantly correlated with internalizing psychopathology such as depression and suicidality, as well as externalizing behaviors such as impulsivity and violence, while alcohol use significantly correlated only with externalizing behaviors. For boys, both drug and alcohol use correlated with externalizing behaviors. For girls, PTSD symptomatology had an independent and significant contribution to the prediction of either problematic alcohol or drug use even when controlling for the joint effects of depression and impulsivity. This finding was not evident in boys.

Summary

Notwithstanding the often contradictory information, and appreciating the lack of comparability between studies, several points emerge:

1. The types of trauma children and adolescents are exposed to differ between genders, with sexual abuse being more common for females and physical abuse for males.

2. Rates of exposure to trauma are inconsistent from study to study while prevalence rates of PTSD are routinely higher among girls than boys.
3. Though trauma predisposes children and adolescents of both genders to develop internalizing and externalizing symptoms, boys have a greater predilection for developing the latter while girls are more prone to the former.
4. Race and age appear to interact significantly with gender in the development of PTSD. For example, females of a particular race (white) may be more predisposed to developing PTSD than females of other races. Older girls may tend to have greater vulnerability to developing PTSD than younger ones.
5. In girls, the impact of PTSD increases drug and alcohol abuse whereas the effect in boys' intake is less clear. In terms of the relationship between specific symptomatology, substance use, and gender, girls who showed either internalizing or externalizing symptoms had a higher incidence of substance use than girls who showed neither symptom cluster, while for boys, only externalizing behaviors correlated with substance use.

As already noted, there are differences of opinion regarding the rate and severity of trauma exposure in boys and girls. However, once exposure does occur, the likelihood of girls developing PTSD is greater. This is one of the most consistent findings in the literature, and may be explained either by the qualitative difference of the traumas or by differences in the way the trauma is experienced.

Berton and Stabb's 1996 study found that the development of PTSD was predicted by the individual's self-reports of exposure to violence rather than the actual exposure. This implies that the interpretation of the experience may be more powerful than what actually happened.

Treatment Implications

Posttraumatic difficulties cannot be predicted based on gender. Children and adolescents of either sex need to be evaluated and closely followed after exposure to a traumatic event. Korol and colleagues (1999) suggested that younger boys and older girls be especially monitored to prevent maladaptive postdisaster responses. Despite differences in how boys and girls manifest the effect of the trauma, the treatment process in all children needs to address the causative factor (i.e. trauma) as well as the manifest symptoms. Further, the clinician needs to be aware of the differential response to trauma that may occur based on gender and have an understanding of how the child is processing the trauma. Girls may be more vulnerable to developing PTSD after trauma exposure because they are likely to either be blamed or blame themselves after being sexually victimized and, therefore, receive less posttrauma support (Kaminer et al., 2000). Therefore, the clinician needs to evaluate for trauma exposure in a female child because of her increased risk for developing PTSD.

In cases where a clear trauma history cannot be elicited, certain symptom pictures should alert a clinician to a child's possible exposure. Children who are exhibiting disruptive behavior symptoms must be carefully assessed for trauma exposure. Failure to diagnose or treat PTSD in a timely fashion can have serious consequences for both boys and girls. As already discussed, untreated PTSD leads to externalizing symptoms, especially disruptive behavior that puts the child on the path to sociopathic behavior and its sequelae. Additional information that substantiates the importance of timely diagnosis and intervention for this population is found in Lipschitz, Rasmusson, and colleagues (2000). They found that girls with PTSD were more likely to fail a class, be suspended from school, and to be arrested. Cauffman and colleagues (1998) found that females were approximately 50% more likely to have current PTSD than an equivalent male population of juvenile offenders. We have already mentioned that in adolescent girls, PTSD is a serious risk factor for substance abuse.

Directions for the Future

While much remains to be learned, the research thus far indicates that the role of gender in PTSD is an important variable, deserving further intensive examination. Longitudinal studies comparing samples of boys and girls matched for severity of trauma and trauma type is essential. Detailed exploration of how trauma is perceived based on gender is also warranted. It is clear that we are only at the beginning of this search for an understanding of how gender is related to PTSD.

References

American Psychiatric Association. (2000). *Diagnostic and Statistical Manual of Mental Disorders, 4th ed., Text Revision*. Washington, DC: American Psychiatric Association.

Berton MW, Stabb S. (1996). Exposure to violence and post-traumatic stress disorder in urban adolescents. *Adolescence*, 31: 489–498.

Breslau N, Chilcoat H, Kessler R, Peterson E, Lucia V. (1999). Vulnerability to assaultive violence: further specification of the sex difference in posttraumatic stress disorder. *Psychological Med.* 29:813–821.

Breslau N, Davis G, Andreski P, Peterson E, Schultz L. (1997). Sex differences in posttraumatic stress disorder. *Arch Gen Psychiatry.* 54:1044–1048.

Breslau N, Kessler R, Chilcoat H, Schultz L, Davis G, Andreski P. (1998). Trauma and posttraumatic stress disorder in the community: the 1996 Detroit area Survey of Trauma. *Arch Gen Psychiatry.* 55:626–632.

Cauffman E, Feldman S, Waterman J, Steiner H. (1998). Posttraumatic stress disorder among female juvenile offenders. *J Am Acad Child Adolesc Psychiatry.* 37:1209–1216.

Cuffe S, Addy C, Garrison C, et al. (1998). Prevalence of PTSD in a community sample of older adolescents. *J Am Acad Child Adolesc Psychiatry.* 37:147–154.

Flannery DJ, Singer M, Wester K. (2001). Violence exposure, psychological trauma, and suicide risk in a community sample of dangerously violent adolescents. *J Am Acad Child Adolesc Psychiatry.* 40(4):435–442.

Giaconia R, Reinherz H, Silverman A, Pakiz B, Frost A., Cohen E. (1995). Traumas and posttraumatic stress disorder in a community population of older adolescents. *J Am Acad Child Adolesc Psychiatry.* 34:1369–1380.

Horowitz K, Weine S, Jekel J. (1995). PTSD symptoms in urban adolescent girls: compounded community trauma. *J Am Acad Child Adolesc Psychiatry.* 34:1353–1361.

Kaminer D, Soraya S, Lockhat R, Stein D. (2000). Violent trauma among child and adolescent girls: current knowledge and implications for clinicians. *Int Clin Psychopharmacol.* 15:S51–S59.

Korol M, Green B, Gleser G. (1999). Children's responses to a nuclear waste disaster: PTSD Symptoms and outcome prediction. *J Am Acad Child Adolesc Psychiatry.* 38:368–375.

Lewis M, King R. (2002). Psychiatric assessment of infants, children and adolescents. In: Lewis M, ed. *Child and Adolescent Psychiatry: A Comprehensive Textbook* (3rd edition). Baltimore, Md: Lippincott, Williams, & Wilkins; 525–540.

Lipschitz D, Grilo C, Fehon D, McGlashan T, Southwick S. (2000). Gender differences in the associations between posttraumatic stress symptoms and problematic substance use in psychiatric inpatient adolescents. *J Nerv Ment Dis.* 188:349–356

Lipschitz D, Rasmusson A, Anyan W, Cromwell P, Southwick S. (2000). Clinical and functional correlates of posttraumatic stress disorder in urban adolescent girls in a primary care clinic. *J Am Acad Child Adolesc Psychiatry.* 39:1104–1111.

Lipschitz D, Winegar R, Hartnick E, Foote B, Southwick S. (1999). Posttraumatic stress disorder in hospitalized adolescents: psychiatric comorbidity and clinical correlates. *J Am Acad Child Adolesc Psychiatry.* 38:385–392.

March J, Amaya-Jackson L, Terry R, Costanzo P. (1997). Posttraumatic symptomatology in children and adolescents after an industrial fire. *J Am Acad Child Adolesc Psychiatry.* 36:1080–1088.

Schwab-Stone M, Ayers T, Kasprow W, Voyce C. (1995). No safe haven: a study of violence exposure in an urban community. *J Am Acad Child Adolesc Psychiatry.* 34:1343–1352.

Schwab-Stone M, Chen C, Greenberger E, Silver D, Lichtman J, Voyce C. (1999). No safe haven II: The effects of violence exposure on urban youth. *J Am Acad Child Adolesc Psychiatry*. 38:359–367.

Vernberg E, La Greca A, Silverman W, Prinstein M. (1996). Prediction of posttraumatic stress symptoms in children after Hurricane Andrew. *J Abnorm Psychol*, 105:237–248.

Warnes H. (1973). The traumatic syndrome. *Can Psychiatr Assoc J*. 17:391–396.

Weaver TL, Clum GA. (1995). Psychological distress associated with interpersonal violence: a meta-analysis. *Clin Psychol Rev*. 15:115–140.

Yule W, Bolton D, Udwin O, Boyle S, O'Ryan D, Nurrish J. (2000). The long-term psychological effects of a disaster experienced in adolescence: I: The incidence and course of PTSD. *J Child Psychol Psychiatry*. 41:503–511.

9

■

Intergenerational Links Between Mothers and Children with PTSD Spectrum Illnesses

L. Oriana Linares and Marylene Cloitre

Mothers and their preschool children who reside in high-crime neighborhoods are likely to witness traumatic events that elicit feelings of fear and hopelessness. As such, these mother–child dyads are a population at risk for developing posttraumatic stress disorder (PTSD), either as a full or partial disorder. Little is known about the relationship between maternal PTSD and pediatric PTSD symptoms in nonclinical or community samples. This chapter examines familial components of PTSD by focusing on the intergenerational relationships of child and maternal exposure to violence, and their associations of child and maternal PTSD symptomatology in a community sample of mother–child dyads residing in high-crime neighborhoods. We examine child and maternal exposure to community violence (CV), and domestic violence (DV), as well as subsequent risk for PTSD in a high-risk sample of 160 disadvantaged dyads in Boston. The presence of a chronic and prolonged stressor in the life of young children—namely exposure to chronic CV in their neighborhoods—was related to child internalizing and externalizing problems, after controlling for socioeconomic differences and exposure to family violence (Linares et al., 2001). In this chapter, we will consider PTSD symptoms regarding child expo-

The authors thank Jennifer Speisman for assisting in the preparation of this manuscript. The study was funded by a National Institutes of Health grant (RO1DA/MH11157).

sure to community violence and to two psychosocial factors that may be associated with increased risk for PTSD in preschool children. These are exposure to maternal trauma and maternal PTSD. We define child exposure to CV as the Criterion A1 event required in the *Diagnostic and Statistical Manual of Mental Disorders, Fourth Edition (DSM-IV)*, in which the child witnessed or experienced, in the presence of the mother, actual or a threat of serious injury. The study of intergenerational PTSD symptoms is an important first step in furthering our understanding of the possible psychosocial mechanisms by which exposure to violent events culminates in adverse psychological consequences for young children.

PTSD Spectrum Among Young Children Exposed to Multiple Violence

Exposure to violence may affect young children across multiple domains of functioning including security of attachment, moral development, readiness to learn, emotional functioning, and psychiatric disorders, particularly PTSD. Since the publication of the *DSM-III* in 1980, PTSD has been recognized as a distinct life span syndrome affecting infants, children, adolescents, adults, and the elderly that is characterized by coexisting cardinal symptom clusters of: reexperiencing the traumatic event, avoidance, and increased arousal. Applying the life span criteria to school-aged children has resulted in elevated PTSD symptomatology following exposure to CV (Cooley-Quille et al., 1996; Cicchetti & Lynch, 1993; Reynolds & Mazza, 1999; Overstreet et al., 1999; Eiden, 1999). For example, Fitzpatrick and Boldizar (1993) in an early study, found that among 7 to 18 year olds exposed to CV, 27% met all three PTSD diagnostic criteria.

However, since the early 1990s, there has been an increasing recognition that the expression of traumatic stress reactions among preschool children may be different than that of adults or school-aged children. The *DSM-IV* criteria, when applied to young children, have been found to rely excessively on verbalizations and subjective experiences. According to Scheeringa and colleagues, the adult criteria may not be developmentally sensitive to capture age-related stress-related dysfunction (Scheeringa et al., 1995, 2001). For example, boundaries between changes in behavior due to normal developmental stages and psychopathology are not always well defined, the thresholds of impairment are unclear, and the onset of symptoms in relation to chronic traumas is also unclear. To ameliorate these methodological difficulties, and based on clinical observations of traumatized young children, an alternate criteria for PTSD suitable for young children was developed by the National Center for Clinical Infant Programs in 1994. It is contained in the *Diagnostic Classification of Mental Health and Developmental Disorders of Infancy and Early Childhood* (Scheeringa et al., 1995). The age-sensitive criteria for PTSD replace symptoms requiring verbalizations or self-reflection with age-specific behavior disruptions or loss of emerging skills. For example, careful attention is given to constriction of play, loss of activities of daily living, and new fears. Validating these new PTSD criteria for early childhood is an emerging key area in child psychiatry (Scheeringa et al., 2001).

Reactions to traumatic events may be manifested through disruptions in stage-salient developmental tasks typical of the preschool age period such as the development of a secure attachment to caregivers, autonomous self-development, and effective peer relationships. Disruption to these through exposure to violence derails the normal process of development and renders achievement of the next stage either impossible or significantly more difficult to achieve. Unlike school-aged children, young children may develop specific, circumscribed symptoms reflecting recurrent recollections of events, not necessarily distressing. These symptoms nevertheless may interfere with the attainment of crucial preschool tasks, thus requiring further clinical attention. Regarding the cardinal PTSD feature of reexperiencing, young children may reenact in play the distressing memories resembling the traumatic event. Terr and her associates (Terr, 1991; Terr et al., 1997) observed that the reexperiencing of traumatic events is often seen during play episodes, and takes the form of *dysregulated play*. Dysregulated play is characterized by disturbances of normal developmental play that reflect the young child's anxiety, fear, or preoccupation with upsetting or potentially traumatic events. Dysregulated play may include 1) *posttraumatic play*, characterized by compulsively repetitive play that is less elaborate and imaginative than usual play, and fails to relieve anxiety (e.g., a child who plays with a car mechanically and with little variation), and 2) *play reenactment* of traumatic events that represents part of the trauma but lacks the monotonous repetition and other characteristics of posttraumatic play (e.g., a child who crushes the car on the boy). This study uses maternal reports to explore the presence of dysregulated play in preschool children.

In addition, consistent with the developmental agendas of the preschool years, young children may display symptoms of avoidance/numbing of responsiveness through avoidance of any type of reminder and social withdrawal as a consequence of experiencing a traumatic event. Unlike older children or adults, traumatized preschool children may experience loss of activities of daily living (toileting, dressing, communication). Hyperarousal symptoms may be shown as sleep disturbances (e.g., difficulty going to sleep, waking up at night), temper tantrums, decreased concentration, and exaggerated startle response. Finally, young children may develop new fears, new separation anxiety, and new aggression.

In spite of differences in expression of stress-related symptoms across the life span, we found that co-exposure to community violence (in which mothers witnessed or experienced community violence in the presence of their children) was related not only to increased child internalizing and externalizing problems, but also to maternal global distress and partial PTSD (Linares et al., 1999, 2001). In our past studies, we demonstrated that, among preschool children, the maternal response to stressful events is crucial to a child's response, independent of the child's exposure to similar circumstances. In this chapter, using maternal reports, we focus on a narrow band of problematic PTSD-related child behaviors associated with exposure to traumatic events, namely developmental disruptions in play, reexperiencing and avoidance symptoms, and the development of new fears.

Similar to the adult literature (Cloitre, Cohen et al., 2002), recent research suggests that children who show subclinical threshold criteria for PTSD (fewer symptoms than are necessary for the disorder) may nevertheless experience substantial functional impairment in their daily lives. (For example, in a study of 59 school-aged children exposed primarily to family violence, Carrion and colleagues [2002] found that a few children [24%] met all of the cardinal symptom triad of PTSD.) Nevertheless, researchers (Carrion et al., 2002) found a substantial functional impairment for children who met only one or two symptom clusters, underscoring the importance of examining child PTSD spectrum, in addition to the full-blown disorder, particularly among young children exposed to pervasive, chronic, levels of interpersonal violence. In the current study, we did not assess the presence or absence of PTSD as a psychiatric disorder by applying *DSM-IV* criteria. Instead, we assessed the frequency of life span cardinal symptom clusters of PTSD (reexperiencing, avoidance/numbing, hyperarousal), as well as preschool-specific symptoms (dysregulated play and new fears), and its associations with trauma exposure history (for the child and mother) and maternal PTSD.

Psychosocial Influences in Familial Transmission of PTSD

From a social ecological perspective on child development (e.g., Bronfenbrenner, 1986), we would expect the children's psychological functioning to affect and be affected by the level of stress and symptoms experienced by their mothers. Maternal and child psychopathology links are well established, especially for maternal depression (Hammen et al., 1991). Mothers' stress-related symptoms affect their children, and traumatized children elicit stress-related symptoms in their mothers (Compas et al., 1989). Recent studies have suggested familial mechanisms—both biological and psychosocial and their interactions—in the etiology of adult PTSD. For the case of pediatric PTSD, the exploration of psychosocial mechanisms that affect the expression of PTSD among children of mothers with the disorder is a new, largely uncharted, area of inquiry. Given child exposure to a Criterion A1 event (exposure to CV), several possible mechanisms of familial transmission are possible, among them: the child may be genetically predisposed to experience high levels of anxiety, fear, or traumatic stress before, during, or after exposure began; the child may be at high risk because he or she is exposed to maternal trauma (namely witnessing CV or DV against the mother); the child may be at higher risk because his or her mother suffers from PTSD. If a parent displays symptoms of distress such as traumatic stress, depression, or anxiety in association with a stressor, this conveys a high degree of threat to a young child. In this study, we consider two possible psychosocial factors in the transmission of the disorder from mother to child: (1) via child exposure to maternal trauma (CV or/and DV), and (2) maternal PTSD.

Child Exposure to Maternal Trauma

The negative impact of exposure to maternal trauma in the form of witnessing DV on a child's development is well known

(Jouriles et al., 1989; Kilpatrick & Williams, 1998; Margolin & Gordis, 2000). In earlier studies, researchers found that children from families with greater physical interparental conflict exhibit more distress when watching videotaped interactions involving anger between two adults (Cummings et al., 1989). This suggests that victimized children develop a cognitive-contextual mind set from which to perceive and make sense of the adult social world (Grych & Fincham, 1990), resulting in an array of mental health outcomes that include separation anxiety, obsessive-compulsive disorder, and conduct disorder (McCloskey et al., 1995). Exposure to domestic violence has been found to "get into the child's skin" via direct means (witnessing) and indirect means (negative parenting) (Grych & Findcham, 1990). Using path coefficient analyses, Margolin and John (1997) found that, although both direct and indirect effects on child depressive and anxiety symptoms were significant, the indirect effect, via impaired parenting, was larger than the direct effects (34% versus 7%), particularly for boys. Thus, although modest in magnitude, prior research indicates that child exposure to DV leads directly to child stress-related symptoms without a causal link between maternal and child psychological dysfunction.

Maternal PTSD

Secondly, maternal PTSD may be a risk factor for child PTSD, although the field addressing the possible mechanisms involved in the familial transmission of PTSD from mother to child is in its infancy. Studies of adult prevalence rates demonstrate that maternal PTSD develops in about 24% to 80% of those exposed, depending upon other factors, on how the disorder is assessed, the type of sample, exposure-related factors, and past morbid history (Breslau & Davis, 1992; Kessler et al., 1995; Norris, 1992). Even after accounting for exposure to high-impact crimes, such as rape and child abuse, mothers who witnessed or experienced CV showed elevated PTSD symptoms, as compared with unexposed mothers (Linares, in press). Individuals with PTSD also commonly suffer from comorbid disorders, particularly concurrent depression (Yehuda, 1999; Cloitre, Koenen, et al., 2002). For example, in a national epidemiological study, depression was seen in 37% of individuals with PTSD (Breslau & Davis, 1992). Also common among PTSD patients are perceptions of bodily pain (Koss, Cloitre, Koenen, et al., 1990) and poor general health (Cloitre et al., 2002; Wolfe et al., 1994; Yule, 2001). Thus, it is important to assess other manifestations of traumatic stress associated with maternal PTSD presentation to distinguish general versus specific effects of maternal psychopathology on child psychopathology.

The impact of a traumatic occurrence, either CV or DV, on a young child can be understood in relation to the parent's reaction to the event and to the parent's availability to help the child make sense of the event (Pynoos, 1994). The parenting ability is likely to be compromised by the mother's own symptoms of reexperiencing, numbing, and hyperarousal. Emerging literature in pediatric PTSD indicates that access to parental support predicts children's PTSD reactions to natural disasters (Vernberg et al., 1996), community violence (Kliewer et al., 1998), and war zones (Dybdahl, 2001). Mothers suffering from PTSD symptoms and related disorders, may be "frightened" or "frightening" to their children (Main, 1996), unable to protect their children from feelings of fear and danger. However, it is important to note that parenting difficulties among PTSD mothers may result from chronic stressors that originate within the family (e.g., marital conflict), or outside the family (e.g., neighborhood, economic conditions), and may not necessarily be the result of PTSD. It is largely unknown whether maternal PTSD per se has an impact on parenting beyond that of chronic stress. Given exposure to DV, it is likely that children of parents with PTSD spectrum are at greater risk for PTSD than children with parents without the disorder.

In recent studies of adult PTSD risk, the notion of intergenerational PTSD transmission was examined by Yehuda and her colleagues (1998, 2001). In these studies, adult children of parents who were victims of the Holocaust reported on their parents' PTSD symptoms and on their own PTSD symptoms. In this sample, Yehuda found support for the hypothesis that trauma exposure in a parent is related to increased prevalence of PTSD in adult children (Yehuda et al., 1998). Yehuda and her associates suggested that parental PTSD more than parental trauma exposure per se may be a specific risk factor for the development of PTSD among offspring of Holocaust victims (Yehuda et al., 1998). That is, it may be possible that maternal symptoms are a type of stressor that triggers PTSD symptomatology in vulnerable individuals in the presence of a Criterion A1 event.

Goals of the Study

In the pediatric literature, there is little direct evidence on the association between maternal PTSD and child risk for PTSD. Our study took a preliminary step in this direction. This intergenerational study of a high-risk sample of dyads exposed to community violence, in which a substantial number of mothers exhibit partial PTSD, may provide us with a rich methodology to examine PTSD risk in young offspring and further our conceptual understanding of the familial role in the development of pediatric PTSD. From a treatment standpoint, it is important to identify mechanisms of familial transmission that may inform prevention studies for high risk child groups—namely young children of mothers with PTSD.

Study participants were mothers and their young children aged 3 to 5 who resided in high-crime neighborhoods in Boston

and who were recruited for an NIMH study of community violence (R01DA/MH11157). The main study examined the direct
and indirect contribution of exposure to community violence on
the emergence of preschool behavior problems (Linares et al.,
2001). The sample was drawn from pediatric patients attending
a primary care clinic at a teaching hospital in Boston. Consistent
with the aims of the main study, the sampling strategy over-
sampled dyads exposed to high levels of community violence.
Families in the study resided in five urban contiguous residential
zip codes with the three highest crime districts rates for seven
serious crimes (e.g., homicide, rape, robbery, simple assault,
aggravated assault, home burglary, and larceny) in Boston during
the years of 1991 to 1995. Detailed methodological descriptions
of the sample are reported elsewhere (Linares et al., 1999;
Linares et al., 2001). Eligible children were preschoolers between
3 and 5 years of age.

Mothers completed self-reports via face-to-face interviews
about exposure and symptoms for themselves and their children.
The study protocol was administered in the home with the
mother alone by one of a two-person trained visiting team.

The majority were in their early 30s, of African American
descent (71%) or Hispanic (22%), and of low to moderate
socioeconomic status. Sixty-three percent were born in the
United States, while the remaining immigrated 11 years ago (on
average) from 21 different countries, reflecting the international
composition of Boston residents. Close to half (42%) completed
high school or a Graduate Education Degree (GED) program,
while 26% had less than a high school diploma and 32% had
post-high school education. Mothers were employed outside of
the home (52%), attend school (20%), or receive financial assistance from the government (i.e., Assistance For Dependent
Children) 45%. Forty percent were single heads of household,

and 69% were currently involved with a partner. Mothers had an average of 2.7 (SD = 1.5) children. The target child mean age was 4.1 years (SD = .86), and 48% were girls.

Exposure to Violence by Mother and Child

"Co-Witnessing Community Violence" is the measure we modeled after the work of Martinez and Richters (1993). It included 11 questions about mother and child co-witnessing potentially traumatic events in their neighborhood in the past year. *Co-witnessing* referred to events in which mother and child were together or in close physical proximity of each other when the event took place. Events included: witnessing someone being murdered, shot or shot at, hit, mugged, beaten up, held at gunpoint, or threatened with physical harm. Events also included hearing gunshots in the past year by somebody who included a stranger or a known friend or relative. Partners or husbands and ex-partners or exhusbands were excluded. In 80% of cases, the perpetrator was a stranger or someone known. Eighty-one percent of mothers and 42% of children witnessed at least one violent event, 21% of children saw three or more events, and 12% saw eight or more events.

"Co-Experiencing Community Violence" is a measure modeled after the screening questions of the Crime Victimization Survey (Bureau of Justice Statistics, 1992), and it included seven questions about mother and child co-experiencing potentially traumatic events in their neighborhood in the past year. *Co-experiencing* referred to events in which mother and child were together or in close physical proximity of each other when the event took place. Events included: robbery by force or threat of force, assault with and without (aggravated) a weapon, or threat of an attack with a weapon.

Domestic Violence Experienced by Mother and Witnessed by Child

The Physical Violence scale from the Conflict Tactics Scale-Revised (Straus, 1990) was used to measure partner physical violence during the past 30 days. Reliability alpha coefficients for these scales were .92. In this sample, 22% of mothers reported partner physical violence toward themselves, while 10% reported partner physical violence toward their child. Partner violence toward mother was related to partner violence toward the child (chi-square [1,160] = 4.98, p < .05). Among mothers who reported physical aggression toward themselves, 20% also reported partner violence toward their child. Among mothers who did not report partner violence toward themselves, 7% did not report partner violence toward the child.

Maternal Symptomatology

The Diagnostic Interview Schedule PTSD-Module, National Women's Study version (Kilpatrick et al., 1989), was used to assess current PTSD symptoms. This module was used to obtain a measure of partial PTSD diagnosis (functional impairment was not assessed in this study). The Kilpatrick measure was prefaced with a non-event-specific probe (i.e., Have you experienced any of the following?). If PTSD symptomatology was reported, we followed up by asking about the nature of the event, and we then rated it as a qualifying or a nonqualifying Criterion A1 event. Current (within the past 6 months) and lifetime (more than 6 months) symptoms reported to qualifying events were entered in data analyses. Responses were coded Y/N and summed across symptoms. For all analyses reported in this chapter, mothers met partial PTSD diagnosis if they reported all of the following: one or more symptoms of reexperiencing, three or more symptoms of avoidance, and two or more symptoms of increased arousal in the Diagnostic Interview Schedule PTSD-Module. There were 50 mothers who met criteria for partial PTSD. The Cronbach alpha coefficient for the maternal PTSD measure was .86.

The General Health and the Bodily Pain scales of the Short Form (SF)-36 Health Survey (McHorney et al., 1994) were selected to evaluate personal health and pain or limitations due to pain in the past 4 weeks. The SF-36 Health Survey is a standardized self-report measure widely use in medical settings. Reliability alpha coefficients for these scales were .58 and .85, respectively.

The depression subscale of the Symptom Checklist (SCL) 90-R (Derogatis, 1994) was used to measure depression symptoms in the past 7 days. Respondents used a 5-point intensity scale, ranging from "not at all" (0) to "extremely" (4) to indicate how distressed they were by each of the depression items. A reliability alpha coefficient for this scale was .85.

Child PTSD Symptomatology

A developmentally appropriate 20-item symptom checklist for preschool children was used to measure posttraumatic stress-related symptoms across four clusters: reexperiencing (including dysregulated play), avoidance/numbing of responsiveness, hyperarousal, and new fears and aggression. Ten items were obtained from the Child Behavior Checklist 2/3 or 4-18 (one reexperiencing; three avoidance; five hyperarousal; one new fears). The remaining 10 items were developed in our laboratory following the alternative criteria PTSD diagnostic classification proposed by Scheeringa and colleagues (1995) and the *Diagnostic Classification of Mental Health and Developmental Disorders of Infancy and Early Childhood* (1994). The new items were constructed using the same three-point Likert scale (0 = not present; 1 = sometimes; 2 = very much or often present) compatible with the Child Behavior Checklist scales. New items included: three reexperiencing; two avoidance; two hyperarousal; three new fears. Posttraumatic stress disorder symptoms were assessed using a non-event-specific probe and addressed symptoms present in the past month. If a mother endorsed a symptom to an event (e.g., plays an upsetting event over and over), we followed up by asking about the nature of the event and subsequently rated it as a qualifying or a nonqualifying event. Only symptoms reported to qualifying events were entered in data analyses. The Cronbach alpha coefficient for this scale was .77. Responses (0, 1, 2) were summed across clusters to create a continuous measure of total child PTSD symptoms (PTSD spectrum). In addition, children were considered positive for PTSD spectrum if their mothers endorsed (sometimes or often present) at least one symptom in each of the four PTSD clusters. There were 27% of children with positive PTSD spectrum.

Study Results

First, using the student t-Test statistic, we examined partial PTSD (n = 50) and no PTSD (n = 110) among mothers by levels of mother's exposure to CV (witnessing and experiencing) and DV. We also assessed maternal PTSD comorbidity by examining mothers with partial PTSD and no PTSD by levels of general health, bodily pain, and depressive symptoms. Second, using correlation coefficients, we showed the associations between child total PTSD symptoms and partial maternal PTSD. Third, we examined child PTSD clusters by level of child exposure to maternal CV and DV and by maternal PTSD.

Maternal PTSD and Intergenerational Exposure to Violence

As seen in Table 1, mothers with partial PTSD (n = 50) reported higher mother and child co-witnessing CV events (p < .004), and mother and child co-experiencing CV events (p < .05) than mothers with no PTSD. No differences in maternal groups (partial and no PTSD) were found for mothers or children experiencing DV.

TABLE 1.
Maternal Posttraumatic Stress Disorder and Exposure to Community Violence

Type of Exposure	Maternal PTSD (n = 50) Mean	(SD)	No PTSD (n = 110) Mean	(SD)	Student's t-Test t (df = 158)	P Value
Mother witnessing CV	3.0	2.19	1.94	1.73	-2.99	.004
Mother experiencing CV	.58	.76	.35	.58	-1.99	.048
Mother experiencing DV	2.32	7.90	.93	3.20	-1.57	.120

CV indicates community violence; DV, domestic violence; P, probability; t, value of the Student's t-Test.

Maternal PTSD and Comorbidity

Mothers with partial PTSD (n = 50) reported higher interference due to Bodily Pain Scale of the SF-36 (p < .02), and higher depressive symptoms in the SCL90-R (p < .001) than mothers with no PTSD (n = 110). No differences in maternal groups (partial and no PTSD) were found for general health (see Table 2).

Type and Frequency of Child PTSD Symptoms

Table 3 presents the percentages of children reported to show dysregulated play, other reexperiencing symptoms, avoidance/ numbing of responsiveness, hyperarousal, and new fears, endorsed "sometimes" or "often." Endorsement of individual items ranged from 7% to 59%. Endorsement of at least one symptom in a cluster ranged from a low 13% for dysregulated play to a high 92% hyperarousal. Other reexperiencing, avoidance, and new fears were commonly endorsed (54%, 53%, and 82%, respectively).

TABLE 2.
Maternal Posttraumatic Stress Disorder and Comorbidity

Cormorbidity	Maternal PTSD (n = 50)		No PTSD (n = 110)		Student's t-Test	
	Mean	(SD)	Mean	(SD)	t	P Value
T-General health (SF-36)*	68.66	14.94	71.11	16.24	.90	ns
T-Bodily pain (SF-36)†	53.54	25.77	64.49	30.05	2.23	.027
T-Depressive symptoms (SCL90-R)	59.65	9.67	50.43	10.32	-5.43	.001

*Higher scores indicate better health.
†Higher scores indicate lack of pain.
P = probability; SCL90-R, Symptom Checklist 90-Revised; SF-36, Medical Short Form 36; t = value of the Student's t-Test.

TABLE 3.
Frequency of Child Posttraumatic Stress Disorder Symptoms

Cluster Items	Sometimes or often present (%)
Reexperiencing Dysregulated Play	
Shows repetitive, monotonous play	8
Plays out an upsetting event over and over	7
Other Reexperiencing	
Has repeated dreams about certain event that happened	8
Talks or ask questions about an upsetting event	30
Nightmares	31
Avoidance/Numbing of Responsiveness	
Shows social withdrawal	13
Stares into space/In a fog	10
Daydreams	22

TABLE 3. *continued*

Shows lack of play	11
Avoids or becomes upset with reminders of the event	15
Avoids going out of the home	11
Hyperarousal	
Startles often; is jumpy	19
Trouble sleeping	15
Wakes up at night	29
Cannot concentrate	47
Irritable	59
Temper tantrums	55
New Fears	
Is afraid of going to sleep alone	41
Is afraid of the dark	49
Shows separation anxiety	41
Shows new fear	37

Child Dysregulated Play, Other Reexperiencing Symptoms, and Exposure to Violence

Because of our interest in the potential diagnostic value of dysregulated play in young children as an age-sensitive expression of traumatic stress to violent events, we explored the associations between dysregulated play, other reexperiencing symptoms, and levels of exposure to community and domestic violence (see Table 4). We found that children with dysregulated play versus those without, reported higher levels of witnessing CV (p < .001) and of experiencing CV (p < .01).

Associations Between Child and Maternal PTSD

No significant associations were found between diagnosis-like maternal (partial PTSD) and diagnosis-like child PTSD (positive PTSD spectrum). As can be seen in Table 5, mothers with partial PTSD reported more reexperiencing symptoms as well as dysregulated play in their children than mothers with no PTSD (p < .05). Avoidance, hyperarousal, and new fears were not significantly related to partial PTSD.

TABLE 4.
Child Dysregulated Play and Intergenerational Exposure to Violence

Type of Child Exposure	Children with Dysregulated Play (n = 21)		Children withoug Dysregulated Play (n = 139)		Student's t Test	
	Mean	(SD)	Mean	(SD)	t	p value
Co-witnessed CV	3.61	1.80	2.07	1.89	-3.50	.001
Co-experienced CV	.76	.70	.37	.63	-2.55	.010
Witnessed DV	2.90	9.52	1.13	4.15	-.83	NS

CV, community violence; DV, domestic violence; NS, not significant; t, value of the conclusions

TABLE 5.
Maternal and Child Posttraumatic Stress Disorder Symptoms

Child Clusters	Maternal PTSD (n = 50)		No PTSD (n = 110)		Student's t-Test	
	Mean	(SD)	Mean	(SD)	t (df = 158)	P Value
PTSD Total	4.06	3.17	3.72	3.00	-.64	NS
Dysregulated play	.36	.74	.15	.58	-1.89	.05
Other Re experiencng	1.08	1.02	.74	.94	-1.99	.05
Avoidance/numbing	.81	.98	.57	.89	-1.46	NS
Hyperarousal	2.62	1.27	2.33	1.49	-1.17	NS
New fears	1.74	1.19	1.86	1.31	.49	NS

NS, not significant; P, probability; t, value of the Student's t-Test.

Conclusions

In this chapter, we examined familial PTSD spectrum in a community sample of mother-child dyads residing in high-crime neighborhoods. We considered child risk for PTSD symptoms in relation to child exposure (witnessing and experiencing) to community violence (Criterion A1 event) and to two psychosocial risk factors that may be associated with the development of PTSD in preschool children: witnessing maternal trauma (DV) and having a mother with partial PTSD.

The data presented here offer a window into the associations between intergenerational exposure to violence and PTSD, as seen through maternal reports. Maternal diagnosis of probable PTSD (partial PTSD) was related to exposure to maternal trauma, to child trauma, and to reexperiencing symptoms, including child dysregulated play.

Although the association between maternal PTSD and exposure to high impact interpersonal trauma, such as rape and child abuse, has been well established (Breslau & Davis, 1992), less is known about the impact of CV on the well-being of mothers of young children. This study contributes to the existing literature by demonstrating that exposure to community violence, via witnessing or experiencing, also is associated with PTSD symptomatology among mothers residing in inner-city poor neighborhoods. Routine exposure to potentially traumatic events such as seeing a dead body, hearing gun shots, seeing knifing, being attacked with a weapon, or being robbed by force contributes to recurrent thoughts about these events, feelings of avoidance, emotional numbing, and hyperarousal. The finding that a substantial number of mothers (31%) met partial criteria for PTSD suggests the need for extensive screening and treatment in settings where mothers are likely to seek services such as: women's health and pediatric clinics, transitional assistance centers, and social service agencies. These symptoms potentially impair the ability of mothers to exercise effective parenting, thus deserving careful clinical attention from providers of child mental health services.

The finding that mothers with partial PTSD also experienced depressive symptoms and suffered from bodily pain further documents the pervasive toll of exposure to CV and suggests the need to provide comprehensive screening not only for the cardinal symptom clusters of PTSD, but also for comorbid psychopathology.

A specific reexperiencing feature of the PTSD, child dysregulated play, was related to child exposure to CV, to exposure to maternal trauma (DV), and to maternal partial PTSD. The specific linkage between maternal PTSD and reexperiencing through play suggests that disruptions of play associated with trauma histories are an important area for future research.

The assessment of play behaviors may be clinically important to the understanding of how young children cope with traumatic events. Although distinctions between the real world and fantasies need careful assessment, young children's inner world of worries and fears may be uniquely expressed in fantastic play that contains elaborate, or fragmented, sequences of fighting and surrender, aggression, and withdrawal. Diagnostic assessment tools need to distinguish between aggressive traumatic play and normative make-believe aggressive play typical of the preschool years.

The clinical assessment for the preschooler's play involves multiple observations over time in collaborative partnership with the child's caregivers and requires clinical training on the part of the observer (Lieberman et al., 1997). Although observations of play are normally considered in the clinical diagnosis of preschool PTSD among children exposed to violence (Groves, 2002), careful descriptions and operationalization of traumatic play behaviors in young children are needed in research studies.

Reliable structured assessments of play behavior are essential in hypothesis testing or outcome studies.

The methodology used here involved a parent-administered dimensional scale comprised of newly developed event-related symptoms and selected items of the Child Behavior Checklist scales (a commonly used tool to assess child problems). New items in this study, intended to be clinically relevant, gave mothers the chance to report on events that were meaningful to them or to their children, and to talk about distressing memories observed in their children. Moreover, there is a need to develop cost-effective screening tools for high-risk groups of children, such as those potentially victimized by CV. Further work in this area is needed.

From all four clusters considered in this study (reexperiencing, avoidance, numbing, and new fears), only maternal endorsement of child reexperiencing symptoms was related to their own PTSD symptoms. Cardinal symptoms clusters such as avoidance, hyperarousal, and new fears, even when considered together, are commonly present in the preschool years and may not have diagnostic value for the assessment of preschool PTSD. For example, irritability, poor concentration, or temper tantrums, which are symptoms of hyperarousal cluster in both *DSM IV* and *Zero to Three* was reported for about half of preschoolers in this sample.

Several limitations in the study are noted. One limitation is that the study relied solely on maternal reports. That is, mothers are the reporters of both exposure and symptoms for themselves and for their children, as is typically the case with large scale studies of preschool children. It is not known whether the associations between symptoms in the mother and the child are due to a bias in reporting or a real adverse effect of symptomatic parent on children's adaptation. Multi-approach assessment is needed to address this problem.

References

Breslau N, Davis G. (1992). Posttraumatic stress disorder in an urban population of young adults: risk factors for chronicity. *Am J Psychiatry*. 4:216–222.

Bronfenbrenner, U. (1986). Ecology of the family as a context for human development research perspectives. *Devel Psychol*. 22:723–742.

Bureau of Justice. (1992). *Criminal victimization in the U.S.* Washington, DC: Department of Justice.

Carrion V, Weems C, Ray R, Reiss A. (2002). Toward an empirical definition of pediatric PTSD: the phenomenology of PTSD symptoms in youth. *J Am Acad Child Adolesc Psychiatry*. 41(2):166–173.

Cicchetti D, Lynch M. (1993). Toward an ecological/transactional model of community violence and child maltreatment: consequences for children's development. *Psychiatry*. 56(1):96–108.

Cloitre M, Cohen LR, Scarvalone P. (2002). Understanding revictimization among childhood sexual abuse survivors: an interpersonal schema approach. *J Cognitive Psychotherapy*. 16:91–112.

Cloitre M, Koenen K, Cohen L, Han H. (2002). Skills training in affective and interpersonal regulation followed by exposure: a phase-based treatment of PTSD related to childhood abuse. *J Consul Clin Psychol*. 70 (5):1067–1074.

Compas BE, Howell DC, Phares V, Williams RA. (1989). Parent and child stress and symptoms: an integrative analysis. *Devel Psychol*. 25:550–559.

Cooley-Quille MR, Turner SM, Beidel DC. (1996). Emotional impact of children's exposure to community violence: a preliminary study. *J Am Acad Child Adolesc Psychiatry*. 34:1362–1368.

Cummings EM, Vogel D, Cummings JS, El-Sheikh M. (1989). Children's responses to different forms of expression of anger between adults. *Child Dev*. 60:1392–1409.

Derogatis, LR. (1994). *SCL90-R Administration, Scoring, and Procedural Manual*. Minneapolis, MN: National Computer Systems, Inc.

Diagnostic Classification of Mental Health and Developmental Disorders of Infancy and Early Childhood. (1994). Washington: Zero to Three.

Dybdahl R. (2001). Children and mothers in war: an outcome study of a psychosocial intervention program. *Child Dev*. 72:1214–1230.

Eiden, RD (1999). Exposure to violence and behavioral problems during early childhood. *J Interpersonal Violence*. 14:1299–1313.

Fitzpatrick KM, Boldizar JP. (1993). The prevalence and consequences of exposure to violence among African-American youth. *J Am Acad Child Adolesc Psychiatry*. 32:424–430.

Groves BM. (2002). *Children Who See Too Much*. Boston: Beacon Press.

Grych, JH, Fincham FD. (1990). Marital conflict and children's adjustment: a cognitive-contextual framework. *Psychol Bull*. 108:267–290.

Hammen C, Burge D, Adrian C. (1991). Timing of mother and child depression in a longitudinal study of children at risk. *J Consult Clin Psychol*. 59:341–345.

Jouriles EN, Murphy CM, O'Leary KD. (1989). Interspousal aggression, marital discord, and child problems. *J Consult Clin Psychol*. 57:453–455.

Kessler RC, Sonnega A, Bromet E, Hughes M, Nelson CB. (1995). Posttraumatic stress disorder in the national comorbidity survey. *Arch Gen Psychiatry*. 52:1048–1060.

Kilpatrick DG, Resnick HS, Saunders BE, Best CL. (1989). *National Women's Study PTSD Module*. Unpublished manuscript. National Crime Victims Research and Treatment Center. Medical University of South Carolina, Charleston.

Kilpatrick KL, Williams LM. (1998). Potential mediators of posttraumatic stress disorder in child witnesses to domestic violence. *Child Abuse Neglect*. 22:319–330.

Kliewer W, Lepore SJ, Oskin D, Johnson PD. (1998). The role of social and cognitive processes in children's adjustment to community violence. *J Consult Clin Psychol*. 66:199–209.

Koss MP, Woodruff WJ, Koss PG. (1990). Relation of criminal victimization to health perceptions among women medical patients. *J Consult Clin Psychol*. 58:147–152.

Lieberman AF, Van Horn PF, Grandison CM, Pekarsky JH. (1997). Mental health assessment of infants, toddlers, and preschoolers in a service program and a treatment outcome research program. *Infant Ment Health J*. 18:158–170.

Linares LO. (In press). Social connection to neighbors, multiple victimization, and current health among women residing in high crime neighborhoods. *J Fam Violence*.

Linares, L.O., Groves, B.M., Greenberg, J., Bronfman, E., Augustyn, M., & Zuckerman, B. (1999). Restraining orders: A frequent marker of adverse maternal health. *Pediatrics*, 104, 249–257.

Linares LO, Heeren T, Bronfman E, Zuckerman B, Augustyn M, Tronick E. (2001). A mediational model for the impact of exposure to community violence on early childhood behavioral problems. *Child Dev.* 72:639–652.

Main M. (1996). Introduction to the special section on attachment and psychopathology: 2. Overview of the field of attachment. *J Consult Clin Psychol.* 64(2):237–256.

Margolin G, Gordis EB. (2000). The effects of family and community violence on children. *Annu Rev Psychology.* 51:445–479.

Margolin G, John RS. (1997). Children's exposure to marital aggression: direct and mediated effects. In: Kanter GK, Jesinski JL, eds. *Out of the Darkness.* Thousand Oaks, Calif: Sage; 446–469.

Martinez P, Richters JE. (1993). The NIMH community violence project: II Children's distress symptoms associated with violence exposure. *Psychiatry.* 56:22–35.

McCloskey LA, Figueredo AJ, Koss MP. (1995). The effects of systemic family violence on children's mental health. *Child Develop.* 66:1239–1261.

McHorney CA, Ware JE, Lu JF, Sherburne CD. (1994). The MOS 36-item short-form health survey (SF-36): III. Tests of data quality, scaling assumptions, and reliability across diverse patient groups. *Med Care.* 32:40–66.

Norris F. (1992). Epidemiology of trauma: frequency and impact of different potentially traumatic events on different demographic groups. *J Consult Clin Psychol.* 60:409–418.

Overstreet S, Dempsey M, Graham D, Moely B. (1999). Availability of family support as a moderator of exposure to community violence. *J Clin Child Psychology.* 28:151–159.

Pynoos RS. (1994). Traumatic stress and developmental psychopathology in children and adolescents. In: Pynoos RS, ed. *Posttraumatic Stress Ddisorder: A Clinical Review.* Los Angeles: University of California Department of Psychiatry & Behavioral Sciences; 65–98.

Reynolds WM, Mazza JJ. (1999). Assessment of suicidal ideation in inner-city children and young adolescents: reliability and validity of the Suicidal Ideation Questionnaire-JR. *School Psychology Rev.* 28:17–30.

Scheeringa MS, Peebles CD, Cook CA, Zeanah CH. (2001). Toward establishing procedural, criterion, and discriminant validity for PTSD in early childhood. *J Am Acad Child Adolesc Psychiatry.* 40:52–60.

Scheeringa MS, Zeanah CH, Drell MJ, Larrieu JA. (1995). Two approaches to the diagnosis of posttraumatic stress disorder in infancy and early childhood. *J Am Acad Child Adolesc Psychiatry*. 34:91–200.

Straus MA. (1990). The Conflict Tactics Scale and its critics: an evaluation and new data on the validity and reliability. In: Straus MA, Gelles RJ, eds. *Physical Violence in American Families*. New Brunswick, NJ: Transaction Publishers; 49–74.

Terr L. (1991). Childhood traumas: An outline and overview. *Am J Psychiatry*. 148:10–20.

Terr, LC, Bloch, DA, Michel, BA, Shi, H, Reinhardt, JA, Metayer S. (1997). Children's thinking in the wake of Challenger. *Am J Psychiatry*. 154:744–751.

Vernberg EM, LaGreca AM, Silverman WK, Prinstein MJ. (1996). Prediction of posttraumatic stress symptoms in children after Hurricane Andrew. *J Abnorm Psychology*. 105:237–248.

Wolfe J, Schnurr PP, Brown PJ, Furey J. (1994). Posttraumatic stress disorder and war-zone exposure as correlates of perceived health in female Vietnam War veterans. *J Consult Clin Psychol*. 62:1235–1240.

Yehuda R. (1999). *Risk Factors for Posttraumatic Stress Disorder*. Washington, DC: American Psychiatric Press.

Yehuda R, Halligan SL, Bierer LM. (2001). Relationship of parental trauma exposure and PTSD to PTSD, depressive and anxiety disorders of offspring. *J Psychiatric Res*. 35:261–270.

Yehuda R, Schmeidler J, Giller EL, Siever LJ, Binder-Brynes K. (1998). Relationship between posttraumatic stress disorder characteristics of Holocaust survivors and their adult offspring. *Am J Psychiatry*. 155:841–843.

Yule W. (2001). Post-traumatic stress disorder in children and adolescents. *Int Rev Psychiatry*. 13:194–200.

10

Assessment of PTSD in Children and Adolescents

Philip A. Saigh

According to the American Psychiatric Association's (APA) *Diagnostic and Statistical Manual of Mental Disorders, Fourth Edition (DSM-IV)*, posttraumatic stress disorder (PTSD) is indicated by exposure to a traumatic incident and characterized by reexperiencing, avoidance, numbing, and arousal symptoms. Although exposure is a prerequisite for the disorder, the majority of individuals who experience traumatic events do not develop PTSD (Acierno et al., 1999; Kulka et al., 1990; Saigh et al., 1999). Epidemiological studies also indicate that the overriding majority of stressors that were studied induced PTSD among a subset of the participants that were examined (Saigh et al., 1999). In view of this and the debilitating symptoms of PTSD, there is a considerable need to obtain reliable and valid information regarding the presence or absence of PTSD among traumatized youth. With these points in mind, this chapter describes procedures to diagnose child-adolescent PTSD. A multisource multimethod assessment paradigm (March, 1999; Saigh & Yasik, 2002) is recommended. The descriptor multimethod means that multiple assessment methods (i.e., clinical interviews, structured interviews) should be used to establish diagnoses. The descriptor multisource designates that several avenues of information (i.e., child, parent, medical records) should be used. It is also recommended that the assessment process involve a team approach, as the diagnostic decisions may be influenced by examinee variance (e.g., an examinee may withhold or acknowledge different symptoms when questioned by different examiners). A team approach is also very helpful in dealing with threshold cases (i.e., a youth whose symptom presentation is very close to the *DSM-IV* standard for meeting or not meeting diagnostic criteria). In these situations, the use of multiple interviewers may significantly contribute to the development of more diagnoses, when appropriate.

Interviews

Interviews are most frequently used to establish inferences in clinical settings. Typically, an interview "involves a series of interactions, frequently in question and answer format, that are used in formulating inferences" (Saigh, 1992, p. 142). With reference to format, interviews generally employ a structured or unstructured format. Structured interviews (also referred to as clinical interviews) involve a discrete process during which examiners ask questions according to a written protocol. Such interviews are characterized by the use of nonstandardized questions that rely on examiner knowledge and impressions. Although unstructured or clinical interviews yields a great deal of information, they are prone to information variance (i.e., differences in the amount and quality of information that is obtained from the same examinee by different examiners) (Saigh, 1992; Saigh & Yasik, 2002; Spitzer et al., 1978). Edelbrock and Costello observed that the use of unstructured interviews "is a universal, and arguably an indispensable, component of clinical assessment of children and youth. Yet, it is one of the least trustworthy assessment procedures, subject to broad variations in content, style, detail, and coverage" (1990, p. 308). Edelbrock and Costello also indicated that "interviewers differ in *what they ask* and *how they ask it*. They undoubtedly influence responses directly through the choice of a particular line and style of questioning and indirectly through their verbal and non-verbal reactions" (1990, p. 308). Given these points, Edelbrock and Costello indicated that the reliability of the child assessment process can be significantly improved by structuring the interview process. In effect, this involves limiting the question and answer interactions between the interviewer and youth being examined. According to Edelbrock and Costello, "this is accomplished by defining the phenomena to be assessed, *limiting* the order and working of questions, and *standardizing* how responses are rated, recorded, combined, and interpreted" (p. 308). Although standardized or clinical interviews augment reliability, the unvaried application of this modality may preclude the derivation of clinically valuable information (Kamphaus & Frick, 2002; Saigh, 1992). As such, it is advised that diagnoses should be derived through the use of both modalities.

Clinical Interviews

Prior to seeing a traumatized youth, examiners should carefully review hospital, school, or agency records that involve the case. Examiners should also review the parents or guardians.

Clinical Interviews for Parents

At these meetings, examiners should determine what happened to the child, when the traumatic event occurred, and how the child behaved during and after the incident. If the child was injured, information about the type of injury, pronosis, and treatment should be obtained. Information involving medical of psychiatric conditions and or academic impairments should also be gathered.

Parents or guardians should be interviewed to determine if traumatized youths meet the diagnostic criteria for PTSD. Whereas there are no hard and fast precepts regarding the provision of clinical interviews, examiners should systematically inquire if a child has been traumatized and if his or her symptoms warrant a PTSD diagnosis.

Clinical Interviews for Children and Adolescents

If possible, primary caregivers should introduce the traumatized youth to his or her examiner. The child's caregivers should not, however, be present when the interview takes place. This recommendation is particularly relevant for cases involving sexual abuse or assault. In these instances, children and adolescents may feel reluctant to discuss their personal experiences in the presence of their parents.

Children and adolescents with an IQ of 79 or less may not understand the meaning of the PTSD symptoms. Likewise, children below the age of 6 years may not be able to understand diagnostic questions, or they may lack the verbal skills to adequately describe their symptoms (Saigh et al., 2002). In these instances, examiners may wish to forgo child interviews and rely on parent or caregiver interviews.

Before the diagnostic interview starts, examiners should establish rapport. Children and adolescents frequently hesitate to discuss traumatic experiences as these discussions generally induce situational distress (Saigh & Yasik, 2002). Examiners should also explain that information involving traumatic experiences and symptoms is used to ascertain if a problem exists. Examiners should also explain that effective treatments (Saigh, 1986, 1987a, 1987b, 1987c, 1992b) are available for youths with trauma-related psychological problems.

Once rapport has been established, examiners should directly inquire if the youth has experienced a very frightening experience. Within this context, examinees should be given the opportunity to tell their story. During this process, it is important to maintain a supportive and professional demeanor. Certainly, examiners should refrain from issuing emotional exclamations or making judgmental statements.

If an examiner has reason to believe that an examinee experienced a traumatic incident and the examinee does not report the incident, the examiner should say: *"Ms./ Mr./ Dr./ My records* [name the referent or agency record] *said/ indicated . . .* [briefly describe the event]. *Can you tell me what happened?"* If the examinee does so, examiners should make it a point to record the actual statement. The interview should be temporarily suspended if the examinee continues to disavow the reported experience. In these situations, examiners should engage examinees in a non-traumatic-related conversation or activity that is intended to allay anxiety. Following this, examiners should again attempt to discuss the reported incident with the examinee. If these efforts are effective, the examinee should be asked to describe the experience. If the examinee disavows the incident, the interview should be terminated. In these instances, caregiver feedback should be used to establish a diagnoses.

After obtaining a description of the traumatic episode from the child, examiners should systematically inquire if the youth is experiencing PTSD systems. Questions reflecting each and every *DSM-IV* PTSD symptom should be presented. As children may not understand the meaning of questions about PTSD symptoms (e.g., Are you avoiding thoughts, feelings, or conversations about what happened?), every effort should be made to present questions in understandable language.

Structured Interviews

While a number of *DSM-IV* based structured interviews for parents have been constructed (e.g., Anxiety Disorders Interview Schedule for *DSM-IV*: Child Version [ADIS]; Albano & Silverman, 1996; Diagnostic Interview Schedule for Children, Version IV [DISC]; Shaffer et al., 2000), information regarding the reliability and validity of their PTSD modules has not been reported. In view of the need to make sound diagnoses, this review only describes instruments with reported psychometric properties.

Structured Interviews for Youths

CHILD AND ADOLESCENT PSYCHIATRIC ASSESSMENT (CAPA)

Costello and associates (1998) administered the CAPA (Angold et al., 1995) PTSD module to 58 youths at a child mental health clinic. They also administered the CAPA PTSD module to a child-adolescent community sample (n = 1,015). A κ coefficient was calculated given the responses of nine participants on three screen symptoms (not symptom clusters). At the overall diagnostic level, a κ of .64 was observed. The intraclass correlation coefficient (ICC) was .94 at the diagnostic level. Data analysis indicated that approximately twice as many clinical participants reported traumatic experiences relative to community participants. A point prevalence of 8.6% was reported for the clinical sample relative to a 0.5% point prevalence for the community sample. The authors represented that the difference in PTSD prevalence supported the differential validity of the instrument.

CLINICIAN ADMINISTERED PTSD SCALE FOR CHILDREN

AND ADOLESCENTS (CAPS-CA)

Newman and colleagues (1998) administered the CAPS-CA (Nader et al., 1996) to 50 incarcerated male adolescents. They reported internal consistency α coefficients of .81, 175, and .79 for the respective reexperiencing, numbing and avoidance, and increased arousal symptom clusters. Information regarding the significant impairment was not reported. Newman and colleagues' unpublished research also yielded a Pearson Product-Moment coefficient of .64 when the Amaya-Jackson and associates (1995) Child PTSD Checklist was correlated with the CAPS-CA.

CHILDREN'S PTSD INVENTORY (CPTSDI)

The guiding principal in the construction of the CPTSDI (Saigh, in press a, in press b; Saigh et al., 2000; Yasik et al., 2001) involved writing test items that indicate the *DSM-IV* PTSD criteria. After an experimental version of the *DSM-IV* version of the CPTSDI was developed, the instrument was field tested with a sample of 50 South African female adolescent rape victims (Heitz & Saigh, 1994). Using an inter-rater reliability format, agreement was observed on 45 of the 50 cases (κ = .80). In terms of internal consistency, Cronbach α coefficients of .80, .83, and .83 were observed for the subtests that reflect PTSD reexperiencing, avoidance, and arousal symptoms. An overall α of .93 was observed for the total CPTSDI score.

Given this information and clinical feedback from the test administrators, a number of items were added, deleted, or revised. The revision was independently reviewed by three experts from the *DSM-IV* PTSD advisory group, a minority school psychologist, two board certified child psychiatrists, a school psychologist, two elementary school teachers, and a minority social worker. Given their informed feedback, additional items were added, modified, and deleted. These efforts led to the development of an instrument that consists of five subtests that parallel the *DSM-IV* PTSD symptom clusters. The first consists of four questions involving potential exposure to traumatic incidents as well as four questions denoting reactivity during stress exposure. The second subtest has 11 questions involving the presence or absence of reexperiencing symptoms. The third subtest has 16 questions involving avoidance and numbing symptoms. The fifth subtest is made up of seven questions denoting increased arousal and the sixth subtest has five questions involving significant distress or functional impairment.

In order to establish the content validity of the instrument (Saigh et al., 2000), three members of the *DSM-IV* PTSD Work

Group independently rated the CPTSDI items for correspondence with the *DSM-IV* PTSD criteria according to a 0 to 100 point Likert-type scale (0 = lowest correspondence, 50 = average correspondence, and 100 = highest correspondence). The Situational Reactivity subtest had a mean rating of 86.67 with a standard deviation of 10. The Exposure, Avoidance and Numbing, Increased Arousal, and Significant Impairment subtests each received a mean rating of 90.00 with a standard deviation of 0.00. These ratings consistently reflected high levels of concurrence between the CPTSDI items and the *DSM-IV* criteria.

The CPTSDI was subsequently administered to 67 stress-exposed and 16 nontraumatized youths at Bellevue Hospital (Saigh et al., 2000). High to moderate Cronbach alphas (.53 to .89) were evident at the subtest level. An α of .95 was evident at the diagnostic level. With reference to inter-rater reliability, 97.6% agreement and 2.4% disagreement was observed at the diagnostic level. Inte-rater ICCs ranged from .88 to .96 at the subtest level and .98 for the diagnostic level. High to moderate κ (1.00 to .65) were reported for inter-rater reliability at the subtest level. An inter-rater reliability κ of .98 was reported at the diagnostic level. In terms of reliability, 96.5% agreement was evident at the diagnostic level. High to moderate κ (1.00 to .67) and ICCs (.93 to .66) were observed. A κ of .87 and an ICC of .88 were observed at the diagnostic level.

The criterion and construct validity of the CPTSDI was assessed by administering the measure to 73 traumatized and 22 nontraumatized youths at Bellevue Hospital (Yasik et al., 2001). Answers to the CPTSDI items were compared to responses derived through clinical interviews as well as the Diagnostic Interview for Children and Adolescents—Revised (DICA-R) (Reich, Leacock, & Shanfeld, 1994) and the Structured Clinical Interview for DSM-IV (SCID) (First et al., 1996) PTSD modules. High to moderate levels of sensitivity (1.00 – .91), specificity (.90 – .97), positive (.68 – .94) and negative (1.00 – .95) predictive power, and diagnostic efficiency (.95 – .92) were observed across the respective criterion measures. Significant correlations with the Revised Children's Manifest Anxiety Scale (r = .74) (RCMAS) (Reynolds & Richmond, 1985), Children's Depression Inventory (r = .65) (CDI) (Kovacs, 1992), and the Junior Eysenck Personality Inventory (JEPI) (Eysenck, 1963) Neuroticism scale (r = .59) clearly supported the construct validity of the instrument. Convergent and discriminant validity were evident through a significant correlation with CBCL Internalizing scale (r = .52) along with a nonsignificant association with the JEPI Extraversion scale (r = .-.08) and CBCL Externalizing scale (r = .19).

DIAGNOSTIC INTERVIEW FOR CHILDREN AND ADOLESCENTS—REVISED (DICA-R)

This broad-based interview (Reich, Leacock, & Shanfeld, 1994) includes a PTSD module that may be used to formulate diagnoses based on the *DSM-III-R* or *DSM-IV* criteria. Reich (personal communication, August 8, 1998) administered the DICA-R to 50 clinically referred youth with a mean age of 11 years and reported an internal consistency α of .79 at the diagnostic level. Reich also compared clinically derived diagnoses to DICA-R PTSD module derived diagnoses and 100% agreement was observed yielding a sensitivity of 1.00 and a specificity of .86. Yasik and colleagues (1998) also administered the DICA-R PTSD module to 37 stress-exposed inner-city youth and reported internal consistency α coefficients of .44, .87, .83, and .87 respectively for the reactivity, reexperiencing, avoidance and numbing, and increased arousal subtests. An α coefficient of .94 was reported for the total item pool. In addition, Yasik and colleagues (1998) reported that the DICA-R correctly identified 9 of 15 cases using clinically derived PTSD ratings as the criterion (sensitivity = .60). Yasik and her colleagues also reported that the DICA-R accurately identified 33 of 34 cases that were diagnosed as PTSD negatives through clinical interviews (specificity = .97). Overall, the DICA-R PTSD module accurately identified the diagnostic status of 85.7% of the examinees. A κ of .94 was reported a indicated by the level of agreement between clinician derived diagnoses and DICA-R PTSD module generated diagnoses (Yasik et al., 1998).

SCHEDULE FOR AFFECTIVE DISORDERS AND SCHIZOPHRENIA
FOR SCHOOL-AGE CHILDREN (K-SADS)

This test (Ambrosini, 2000) is available in several different versions (e.g., Epidemiologic version, Present/Lifetime version, Present State-IV-Revised) and contains a PTSD module that corresponds to the *DSM-III-R* and *DSM-IV* diagnostic criteria. The test instructions specify that parents and children should be independently interviewed and that diagnoses should be made on the basis of the combined input. Given this process, Kaufman and colleagues (1997) administered the K-SADS PTSD module to 20 youths and their parents and observed a κ of .67 for a current diagnosis and a κ of .60 for a lifetime diagnosis.

Structured Interviews for Parents

Several *DSM-IV* based PTSD parental interviews have been constructed. As in the case of the child-adolescent structured interviews, most of these measures lack empirical information to support their use. As such, this section of the chapter only describes instruments with psychometric properties.

CHILD AND ADOLESCENT PSYCHIATRIC ASSESSMENT (CAPA)

The parent version of the CAPA (Angold et al., 1995) was administered to the parents of nine youths who responded positively to screening items that were thought to be conceptually related with PTSD (Costello et al., 1998). As based on the responses of this sample, a α coefficient of .54 and an ICC of .99 were reported for the diagnostic module. Evidence supporting the discriminant validity of the instrument was reported in terms of the differential PTSD prevalence estimates among clinical and community samples. While 5.3% of clinic participants who were tested were diagnosed with PTSD based, only 0.4% of the community participants were diagnosed.

CHILDHOOD PTSD INTERVIEW—PARENT FORM

Fletcher (1996) developed the interview and administered it to the parents of 30 children (10 traumatized clinic youths and 20 nontraumatized community youths). The KK-20 internal consistency estimates for the stress-exposure, reexperiencing, avoidance and numbing, and increased arousal symptom clusters were .60, .86, .86, and .83, respectively. The internal consistency for the scale was .94. Moderate correlations ($r = .78$) between the Childhood PTSD Interview—Parent Form ratings and parental ratings on the Wolfe and associates (1989) proposed Child Behavior Checklist (Achenbach, 1991) PTSD index were reported. Fletcher also observed a significant difference between the number of symptoms that were endorsed by traumatized clinic youth and the nontraumatized community sample.

Summary

The position advocated herein supports the use of a multisource multimethod assessment paradigm. The descriptor multimethod means that multiple assessment methods (i.e., clinical interviews and structured interviews) should be used to establish diagnoses. The descriptor multisource designates that several avenues of information (i.e., child, parent, medical records) should be used. It is also recommended that the assessment of traumatized youth should involve a team approach, as the diagnostic process may be influenced by examinee variance.

While it is apparent that a number of *DSM-IV* based child-adolescent PTSD structured interviews have been developed, the psychometric properties of most of these interviews have not been extensively researched. With reference to the child interviews, only four studies reported information regarding internal consistency (Newman et al., 1998; Reich, personal communication, 1998; Saigh et al., 2000; Yasik et al., 1998), two studies reported information on stability over time (Costello et al., 1998; Saigh et al., 2000), and one study reported information on inter-rater reliability (Saigh et al., 2000). Moreover, only one study (Saigh et al., 2000) offered empirical evidence to support content validity relative to the DSM-IV PTSD criteria.

The paucity of research involving content validity across measures presents a serious challenge to the classification process. Certainly, researchers and clinicians must not assume that an instrument reflects the current diagnostic nomenclature without empirical verification (Kamphaus & Frick, 1996). Given the exceptionally limited content validity information, it is advised that researchers and practitioners actually compare the DSM-IV PTSD criteria against the items from tests that reportedly reflect these criteria.

To date, only four authors have reported information regarding criterion-related validity of the child measures (Newman et al., 1998; Reich, 1998; Yasik et al., 1998; Yasik et al., 2001), and only two investigations have addressed the question of construct validity (Costello et al., 1998; Yasik et al., 2001). It is also of exceptional concern to observe that the psychometric properties of almost all of child-adolescent PTSD structured interviews have not been published in peer-reviewed journals. Indeed, only the CAPA and the CPTSDI have had their psychometric properties described in peer-referred journals (Costello et al., 1998; Saigh et al., 2000; Yasik et al., 2001).

As in the case of the child-adolescent PTSD interviews, the majority of the parent interviews lack empirical support. The developers of the CAPA and the Childhood PTSD Interview— Parent Form have, however, reported information regarding internal consistency and construct validity. On the other hand, information regarding content and criterion-related validity is not available.

Clearly, researchers should address unanswered questions about the psychometric properties of many of the child-adolescent and parent interviews that have been developed. Until that time, test adoption decisions should be made on basis of the scientific merits of the instruments that have been developed to diagnose child-adolescent PTSD.

References

Achenbach TM. (1991). *Manual for the Child Behavior Checklist and Revised Child Behavior Profile*. Burlington: University of Vermont, Department of Psychiatry.

Acierno R, Kilpatrick DG, Resnick HS. (1999). Posttraumatic stress disorder in adults relative to criminal victimization: prevalence, risk, factors, and comorbidity. In: Saigh PA, Bremner DJ, eds. *Posttraumatic Stress Disorder: A Comprehensive Text*. Needham Heights, Mass: Allyn & Bacon; 44–68.

Albano AM, Silverman WK. (1996). *Anxiety Disorders Interview Schedule for the DSM-IV: Clinician manual*. New York: Psychological Corporation.

Amaya-Jackson L, McCarthy G, Cherney MS, Newman E. (1995). *Child PTSD Checklist*. Duke University Medical Center, North Carolina. Unpublished manuscript.

Ambrosini PJ. (2000). Historical development and present status of the Schedule for Affective Disorders and Schizophrenia for School Age Children. *Am J Child Adolesc Psychiatry*. 28:723.

American Psychiatric Association. (1994). *Diagnostic and Statistical Manual of Mental Disorders* (4th ed.). Washington, DC: American Psychiatric Associatioin.

Angold A, Prendergast M, Cox A, Harrington R, Simonoff E, Rutter, M. (1995). The Child and Adolescent Psychiatric Assessment (CAPA). *Psychological Med*. 25:739–753.

Costello EJ, Angold A, March J, Fairbank J. (1998). Life events and post-traumatic stress: the development of a new measure for children and adolescents. *Psychological Med*. 28:1275–1288.

Edelbrock C, Costello AJ. (1990). Structured interviews for children and adolescents. In: Goldstein G, Hersen M, eds. *Handbook of Psychological Assessment* (2nd ed.). New York: Pergamon; 308–323.

Eysenck SB. (1963). *Junior Eysenck Personality Inventory*. San Diego, Calif: Educational and Industrial Testing Service and Human Services.

Fletcher KE. (1996, November). *Measuring school-aged children's PTSD: preliminary psychometrics of four new measures*. Paper presented at Annual Meeting of the International Society for Traumatic Stress Studies; San Francisco, Calif.

First M, Gibbon M, Williams JB, Spitzer RL. (1996). Structured Clinical Interview for the DSM-IV (SCID). New York: New York State Psychiatric Institute, Biometrics Research Department.

Heitz B, Saigh PA. (1994). *The psychometric properties of the Children's PTSD Inventory among a sample of South-African females*. Unpublished data.

Kamphaus RW, Frick PJ. (1996). *Clinical Assessment of Child and Adolescent Personality and Behavior*. Needham Heights, Mass: Allyn & Bacon.

Kaufman J, Birmaher B, Brent D, et al. (1997). Schedule for Affective Disorders and Schizophrenia for School-Age Children—Present and Lifetime Version: Initial reliability and validity data. *J Am Acad Child Adolesc Psychiatry*. 36:980–988.

Kovacs M. (1992). *The Children's Depression Inventory*. North Tonowanda, NY: Multi-Health Systems.

Kulka RA, Schlenger WE, Fairbank JA, et al. (1990). *Trauma and the Vietnam War Generation*. New York: Brunner/Mazzel.

March J. (1999). Assessment of pediatric posttraumatic stress disorder. In: Saigh PA, Bremner, JD, *Posttraumatic Stress Disorder: A Comprehensive Text*. Needham Heights, Mass: Allyn & Bacon; 199–218.

Nader KO, Kriegler JA, Blake DD, Pynoos RS, Newman E, Weathers FW. (1996). Clinician-Administered PTSD Scale for Children and Adolescents for DSM-IV. Boston, Mass: National Center for PTSD, Boston Veterans Administration Medical Center.

Newman E, McMackin, RA, Morrissey C, Erwin BA, Kaloupek DG, Keane TM. (1998). *PTSD among incarcerated male adolescents at secure juvenile treatment facilities*. Unpublished raw data.

Reich W, Leacock N, Shanfeld C. (1994). *Diagnostic Interview for Children and Adolescents (DICA-R)*. St. Louis, Mo: Washington University.

Reynolds CR, Richmond BO. (1985). *Revised Children's Manifest Anxiety Scale Manual.* Los Angeles, Calif: Western Psychological Services.

Saigh PA. (1986). In vitro flooding of a 6-year-old boy's posttraumatic stress disorder. *Behav Res and Ther.* 24:685–689.

Saigh PA. (1987a). In vitro flooding of an adolescent posttraumatic stress disorder. *J Clin Child Psychology.* 16:147–150.

Saigh PA. (1987b). In vitro flooding of a childhood posttraumatic stress disorder. *School Psychology Rev.* 16:203–211.

Saigh, PA. (1987c). Structured clinical interviews and the inferential process. *Journal of School Psychology.* 30:141–149.

Saigh, PA. (1992). The behavioral treatment of child and adolescent posttraumatic stress disorder. *Advances in Behav Res Ther.* 14:247–275.

Saigh PA. (in press a). *Children's PTSD Inventory.* San Antonio, Tex: Psychological Corporation.

Saigh PA. (in press b). *Test Manual for the Children's PTSD Inventory.* San Antonio, Tex: Psychological Corporation.

Saigh PA, Bremner JD, eds. (1999). *Posttraumatic Stress Disorder: A Comprehensive Text.* Needham Heights, Mass: Allyn & Bacon.

Saigh PA, Yasik A. (2002). Diagnosing child-adolescent posttraumatic stress disorder in children. In: Brock SE, Lazarus P, eds. *Best Practices in School Crises Pevention and Intervention.* Bethesda, Md: National Association of School Psychologists; 619–638.

Saigh PA, Yasik AE, Mitchell P, Armenian H, Blanchard EB, Abright R. (2002, November). *Teacher ratings of the psychological functioning of preschoolers after September 11, 2001.* Poster presented at: Annual Meeting of the International Society for Traumatic Stress Studies, Baltimore, Md

Saigh PA, Yasik AE, Oberfield RA, et al. (2000). The Children's PTSD Inventory: development and reliability. *J Traum Stress.* 3:369–380.

Saigh PA, Yasik AE, Sack W, Koplewicz H. (1999). Child-adolescent posttraumatic stress disorder: prevalence, comorbidity, and rish factors. In: Saigh PA, Bremner JD, eds. *Postraumatic Stress Disorder: A Comprehensive Text.* Needham Heights, Mass: Allyn & Bacon; 19–43.

Shaffer D, Fisher P, Lucas CP, Dulcan M, Schwab-Stone M. (2000). NIMH Diagnostic Interview Schedule for Children, Version IV: description, differences from previous versions, and reliability of some common diagnoses. *J Am Acad Child Adolesc Psychiatry.* 39:28–38.

Spitzer RL, Endicott J, Robins E. (1978). Research diagnostic criteria: rationale and reliability. *Arch Gen Psychiatry.* 23:41–55.

Wolfe VV, Gentile C, Wolfe DA. (1989). The impact of sexual abuse on children: a PTSD formulation. *Behav Ther.* 20:215–228.

Yasik AE, Saigh PA, Oberfield RA, Green B, Halamandaris P, McHugh M. (2001). The validity of the Children's PTSD Inventory. *J Traum Stress.* 14:81–94.

Yasik AE, Saigh PA, Oberfield RA, et al. (1998, November). *The reliability and validity of the Diagnostic Interview for Children and Adolescents—Revised PTSD module.* Poster presented at: Annual Meeting of the International Society for Traumatic Stress Studies Conference; Washington, DC.

Correspondence concerning this chapter should be addressed to Professor Philip A. Saigh, Doctoral Program in Educational Psychology, Graduate School and University Center, City University of New York, 365 Fifth Avenue, New York, NY 10016. Electronic mail may be sent to PASaigh@aol.com.

11

Differential Diagnosis of PTSD in Children

Mia Pappagallo, Raul R. Silva, and Veronica M. Rojas

Among children and adolescents, special challenges exist in diagnosing any disorder. Several symptoms, such as irritability and poor school performance, can point to any number of Axis I diagnoses. These range from attention deficit hyperactivity disorder (ADHD) to disruptive behavior disorders to psychotic, anxiety and mood disorders. Posttraumatic stress disorder (PTSD), in particular, is a diagnosis for which there are special challenges.

Some disagreement exists about the validity of PTSD criteria, even for adults. There is significant symptom overlap with other disorders, which is further complicated by psychiatric comorbidity. In addition, there are a number of variables that must come together to create the disorder, beginning with the stressor itself. The clinician must be aware of this stressor and its many characteristics in order to make the diagnosis. Finally, we are faced with the challenge of interpreting symptoms in children within the context of the criteria, keeping in mind that children and adolescents naturally manifest symptoms differently at various developmental stages.

Important Issues to Consider when Approaching the Diagnosis of PTSD in Children and Adolescents

There are a number of issues that clinicians should reconcile when approaching a child with PTSD. These can include the challenges posed by the repertoire of varying capacities at different developmental stages. In addition, clinicians must also understand that the complexities of the triad of reexperiencing, avoidance, and hyperarousal can be confounded by similarities with other childhood disorders. We will elaborate on these issues below.

Developmental Issues

We can count on children and adolescents to be dynamic, changing characters. Although this can be one of our most powerful allies in treatment, it can also pose significant challenges for a clinician who is trying to make a sensible differential diagnosis. It is essential to keep a developmental framework in mind. Children can manifest the same disorder, but with different symptoms at different developmental stages.

Each individual has a unique way of reacting to stress. With children and adolescents, there is a somewhat different backdrop for these individual differences. Developmental stages play a crucial role in the way a child or adolescent perceives and reacts to a given traumatic event. For example, very young children may perceive a brief separation from their parents as more traumatic than witnessing the World Trade Center twin towers come down, while adolescents, with their more mature cognitive development, may be more likely to recognize the separation as temporary, but may understand the gravity of the September 11, 2001, terrorist attack and experience the opposite reaction.

When approaching stressors from a developmental frame-work, it helps to understand what normal children tend to fear. Normal children have various age-appropriate fears at different developmental stages. It would follow that children of different developmental stages are susceptible to different types of anxiety and fears. Infants tend to become anxious when they do not feel physically secure, or when loud noises and threatening, looming objects challenge them. We are all familiar with *stranger anxiety* which peaks at approximately 8 months, and separation anxiety, which peaks at approximately 10 to15 months. Young toddlers may fear such external elements as storms, animals, and darkness, while preschoolers may be more fearful of imagined threats such as ghosts and monsters. School-aged children and adolescents tend to fear both internal and external reality-based threats such as injury, burglars, punishment, failure, and social embarrassment (Dulcan & Martini, 1999).

Children and adolescents respond to trauma in a variety of ways, many of which can mimic other diagnoses. A careful clini-cian is aware of the diagnostic criteria as well as the many ways they can manifest at a variety of developmental stages. Even pre-verbal children experience trauma and show symptoms of post-traumatic stress (Scheeringa et al., 1995).

The clinical presentation of PTSD and posttraumatic signs and symptoms (PTSS) can vary substantially at different devel-opmental stages. This extends to each of the three core symptom clusters—reexperiencing, avoidance, and hyperarousal. Based on a literature review and their own studies of children and adoles-cents who survived various types of trauma, Perrin and col-leagues (2000) present the reactions commonly observed in traumatized youth to place various criteria sets for PTSD (*Diag-nostic and Statistical Manual*, 3rd Edition; *International Classifica-tioin of Diseases*, 10th edition) into proper perspective.

Reexperiencing

The way a given child is likely to reexperience the event may change with age and maturity. In all age groups, children and adolescents who have experienced a significant traumatic event do often experience repetitive and intrusive thoughts about the trauma, often during quiet times such as bedtime. Children may also reexperience the trauma through nightmares, although the content of nightmares may or may not be specifically related to a given traumatic event (Drell et al., 1993). The child may not spontaneously report these thoughts and nightmares, so the clinician must take a careful history with emphasis on the child's thought content and play.

Preschoolers and young school-aged children may reenact the trauma through drawings and play (Scheeringa et al., 1995). Play themes may be directly related to the trauma, but it is important to remember that they may also be nonspecific. In our own clinic, several children who were affected by the attacks on the World Trade Center spent many therapy sessions building and destroying "twin towers," while others who were equally affected showed play themes centering on monsters and dragons.

Reenactment can also take the form of behavior changes, which may, in turn, mimic various other disorders, such as disruptive behavior disorders. Terr (1985) reported on a young child who was kidnapped at the age of 7 and who later reenacted the trauma by running away from home at age 10. Although Terr suggested that younger children may not experience visual flashbacks, dissociation, and numbing with the same frequency as adults and adolescents, such symptoms are possible and, when present, may even mimic psychotic disorders.

Avoidance

In addition to avoiding overt discussions of the trauma and specific reminders of the trauma, fear and avoidance can manifest in a more nonspecific manner. As previously stated, preschoolers may demonstrate nonspecific fears and anxiety, the content of which is not directly related to the specific trauma (Drell et al., 1993). Such children may show fear of monsters and the dark and report nightmares about monsters (Benedek, 1985). Another manner in which avoidance may be observed is that children and adolescents demonstrate new anxiety about being separated from their caregivers, which may also cause them to appear quite irritable. They may refuse to attend school or to go to places that cannot be ostensibly connected with the trauma. Such avoidant behaviors may be misinterpreted as oppositionality, depressive disorders, separation anxiety disorder, or other anxiety disorders and, therefore, must be carefully evaluated in context.

Increased Arousal

Increased arousal may present in a variety of ways. Disrupted sleep cycles are common in adults and children. Nightmares and waking throughout the sleep cycle may be of particular importance in young children (Benedek, 1985). Hyperarousal may present in the form of irritability, distractibility, and decreased concentration. For children, a combination of poor sleep and lack of concentration may first become apparent as a decline in academic performance (Rust & Troupe, 1991). Symptoms of hyperarousal can mimic ADHD, depression, or other disruptive behavior disorders. Delaney-Black and associates (2002) set out to examine the relationship between exposure to violent trauma and IQ test performance in a set of first graders in an urban setting. They found decreased IQ scores and lower reading achievement in children who were exposed to violent trauma.

As children mature through adolescence, they are more likely to show symptoms that are similar to those of adults and may more closely approximate the *DSM-IV* criteria (Pynoos et al., 1995).

DSM Criteria

Several clinicians have questioned the validity of the diagnostic criteria in DSM-IV-TR, especially as they apply to children. The DSM-IV-TR describes six criteria: a traumatic event, a time frame, symptoms of reexperiencing, avoidance, and hyperarousal, as well as clinically significant dysfunction.

It is very likely that heterogeneous psychopathologies underlie this cluster of signs and symptoms (Perry & Azad, 1999). Perrin and colleagues (2000) pointed out that, irrespective of criteria revision for PTSD, they have never been very useful in very young traumatized children. Limited as the criteria may be, though, they may be helpful in identifying the ways people react to stress and may be used as a guideline. While it appears that the criteria do have some applicability, there continues to be room for improvement.

Proposed Revisions of the Criteria

Perry and Azad (1999) noted that twice as many children present with posttraumatic signs and symptoms (PTSS) as meet full PTSD criteria. These symptom clusters arguably share similar outcomes to the full disorder in childhood. This illustrates a relative weakness of the current diagnostic system and has several clinical implications. We need to be able to identify pertinent signs and symptoms, irrespective of how they may manifest. This will ostensibly increase our sensitivity in making the diagnosis in general, and particularly in children and adolescents, and it may well improve our ability to treat PTSD.

Following the observation of the frequency of PTSS, there is the suggestion that, similar to generalized anxiety disorder, we may need to decrease the number of symptoms required to diagnose a child versus an older adolescent or adult with PTSD. Similarly, Herman (1992) proposed a new diagnostic category of disorders of extreme stress not otherwise specified (DESNOS) to cover the children and adolescents whose symptomatology is certainly severe enough to warrant clinical attention, but who do not strictly meet adult criteria. His proposed revision would also address sexual abuse and its long-term effects. Lonigan and colleagues (1998) suggested that some symptoms, such as avoidance, are more essential to the diagnosis of PTSD in children and should be considered with more emphasis.

Perhaps the most structured of the proposed revisions is the set of criteria proposed by Scheeringa and associates (1995). Taking the above into account, they suggested an alternate set of PTSD criteria for children and adolescents, with particular relevance for preschool-aged children. They used *DSM-IV* as a base, but attempt to expand and alter the criteria to become more developmentally sensitive. These criteria are still under investigation and are not in common use. However, they underscored that PTSD can present differently in children and that perhaps we should expand our conceptualization of what qualifies as PTSD, especially in children.

Scheeringa and colleagues proposed revisions of the definition of trauma, the level of observed impairment, and the specific symptoms necessary within each of the core clusters of reexperiencing, avoidance, and hyperarousal. First, they suggested that a child needs only to experience a traumatic event and not necessarily report the intense fear the *DSM-IV* requires. They also suggested that, since children and adolescents may not demonstrate the same degree of impairment seen in adults, that criterion may be dropped.

The reexperiencing criteria are fleshed out to present a more developmentally sensitive approach to children and adolescents. The revised crittteria require only one symptom to be present and focus on examining the nature of play, nightmares, and intrusive recollections. They also reminded clinicians that children do not

necessarily show observable levels of distress during such recollections and play.

Scheeringa and associates also added night terrors and nonspecific sleep difficulties to the criteria of increased arousal, and
emphasized that a decline in concentration, which may be more
evident in children, is a readily accessible gauge for monitoring.

They revised the avoidance criteria by focusing on play and
development, and suggested that only one, and not three, of the
following need be present: (1) in the realm of play, it may present
more like reenactment or be posttraumatic in nature; (2) social
withdrawal; (3) reduced affective expression; (4) loss or regression
of developmental skills, especially in language or toilet training.

Finally, Scheeringa and colleagues (1995) added a new
cluster of symptoms, which reflect the multiple different ways
children specifically react to trauma and stress. This cluster
included new onset of aggression, new separation anxiety, fear of
toilet training, fear of the dark, and new fears of situations and
things that are not trauma-specific.

Overall, these criteria reflect a desire to move toward a more
developmentally sensitive approach to the diagnosis of this disorder and to expand how we think about PTSD and its many
manifestations in children of all ages.

Clinical Presentation in Children and Adolescents and Making the Diagnosis

There are a number of challenges clinicians confront in the differential diagnosis of PTSD. It is important to weigh elements of
history and presentation.

Again, it is vital to approach differential diagnosis of PTSD
and all disorders in children and adolescents from a developmental perspective, considering the child or adolescent's cogni-

tive, social, and emotional maturity. A clinician begins with a familiarity with the diagnostic criteria as well as an awareness of the many ways these symptoms can manifest at a variety of developmental stages.

The first task is to take a careful history. Overall, it is the clinician's challenge to place the current symptoms in a context, which will assist in making a final diagnosis.

At the most basic level, by definition, PTSD requires that a traumatic event predate the symptoms, so the clinician must elicit a history of a precipitating stressor. This is one diagnosis that depends, by definition, upon an outside event to precipitate the disorder, and that complicates things. Individual patients may differ in their perception of what is traumatic and what is not. This stems from a wide variety of factors, such as individual temperament, coping skills, past experience, environmental support, and cultural factors.

Some cases are more clear-cut, with an immediately discern-able event. In some cases, this may even be the parent or child's identified reason for presenting for an evaluation, as they may already discern a link between the event and the presenting symptoms. In other cases, the event may not be readily apparent. Often, the event may not be perceived as a trauma in the eyes of the parent. In some cases, parents may be unaware of the event and the child or adolescent may not report the event for a variety of reasons. Children may be preverbal or lack the verbal skills to report an event. Depending on the nature of the event, they may be frightened or ashamed to report. All of these must be teased out, identified, and considered in the initial history. This is one reason that PTSD and PTSS are often misdiagnosed, as we shall see in the case of K that follows. A patient and family may fail to make the association between a prior event and the present symptoms and so do not report it. Some clinicians prefer to use structured or semistructured interviews so that they do not miss this diagnosis. There are, however, limitations to the available scales. Most available PTSD scales have been developed relatively recently and require much further development prior to their regular clinical use (Ohan et al., 2002).

After identifying a traumatic event, we need to examine the nature of the event and the manner in which that particular child perceived it. Some types of traumatic events are more likely to lead to PTSD symptoms than others. It's also important to get a history of previous psychiatric diagnoses and a child's general temperament and coping style.

Finally, it is important to go through a careful assessment of each of the criteria, keeping in mind the developmental differences in presentation, which are discussed in the previous section.

Case History

We are including a case history to illustrate the various points we touched on thus far in this chapter:

K is a 8½-year-old by who presented in our clinic for evaluation. He had a history of general poor sleep, poor concentration, "zoning out," isolativeness, and dysphoric mood since the age of 6. He had been hospitalized three times for "auditory hallucinations and depressive symptoms." Prior to age 6, there were no developmental abnormalities, and K was described as a "happy and engaging baby and toddler." He came to our clinic approximately 1 month after his most recent hospitalization at a local hospital and carried a diagnosis of psychotic disorder—not otherwise specified. He had been treated with fluoxetine and olanzapine and his baseline functioning between episodes was reported to be good in social and academic spheres. His mother did report, though, that even at his best K was an anxious and hypervigilant child.

His chief complaint at the time of presentation was poor sleep, hypervigilance, easy startle, general nightmares, and recurrent, intrusive thoughts about a boy who had touched him and threatened to kill him during his most recent hospitalization. The investigative work of an initial interview was to begin.

One crucial detail that was not in his hospital records proved critical in arriving at a diagnosis and treatment plan. During the intake interview, K and his mother were asked if they could remember anything that was particularly stressful at the time of onset of K's symptoms. His mother revealed that K's psychiatric history appeared to begin after the child, at age 6, witnessed the violent murder of his maternal aunt. Within a month after that event, K became isolative and quiet, he often zoned out, and his sleep was disrupted by nightmares. His concentration in school was poor. He remained quiet and dysphoric and complained of hearing voices saying "bad things." K's mother stated that she wondered if witnessing the murder had anything to do with K's illness, especially because K did not specifically talk about the event.

The mother also revealed that she, herself, had a history of severe physical abuse and had experienced PTSD-like symptoms in the past. There was also a history of an anxiety disorder in the patient's teenaged cousin.

The importance of obtaining a complete history, with specific inquiry about traumatic events, must be underscored. In this case, an essential piece of the final picture was initially missed. Because 8½-year-old K never specifically talked about his aunt's death, his mother did not think to report it as a stressor, although the event was a fairly clear precipitant and certainly met the criteria laid out by the DSM, both in nature and severity.

The previous clinicians had explained the isolativeness, zoning out, and nightmares in the context of a psychotic prodrome. After eliciting the history of a severe stressor, we were able to place the symptoms in a different context. His isolativeness may have been avoidance. His zoning out may have been dissociation. His poor concentration, hypervigilance, and increased startle were symptoms of increased arousal. The voices and nightmares were his ways of reexperiencing the trauma. Recall that the content of children's nightmares in PTSD is not always specific to the stressor.

It may be a sign of avoidance that K never talked about the stressor, or it may be a reflection of his age and developmental level at the time of the stressor.

We can note, also, that K had several risk factors. There is a family history of anxiety disorders and his mother had a history of PTSD-like symptoms. Also, let us turn to one of his presenting complaints—intrusive thoughts about a more recent stressor, a boy touching him and threatening to kill him. K likely perceived this as a significant threat and was experiencing an acute stress response. While the time frame prohibited a diagnosis of PTSD, we can say that he was having an acute stress reaction and that he may be more prone to PTSD from this new stressor, considering his history of past trauma.

It is also possible that K was suffering from a comorbid depressive disorder, which may have been contributing to his psychotic features and general symptomatology.

Comorbidity of PTSD

As we have previously mentioned, a fair amount of overlap exists among psychiatric disorders, and this is especially true with PTSD.

This overlap tends to make the margins among PTSD and other entities, namely depression, other anxiety disorders, substance abuse, personality disorder formation, disruptive behavior disorders, and cognitive disorders, difficult to clearly separate. This becomes particularly difficult with children due to the fact that their symptoms may vary with their level of emotional, physical, and psychological development.

As we cited above, many clinicians have deliberated over the issue of adapting PTSD criteria to children and adolescents (Herman, 1992; Terr, 1991), taking into account their developmental level and symptomatology.

A number of authors (Scheeringa et al., 1995; Rust & Troupe, 1991; Delaney-Black et al., 2002) have presented some of the elements that confound the interpretation of presenting symptoms and complicate the establishment of a definitive diagnosis from the differential diagnostic options. These include the lack of complete recollection of the traumatic event, and the need to disentangle avoidance and separation anxiety. Flashbacks may not occur, yet a child may experience nightmares or night terrors that are not directly related to the event. Certain symptoms such as irritability, distractibility, and problems in concentration are frequently identified in hyperactive children and may occur denovo in a very young child, or these symptoms may be accentuated in another child.

All of these symptoms tend to perplex clinicians, teachers, parents, and the children themselves. Perrin and colleagues (2000) proposed that a potentially useful approach to this dilemma would be a multifaceted evaluation that would include culturally sensitive information and incorporate the use of semi-structured interviews and self-reports for data collection purposes. He based this concept on the varying symptomatology and comorbidity that children with PTSD present with. Moreover, he reinforced the importance of clinicians being acquainted with the concept of PTSD presenting in children with polymorphously diverse symptomatology.

The approach is sound when one considers Yule's notion (2001) that the diagnostic process of the *DSM-IV* actually promotes making multiple diagnoses and thus encourages comorbidity.

Perry and Azad (1999) reported that, using structured diagnostic interviews, the majority of children met criteria for three or more *DSM* diagnoses in addition to PTSD. This is consistent with the findings of others (Silva et al., 2002; Brent et al., 1995), which have reported that some children with comorbid and pre-existing diagnoses may be predisposed to the development of PTSD. Silva described anxiety prior to the traumatic event as a substantial risk factor for the development of PTSD. Brent described depression as a potential vulnerability factor and agrees with the concept that both depression and anxiety have symptoms in common with PTSD.

We should also take into account that other psychiatric and even medical disorders may follow the development of PTSD. These may include substance abuse, depression, anxiety, phobia, and symptomatic pain. The lack of timely diagnosis of PTSD and the consequent lack of treatment may also be causal in the persistence of some symptoms and the development of new ones.

Regardless of preexisting factors or comorbid symptoms, clinicians should reconcile the potential of multiple comorbities existing and take these into account when formulating a treatment plan for these children. According to the *DSM-IV-TR*, the differential diagnoses of PTSD that should be entertained include adjustment disorders, acute stress disorder, mood disorder, anxiety disorders, obsessive-compulsive disorder, schizophrenia, other psychotic disorders, substance induced disorder, psychotic disorder due to a general medical condition, and malingering.

Although the *DSM-IV-TR* presents a thorough list, it does not include certain childhood disorders that we believe might also be confused with PTSD. These diagnoses include elements of separation anxiety disorder, attention deficit hyperactivity disorder, other disruptive behavior disorders, and sleep disorders.

Differentiating each disorder from PTSD in children presents difficulties. At times, this is due to overlapping symptoms, or due to the ambiguity of information provided by the child or legal guardian. We will now attempt to review the major points in differentiating PTSD from the above listed diagnoses.

We may differentiate PTSD from adjustment disorder by evaluating the nature and intensity of the event (stressor) and by considering the criteria for trauma. Also, the symptoms in an adjustment disorder are generally less severe. Symptoms may emerge within 3 months of the event and should not continue for more than 6 months after the stressor.

In the case of acute stress disorder, although it occurs after a traumatic event, it can be differentiated on the basis of duration of symptoms, which tend to be shorter (2 days to 4 weeks) than PTSD, which requires the persistence of symptoms beyond 4 weeks.

Depression and PTSD have common diagnostic characteristics. These disorders are not mutually exclusive and their comorbity is often evident. Furthermore, as we mentioned above, one disorder could induce the other.

When discussing anxiety disorders, according to the *DSM-IV-TR*, generalized anxiety disorder (GAD) shares four symptoms (sleep disturbances, difficulty concentrating, hypervigilance, and irritability) with PTSD. Clearly, the context of the symptoms, such as onset after an identified stressor, may help clarify diagnostic dilemmas between PTSD and GAD.

Obsessive-compulsive disorder (OCD) differs from PTSD as individuals with the former diagnosis experience frequent and repetitive thoughts, referred to as obsessions, which are not particularly related to a traumatic event. Conversely, the intrusive thoughts that accompany PTSD are usually related to a traumatic event, although the intrusive thoughts may be more general in nature in younger children. In should be noted that in some cases, OCD symptoms may follow a traumatic event.

Phobias are characterized as anxiety secondary to exposure to a feared object or situation and can culminate in avoidant behavior (*DSM-IV-TR*). Phobias can be differentiated from

PTSD in that they should not present with the intrusive or increased arousal cluster of symptoms.

Panic attacks are characterized as circumscribed periods during which the patient experiences the precipitous onset of intense apprehension, terror, or doom (*DSM-IV-TR*). In comparing the two disorders, symptoms of increased arousal are shared by both.

Disruptive behavior spectrum symptoms occur more often in boys. They manifest with varying combinations of aggression, impulsivity, inattention, and hyperactivity. However, as previously discussed, the presentation of these symptoms can often be observed in children with either PTSD or disruptive behavior disorder.

Regarding separation anxiety symptoms, Vogel and colleagues (1993) in their review of children's response to disasters, found that children respond to disaster with symptoms of fear, separation anxiety, regression, and sleep difficulties.

Psychotic disorders, namely schizophrenia and any other perceptual disorder may share with PTSD the spontaneous recurrence of certain images or *flashbacks*. As discussed in the case of K presented earlier, the interpretation of symptoms can confound the establishment of the PTSD diagnosis.

With respect to the differential between PTSD and sleep disorders, Criterion D of PTSD in the *DSM-IV-TR* establishes that there might be unrelenting difficulty falling or staying asleep as part of persistent symptoms of increased arousal. Once again, in differentiating these symptoms, the clinician could easily confuse this presentation with a sleep disorder of the insomnia type. Furthermore, Criterion B of PTSD in the *DSM-IV-TR* also states that children might have distressing dreams without identifiable content, which can also be inaccurately classified as a sleep terror disorder in a young child.

In comparing the common elements of PTSD and dissociative disorder, dissociation generally displays a progression of a synchronized set of actions, thoughts, attitudes, or emotions that become separate from the rest of the person's personality. The presence of dissociation is also included as part of Criterion B in PTSD.

Enuresis and encopresis are other diagnoses that can be seen in children with PTSD, especially when the children tend to suffer regression of their behavior as a result of the trauma.

The AACAP practice parameters (1998) reported that when symptom patterns of other mental disorders such as major depression, attention deficit hyperactivity, and substance abuse occur in response to a stressor, these disorders should be used instead of PTSD. Nonetheless, when the trauma obviously predated the onset of PTSD symptoms, and the symptoms of other diagnoses coexist, AACAP indicates that both diagnoses should be made. This is a significant concept to consider when making diagnostic decisions regarding comorbid psychiatric entities and PTSD.

Conclusions

PTSD shares signs and symptoms with many other psychiatric disorders, particularly in children and adolescents, who present an additional challenge. One of the long-term sequelae of suffering a traumatic event is that the suffering perpetuates chronic manifestations of PTSD and maladaptive coping mechanisms. Therefore, it is essential to identify the presenting features, establish a diagnosis and provide treatment as early as possible.

We recommend a developmentally sensitive approach when assessing children and adolescents that considers developmental stages, comorbidity patterns, and the overlap of symptoms with other disorders. Finally, a careful review of the child's history is crucial.

References

American Academy of Child & Adolescent Psychiatry. (1998). *Practice Parameters for the Assessment and Treatment of Children and Adolescents with Posttraumatic Stress Disorder.* 37(suppl October):10.

Benedek EP. (1985). Children and disaster: emerging issues. *Psychiatric Ann.* 15:168–172.

Brent DA, Perper JA, Moritz G, et al. (1995). Posttraumatic stress disorder in peers of adolescent suicide victims. Predisposing factors and phenomenology. *J Am Acad Child Adolesc Psychiatry.* 34:209–215.

Delaney-Black V, Covington C, Ondersma SJ, et al. (2002). Violence exposure, trauma, and IQ and/or reading deficits among urban children. *Arch Pediatr Adolesc Med.* 156(3):280–285.

Drell MJ, Siegel CH, Gaensbauer TJ. (1993). Posttraumatic stress disorder. In: Zeanah CH, ed. *Handbook of infant mental health.* New York: Guilford Press; 291–304.

Dulcan MK, Martini D. (1999). *Concise Guide to Child and Adolescent Psychiatry.* Second Edition. Washington, DC: APA Press Inc.; 128–129.

Herman JL. (1992). Complex PTSD: a syndrome in survivors of prolonged and repeated trauma. *J Trauma Stress.* 5:377–391.

Lonigan CJ, Anthony JL, Shannon MP. (1998). Diagnostic efficacy of posttraumatic stress symptoms in children exposed to disaster. *J Clin Child Psychol.* 27(3):255–267.

Ohan JL, Myers K, Collett BR. (2002). Ten-year review of rating scales IV: scales assessing trauma and its effects. *J Am Acad Child Adolesc Psychiatry.* 41(12):1401–1421.

Perrin S, Smith P, Yule W. (2000). Practitioner review: the assessment and treatment of post-traumatic stress disorder in children and adolescents. *J Child Psychol Psychiatry.* 41(3): 277–289.

Perry BD, Azad I. (1999). Posttraumatic stress disorders in children and adolescents. *Curr Opinion Pediatr.* 11:310–316.

Pynoos RS, Steinberg AM, Wraith RA. (1995). Developmental model of childhood traumatic stress. In: Cicchetti D and Cohen D, eds. *Manual of Developmental Psychology* (vol.2). New York: Wiley; 72–95.

Rust JO, Troupe PA. (1991). Relationship of child sexual abuse with school achievement and self-concept. *J Early Adolescence.* 11:420–429.

Scheeringa MS, Zeanah CH, Drell MJ, Larrieu JA. (1995). Two approaches to the diagnosis of posttraumatic stress disorder in infancy and early childhood. *Am Acad Child Adolesc Psychiatry.* 34(2):191–200.

Shalev AY. (2001). What is posttraumatic stress disorder? *J Clin Psychiatry*. 62 (suppl 17):4–10.

Silva RR, Alpert M, Munoz DM, et al. (2002). Stress and vulnerability to posttraumatic stress disorder in children and adolescents. *Am J Psychiatry*. 157:1229–1235.

Terr LC. (1991). Childhood traumas—an outline and overview. *Am J Psychiatry*. 148:10–20.

Terr LC. (1985). Psychic trauma in children and adolescents. *Psychiatric Clinics North Am*. 8(4): 815–835.

Vogel JM, Vernberg EM. (1993). Task force report: Part I. Children's psychological responses to disasters. *J Clin Child Psychol*. 22:464–484.

Yule W. (2001). Posttraumatic stress disorder in the general population and in children. *J Clin Psychiatry*. 62 (suppl 17):23–28.

12

▪

Childhood vs. Adult PTSD

Veronica M. Rojas and Tal N. Lee

Posttraumatic stress disorder (PTSD) is a condition in which an antecedent traumatic event—imminent loss of life or physical integrity—is followed by certain characteristic symptoms of reexperiencing, avoidance of stimuli, and hyperarousal.

Certain symptoms are known to be specific to PTSD in adults, others are distinctive to children, and some are characteristic of both. In general, children process stimuli differently than adults due to several factors: their developmental stage, their brain development, their environment, and familial-genetic factors.

In this chapter, we will discuss the difference between PTSD symptoms in children and adults. It is of essence to understand the reasons for these differences, and to attempt to increase our cognizance about the children's subjective experience and processing of the trauma within the context of development. The manner in which children experience and process trauma may be inferred by appreciating characteristic behaviors found in traumatized children as juxtaposed with normal developmental behaviors and milestones in children, vis-à-vis models such as psychodynamic, developmental, and neurobiological theories.

Historical Overview of the Diagnosis

It has long been recognized that some soldiers who were exposed to the atrocities of war experienced "shell shock" or "battle fatigue" that manifested in various physical and mental symptoms. In the 1920s, Sigmund Freud defined trauma as an event that has exceeded the adaptive coping mechanisms available to the individual (1920/1955). He believed that trauma overwhelms the individual, thus causing a powerful need to repeat and reenact the traumatic event, even if the reenactment itself is distressing (1926/1959).

Many studies made in the 1940s established a foundation for the study of childhood trauma, but the onset of the movement to understand the condition did not begin until the 1960s and 1970s. In 1952, the first *Diagnostic and Statistical Manual* named the condition *gross stress reaction*, a designation that was replaced in the *DSM-II* of 1968 by the term *transient situational disturbance*.

The importance of traumatic experiences in children was not recognized as a diagnostic category until the publication of the *DSM-III–R*, which identified some of the differences between child and adult PTSD symptoms. In a review of PTSD in children of the past 10 years, Pfefferbaum (1997) described that despite greater exposure of children to increasingly hostile environments, the recognition of PTSD in children lags behind that in adults.

The classification of posttraumatic stress disorder in the psychiatric taxonomy of mental disorders has facilitated increased congruence in diagnosis and treatment of the disorder among clinicians, researchers, and diagnosticians. The categorization refers to a cluster of symptoms that emerges as a result of acute or chronic trauma.

The *DSM-IV-TR* recognizes the differences in definition of trauma and symptomatology between children and adults and delineates them in special notations. Children, for instance, may demonstrate disorganized or agitated behavior (A2), instead of fear, horror, or helplessness seen in adults. They may exhibit repetitive play (B1) that reenacts trauma-specific themes (B3), as opposed to the symptoms of intrusive recollections exhibited by adults. Furthermore, in lieu of distressing dreams about the trauma that are experienced by adults, children may have frightening dreams without recognizable content (B2) (American Psychiatric Association, 1994).

Notwithstanding this acknowledgement by the American Psychiatric Association (APA), the authors of this chapter contend that children's posttraumatic stress disorder varies significantly from that of adults in at least two distinct domains—the *experiential impression* of the trauma, and the PTSD *symptoms* exhibited.

Children's Experience of Trauma

As mentioned above, children's experiential impression of trauma may vary considerably from that of adults. This section focuses on children's experience of trauma in context of their developmental stages, personality formation, attachment patterns, and caregivers' response to the trauma. It is important to note that the objective importance and bulk of the stressor is directly related and proportional to the risk of developing PTSD (March 1993; McNally 1993), and if a traumatic event is intense enough, any child could be traumatized (Pynoos et al., 1987; Terr, 1979).

Relationship Between Developmental Factors and the Experience of Trauma

Responses to traumatic stressors vary across the developmental span of childhood and adolescence. Individuals experience stressors differently, thus their memories, emotional reactions, behaviors, relatedness, and capacity of organizing the experience vary by developmental stage.

Children exposed to a traumatic event before being able to organize the experience verbally differ greatly in their perception of the event from children who experienced it at an older age.

The former, as we mentioned above, may not have the same sense of the traumatic event since they may not have the narrative recollection. Rather, they may experience intense feelings or sensations.

Van der Kolk (1994) discussed Janet's postulation that intense emotional reactions make events traumatic by interfering with the integration of the experience into existing memory schemes. The intensity may cause memories of particular events to disengage from consciousness and to be stored instead as visceral sensations (i.e., anxiety and panic) or visual images (i.e., nightmares and flashbacks). Terr (1988) noted similarly that children younger than three years of age may be unable to narrate their trauma as a chronological description or even have full verbal recollection, because their language is still in the process of development.

Relationship Between Attachment Patterns and the Experience of Trauma

The attachment pattern of an infant to its caregiver is essential for the understanding of its effects on the perception and reaction to trauma. Ainsworth and colleagues' study of the "strange situation" (1978) examined infants' behavior during periods of separation and reunification with their caregivers, and classified the attachment patterns as "secure" or "insecure." The latter classification was further subcategorized as "avoidant," "resistant," and "disorganized" types of attachment. These attachment patterns between infants and primary caregiver appear to have long-lasting implications on the development of the infants' personality.

Siegel (1999) stated that the caregiver's attachment security carries a form of resilience to the infant, which could be sustained even during times of loss or trauma. He also noted "longitudinal research on attachment suggests that certain early relationship experiences promote emotional well-being, social competence, cognitive functioning, and resilience in the face of adversity" (1999, p. 84). Sroufe and associates (1983) suggested that disorganized attachment stemming from child maltreatment may affect child's relationships with other adults, and consequently may impair future social competence.

It is also of essence to examine the manner in which pretraumatic attachment patterns may change if the trauma occurs at a young age. Particularly if the trauma involved the child's caregivers, pretraumatic attachment patterns could possibly be altered to a different posttraumatic attachment pattern. Moreover, it may affect the child's perception, coping, and memory of the trauma and the symptoms he or she exhibits.

Parent Experiences of and Responsiveness to the Trauma and Their Effects on the Child's Experience of the Trauma

Children generally use *social referencing*—take cues from caregivers—to gauge their own response to stimuli. It has been well documented in the literature that children tend to respond to traumatic events based on their parents' responsiveness. (Bingham & Harmon, 1996; Bloch et al., 1956; Earls et al., 1998; Green et al., 1991; Jensen & Shaw, 1993; Sach et al., 1995; Sullivan et al., 1991).

Supporting this notion, Wolmer and colleagues' study (2000) examined the relationship of the three posttraumatic clusters of symptoms (numbing, avoidance, and intrusive symptoms) between mothers and their preschool children 30 months after the end of the Persian Gulf War. They found that these posttraumatic symptom clusters were mostly related with the mothers' general pathological reaction, such as aggression, paranoia, depression, anxiety and phobia, rather than with children's specific posttraumatic symptoms.

They also found that these were correlated with the children's age at the time of the traumatic event—the younger the children, the higher the relationship to their mothers' general symptomatology. In addition, Wolmer and colleagues study elucidates the importance of the children's developmental stage when traumatized. Bingham and Harmon (1996) described that the parents are the main shields for a young child. However, when child and/or parent are exposed to a threatening traumatic event toward the child, then they are challenged together to reestablish the child's safety.

McFarlane (1987) studied the effects of the Australian bush fires on family reactions and the relationship of those reactions to children's functioning. On an 8-month follow-up, he found that the effects of child-to-caregiver reactions were not unidirectional but reciprocal, and that the families who shared similar immediate response to the trauma had better adjustment rates.

Furthermore, there is an association between family environment and children's responses to trauma. As Laor and colleagues (1996) reported, there is a parallel between the unity and warmth of the family and individual symptoms in children. This correlation seems to be a protection from the development of further symptoms in children, particularly preschoolers, who were exposed to traumatic events.

Moreover, Laor and colleagues (1996) contended that the parent-child dyad helps the child regulate both external and internal stimuli and has a buffering effect on the traumatic response. He states that younger children are more dependent on their parents and have amplified sensitivity to the parents' immediate response to the traumatic events. This sensitivity, in turn, may increase or decrease their susceptibility to PTSD symptoms, depending on the parents' immediate reaction.

Developmental Reexperiencing of Trauma

Terr (1990) described trauma being rethought and reexperienced emotionally from the children's new developmental stage. Furthermore, Russell (1986) contended that children who were traumatized can be retraumatized because they may "unconsciously reenact" the traumatic event. Young children who have experienced trauma often repress its memory, but as they experience certain developmental milestones or encounter triggering cues, they may reexperience the traumatic affect and become symptomatic.

Both Freud (1919/1954) and Pavlov (1926) explained the lingering effects of trauma as biologically based. The latter described the hypervigilance and irritability of patients who had been repeatedly traumatized in terms of conditional and unconditional stimuli and responses. Triggering cues of perceived threats that may or may not be inherently related to the original repeated traumatic stimuli, Pavlov argued, elicit a reflexive *defense reaction* response.

Freud (1919/1954) described a similar condition, *deferred action* or *Nachtraglichkeit*, in which an individual experiences two events. The first was traumatic but was not experienced as such at the time. The second event, which may not be traumatic in and of itself, becomes traumatic by activating a deferred affective reaction to the original event. Thus, the memory of the first event remains repressed, and the emotional reaction continues to be consciously attached to the second. He wrote, "Indeed the great majority of instances we find that a first trauma has left no symptom behind, while a later trauma of the same kind produces a symptom, and yet the latter could not have come into existence without the co-operation of the earlier provoking cause; nor can it be cleared up without taking all the provoking causes into account."

Phenomenology of Intrafamilial Abuse

Children who have experienced intrafamilial trauma often experience additional relational and emotional sequelae that transcend the trauma itself. The inherent characteristics of childhood—dependency on adults, inchoate personality development, inefficient utilization of resources, and paucity of previous experiences on which to base judgment—invariably render children more vulnerable than adults.

Traumatized children may experience a profound sense of betrayal by their caregivers and a lingering ambivalence about dependence on the perpetrators. In addition to the sense of relational precariousness, there may also be a significant deterioration of existential security. The children, particularly in cases of chronic traumatization, may have difficulty gauging their safety within their unpredictable environment, which subsequently may lead to a sense of learned helplessness, confusion, and isolation.

Another relational factor that significantly affects the children's experience of trauma is their tendency to view their parents as all-powerful, a notion that is shattered when the parents fail to protect them against the trauma. The attempt to reconcile the notion of the fallibility of the omnipotent caregiver requires substantial emotional resources by the children and may subsequently affect their sense of trust and security.

Symptoms

Clinicians and researchers continue to question the appropriateness of adapting the adult definition of PTSD to children. Younger children present an additional logistical dilemma regarding PTSD diagnosis, which is the clinical difficulty in detecting their symptoms.

PTSD Symptoms in Children

Scheeringa and colleagues (2001) studied the aspects of diagnosis and assessment of PTSD in infants and young children and stated that their study demonstrated the significance of relying on caregivers' reports for accurate diagnosis of young children. Their study concluded "observational/interaction sequences with the children allowed raters to detect only 12% of the diagnostic criteria in a traumatized symptomatic sample" (2001, p. 58). This issue illustrates the importance of comprehensive trauma assessment during interviews, which should include observation and interaction with the child, as well as in-depth interview of the caregiver.

Children and adults share some of the symptoms, but they rarely meet the *DSM-IV-TR* criteria of PTSD, as they might exhibit different symptomatology. Some symptoms in children and adults overlap, such as self-blame, survivor's guilt, dependency, emotional numbing, and impulsivity. However, children may incorporate these symptoms into their personality and subsequently have long-term disturbances to their social, cognitive, and emotional development.

The *DSM-IV-TR* reflects some of these differences by stating that young children's reexperiences of the trauma can be manifested as repetitive play rather than recurring images, thoughts, or perceptions, which are predominantly adult symptoms. This is based on the belief that young children do not have the sense of reliving the past, but rather relive it as the present, as exemplified in symptoms such as regression and posttraumatic play (APA, 1994).

REGRESSION

Regression is an unconscious endeavor to return to an earlier libidinal phase of functioning in order to elude the tension and conflict evoked at the present level of development (Freud, A, 1966). Young children may exhibit loss of previously acquired developmental skills, such as toilet training and language capacities, as well as regression of emotional growth, thus becoming more infantile in their language and behaviors (i.e., thumb sucking, enuresis). Regression is a more prominent PTSD symptom in children than in adults. It is probably used as a means of getting comfort and avoiding anxiety by reverting to earlier modes of response or a safer developmental stage. Furthermore, it may function as a means of receiving additional positive or negative attention from caregivers when facing anxiety-inducing stressors.

POSTTRAUMATIC PLAY

Younger children with PTSD may reexperience the traumatic event in the form of repetitive play instead of the more explicit flashbacks and distressing intrusive memories experienced by older children and adults. These children may use traumatic play, which entails reenacting dramatization with elements or themes of the event, or they may alter the action of the event, and use symbolic dangers (e.g., monsters) or violent, suicidal, or sexually precocious elements (Terr, 1990).

RELATIONSHIP BETWEEN DEVELOPMENTAL FACTORS AND PTSD SYMPTOMS

As mentioned above, developmental stages are important factors to consider in the diagnosis of PTSD. Children may display symptoms such as fear of the dark, fear of separation from caregivers, and nightmares (Yule, 1994), posttraumatic play re-enactment, or a sense of foreshortened future (Terr, 1988).

In reviewing these data, we could infer that young children are often misdiagnosed due to their PTSD presentation that is distinctive and inconsistent with that of adults. For example, Green and colleagues (1991) stated that children—who do not manifest appreciable avoidance symptoms—would qualify as having fewer PTSD symptoms, and therefore might not be diagnosed as such. Other symptoms, such as fear of the dark or of being away from a caregiver could potentially be misdiagnosed as separation anxiety disorder or a phobic disorder.

Preschoolers may exhibit other manifestations as a result of trauma that could affect them in a significantly different way than older children and adolescents. In the Buffalo Creek inci-dent, in which a dam collapsed in West Virginia and caused flooding and loss of life on a large scale, Newman (1976) found that the children had an altered sense of reality and self, height-ened sensitivity to stress (hypervigilance), and early perception of fragmentation and death.

Adolescents and adults, on the other hand, have similar PTSD symptomatology, but also have some significant differ-ences. Adolescents are more vulnerable due to their underdevel-oped integration of personality-identity. Even normal development during adolescence entails confusion, social and academic pressures, sexual development, individuation, and fric-tion with family. These are further confounded and exacerbated by traumatic experiences.

According to Cuffe and colleagues (1998), the most common PTSD symptoms in a sample of subjects aged 16 to 22 years were distressing recollection (re-experience), efforts to avoid activities that facilitate recollections (avoidant/numbing), and efforts to avoid thoughts and feelings. Adolescents may experience flash-backs similar to those of adults (Horowitz, 1976; Terr, 1979), but also they may undergo increased sleeplessness, inattentiveness, and irritability when compared with latency-age children.

PERSONALITY FORMATION

Rutter (1979) stated that the preexisting characteristics of a per-sonality, such as intelligence, humor, and relatedness, are a fun-damental protective barrier against development of posttraumatic stress disorder. However, trauma has long-term consequences on children due to their inchoate personality development. It may have tremendous effects on the trajectory of a child's personality formation, which may range in manifestation from benign idio-syncrasies to debilitating and maladaptive pathologies.

The effects of trauma, particularly abusive caregiving, may radically alter the course of normal personality formation, particularly the development of morality, sense of self, and capacity for intimate relationships. Chronic maltreatment of children may manifest later in life in such characterological disorders as borderline personality disorder or antisocial personality disorder.

One of the most pronounced possible effects of trauma on personality development may be dissociative identity disorder, in which the traumatized child cannot endure the pain of chronic trauma, and alter identities are created. At the time of trauma, these alter identities function as a defense in order to diffuse and isolate the emotional content of the experience. However, as these children mature, they continue to use this complex form of dissociation to cope with stressors, which invariably causes maladaptive functioning as adults.

NEUROBIOLOGICAL FACTORS

There is a paucity of research on the neurobiological effects of trauma and PTSD in developing children, although significant neurobiological and physiological changes occur in response to trauma. However, some available data helps us to better understand how children process trauma. For example, Terr (1988) described that some infants and toddlers have nonverbal experiences (due to their inability to use a verbal language at the time). Nevertheless, she reported that these children have *implicit memories* of their traumatic event.

Implicit memory, according to Siegel (1996), is the way in which the brain processes an experience and influences later behavior without requiring conscious awareness, recognition, or recall of inner experience of a retrieved memory. Siegel further proposes that trauma may involve inhibition of hippocampal functioning at the time of experience, thus blocking the encoding process of explicit memory. Consistent with this concept, Freud (1912/1958) used *free association* to make repressed unconscious memories become conscious in order to retrieve and process early traumatic memories.

From this point of view, a developing brain is less likely to process information than would a fully developed brain would. Perry and colleagues (1995) reported that the response observed in adults might be less adaptive in young children. This is possibly because the brain is in a continuity of development until age 20, when it reaches its adult levels.

When young children experience a traumatic event, they may initially respond with increased activity or hyperarousal. This could make the caretaker become more attentive and understand the child's need for attention and care. However, if the traumatic event persists, the child's response frequently might be immobilization or freezing and subsequent dissociation and surrendering.

When a child suffers a traumatic event, there is an over-stimulation of the central nervous system (CNS) that involves an underproduction of synapses and overpruning. This may create permanent neuronal changes that significantly affect the child's capacity for learning, habituation, and stimulus discrimination (Kolb, 1987; Siegel, 1999). Siegel stated that "in addition to damaging the hippocampus, early childhood maltreatment may directly affect circuits that directly link bodily response to brain function: the autonomic nervous system, the HPA [hypo-thalamic-pituitary-adrenal] axis, and the neuroimmune process" (1996, p. 52).

According to several studies (Shalev, et al.,1992; Davis, 1984; Ornitz & Pynoos, 1989) people who have PTSD often present with an abnormal acoustic startle response, which exemplifies neuronal changes. These studies have also examined acoustic startle response and found abnormal habituation.

Diagnostic Considerations

It our contention that some diagnoses of personality and behavior disorders in children may have originated in misconceptualization and misdiagnosis, in part because the significance of their trauma-related etiology has been underestimated. In order to illustrate this line of reasoning, we will consider three categories—behavioral, emotional, and learning—and their impact on the long-term development of the child.

BEHAVIORAL REGULATION

The *DSM-IV-TR* states that young children might not demonstrate diminished interest in activities and constriction of their affect. It is possible that children could exhibit other symptoms, such as disorganized and agitated behavior, which could be misdiagnosed as a different disorder, such as attention deficit hyperactivity disorder (ADHD) or oppositional defiant disorder.

Glod and Teicher (1996) examined the relationship between activity level of abused children with PTSD, abused without PTSD symptoms, and normal children. She found that abused children were 10% more active than normal children but displayed low levels of daytime activity. Furthermore, abused children with PTSD had significantly higher level of activity than even their non-PTSD abused counterparts.

Also, abused preschool children might demonstrate diminished capacity for pro-social behavior, as they may respond aggressively to peers, avoid people who make friendly overtures toward them, and repeat abusive patterns toward nonabusive adults in their environment (Rutter et al., 1995).

This aggressive presentation of the child may be misdiagnosed as oppositional defiant disorder or intermittent explosive disorder. Aggression, hostility, and defiance can be prevalent behaviors of survivors of childhood trauma, because the difficulty in regulating behavior may be ingrained in their nascent personality. The manifestation of externalized anger may be the result of *identification with the aggressor*, in which the victim incorporates traits of the aggressive offender in an attempt to master the fear that aggressor induces. However, the anger may also be the child's inability to process the trauma. Their dysregulation of behavior is thus manifested by these acting-out behaviors.

EMOTIONAL REGULATION

Children with PTSD often make conscious attempts to avoid traumatic reminders—namely thoughts, feelings, or activities— that precipitate distressing recollections of the event. Cognitive suppression, distraction, and behavioral avoidance are particularly common.

Due to the egocentricity of certain developmental stages, children may assume that they have effectuated their trauma, which subsequently may elicit feelings of internalized anger. This frequently presents as guilt, shame, and self-reproach. These symptoms may be misdiagnosed as depression, when in fact they are masking PTSD.

LEARNING

Traumatized children frequently display inattentiveness, disorganization, poor academic achievement, and language deficits. These may be a result of dissociation, flashbacks, tiredness (due to nightmares), irritability, separation anxiety, memory problems, and difficulties with concentration. These symptoms might make the child seem to be suffering symptoms of a learning disability, or the child may be misdiagnosed as having PTSD.

As a result of misdiagnosis, a child may be misclassified at school and not receive appropriate academic services. More egregiously, the child may fail to receive appropriate therapeutic treatment.

Conclusions

The experiences and symptoms of trauma in children differ significantly from those of adults. The two groups vary in their ability to comprehend trauma and process it, and in the manifestations of their distress. Children and adolescents are in the midst of a development process, which limits their physical, emotional, cognitive, and social abilities to deal with traumatic events in an adaptive manner. Furthermore, children's dependency on their family and environment is more profound than for adults, which may exacerbate their vulnerability and tenuous sense of control.

Since the catastrophic terrorist attacks of September 11, 2001, the public and mental health professionals have become more aware of the importance of conducting further research about the effects of trauma on individuals and the development of posttraumatic stress disorder symptoms. It is essential to continue exploring the ramifications of traumatic events, especially in children and adolescents, because such events have immense impact on their emotional and psychological development, academic and social abilities, and their personality formation.

It also seems crucial to reevaluate the current conceptualization of the PTSD diagnosis as it applies to children and adolescents. Research and clinical evidence demonstrate an experiential and symptomatological incongruity between adult and childhood PTSD diagnoses. We believe that in order to improve accuracy and efficacy of diagnosis and treatment of childhood PTSD, the condition must be examined through the lens of children's development stages and their unique experience of trauma.

References

Ainsworth MDS, Blehar MC, Waters E, Wall S. (1978). *Patterns of Attachment: Psychological Study of the Strange Situation*. Hillsdale. NJ: Erlbaum.

American Psychiatric Association. (1994). *Diagnostic and Statistical Manual of Mental Disorders* (4th ed.). Washington, DC: American Psychiatric Association.

American Psychiatric Association. (2000). *Diagnostic and Statistical Manual of Mental Disorders* (4th ed., text rev.). Washington, DC: American Psychiatric Association.

Bingham RD, Harmon RJ. (1996). Traumatic stress in infancy and early childhood: Expression of distress and developmental issues. In: Pfeffer C, ed. *Severe Stress and Mental Disturbance in Children*. Washington, DC: American Psychiatric Association Press; 499–532.

Bloch DA, Silber E, Perry SE. (1956). Some factors in the emotional reaction of children to disaster. *Am J Psychiatry*. 113:416–422.

Cuffe SP, Addy CL, Garrison CZ. (1998). Prevalence of PTSD in a community sample of older adolescents. *J Am Acad Child Adolesc Psychiatry*. 37:147–154.

Davis M. (1984). The mammalian startle response. In Eaton RC, ed. *Neural Mechanisms of Startle Behavior*. New York: Plenum Press.

DeBellis MD, Baum AS, Birmaher B, et al. (1999). Developmental traumatology, Part I: Biological stress systems. *Biol Psychiatry*. 45:1259–1270.

DeBellis MD, Keshavan MS, Clark DB, et al. (1999). Developmental traumatology, Part II: Brain development. *Biol Psychiatry*. 45:1271–1284.

Earls F, Smith E, Reich W, Jung KG. (1988). Investigation psychopathological consequences of a disaster in children: a pilot study incorporating a structured diagnostic interview. *J Am Acad Child Adolesc Psychiatry*. 27:90–95.

Freud A. (1966). *Ego and the Mechanism of Defense*. Madison, Conn.: International University Press

Freud A, Burlingham D. (1944). *War and Children*. New York: International University Press.

Freud S. (1955). *Beyond the Pleasure Principle*. In Strachey, J. (Ed. & Trans.), *Standard Edition of the Complete Psychological Works of Sigmund Freud*. (Vol. 18, pp. 1–64). London: Hogarth Press. (Originally published 1920)

Freud S. (1958). *The Dynamics of Transference*. In Strachey, J. (Ed. & Trans.), *Standard Edition of the Complete Psychological Works of Sigmund Freud*. (Vol. 12, pp. 97–108). London, Hogarth Press. (Originally published 1912)

Freud S. (1959). *Inhibitions, Symptoms, and Anxiety*. In Strachey, J. (Ed. & Trans.), *Standard Edition of the Complete Psychological Works of Sigmund Freud*. (Vol. 20, pp. 75–175). London: Hogarth Press. (Originally published 1926)

Freud, S. (1954). *Introduction to Psycho-analysis and the war neuroses.* In J. Strachey (Ed. & Trans.), *Standard Edition of the Complete Psychological Works of Sigmund Freud* (vol. 17, pp. 205–216). London: Hogarth Press. (Original work published in 1919).

Freud S, Breuer J. (1955). *Studies on Hysteria.* In Strachey J (Ed. & Trans.), *Standard Edition of the Complete Psychological Works of Sigmund Freud.* London: Hogarth Press. (Originally published 1895)

Glod CA, Teicher MH. (1996). Relationship between early abuse, posttraumatic stress disorder, and activity levels in prepubertal children. *J Am Acad Child Adolesc Psychiatry.* 35(10):1384–1393.

Green BL, Korol M, Grace MC, et al. (1991). Children and disaster: age, gender and parental effects on PTSD symptoms. *J Am Acad Child Adolesc Psychiatry.* 39:945–951.

Horowitz M. (1976). *Stress Response Syndromes.* New York: Aronson.

Jensen PS, Shaw J. (1993). Children as victims of war: current knowledge and future research needs. *J Am Acad Child Adolesc Psychiatry.* 32:697–708.

Kolb LC. (1987). Neurophysiological hypothesis explaining posttraumatic stress disorder. *Am J Psychiatry.* 144:989–995.

Laor N, Wolmer L, Mayes L, et al. (1993). Israeli preschoolers under SCUD missile attacks: a developmental perspective on risk-modifying factors. *Arch Gen Psychiatry.* 53(5):416–423.

Laor N, Wolmer L, Mayes LC, et al. (1996). Israeli preschoolers under Scud missle attacks: a development perspective on risk-modifying factors. *Arch Gen Psychiatry.* 53:416–423.

March J. (1993). What constitutes a stressor? The "Criteria A" issue. In: J Davidson, E Foa, eds. *Posttraumatic Stress Disorder: DSM-IV and Beyond.* Washington, D.C.: American Psychiatric Press; 37–54.

McFarlane AC. (1987). Family functioning and overprotection following a natural disaster. *Aust N Z J Psychiatry.* 21:210–218.

McNally RJ. (1993). Stressors that produce posttraumatic stress disorder in children. In: J Davidson, E Foa eds. *Posttraumtic Stress Disorder: DSM-IV and Beyond.* Washington DC: American Psychiatric Press; 57–74.

Newman C J. (1976). Children of disaster: clinical observations at Buffalo Creek. *Am J Psychiatry.* 133:306–312.

Ornitz EM, Pynoos RS. (1989). Startle modulation in children with post traumatic stress disorder. *Am J Psychiatry.* 146:866–870.

Pavlov, IP. (1926). *Conditioned Reflexes: An Investigation of the Physiological Activity of the Cerebral Cortex* (GV Anrep, Trans. & Ed.). New York: Dover.

Perry BD. (1994). Neurobiological sequelae of childhood trauma: PTSD in children. In: Mumberg, ed. *Catecholamine Function in Posttraumatic Stress Disorder: Emerging Concepts.* Washington, DC: American Psychiatric Press; 233–255.

Perry BD, Pollard RA, Blakley TL, Baker WL, Vigilante D. (1995). Childhood trauma, the neurobiology of adaptation and use-dependent development of the brain: how states become traits. *Infant Ment Health J.* 16:271–291.

Pfefferbaum B. (1997). Posttraumatic stress disorder in children: a review of the past 10 years. *J Am Acad Child Adolesce Psychiatry.* 36(11):1503–1511.

Pynoos RS, Frderick CJ, Nader K, et al. (1987). Life threat and posttraumatic stress in school-age children. *Arch Gen Psychiatry.* 44(12):1057–1063.

Russell D. (1986). *The Secret Trauma.* New York: Basic Books.

Rutter M. (1979). Protective factors in children's responses to stress and disadvantage. In: Kent, MW, JE Rolf. *Primary Prevention of Psychopathology, Vol. 3: Social Competence in Children.* Hanover, NH: University Press of New England; 49–74.

Rutter M, Taylor E, Hersov L. (1995). *Child and Adolescent Psychiatry: Modern Approaches.* Cambridge, Mass: Blackwell Science, Inc.

Sach WH, Clarke GN, Seeley J. (1995). Posttraumatic stress disorder across two generations of Cambodian refugees. *J Am Acad Child Adolesc Psychiatry.* 34:1160–1166.

Scheeringa M, Peebles C, Cook C, Zeanah C. (2001). Toward establishing procedural, criterion, and discriminant validity for PTSD in early childhood. *J Am Acad Child Adolesc Psychiatry.* 40(1):52–60.

Shalev A, Rogel-Fuchs Y, Pitman R. (1992). Conditioned fear and psychological trauma. *Biol Psychiatry.* 31:863–865.

Siegel DJ. (1999). *The Developing Mind: Toward a Neurobiology of Interpersonal Experience.* New York: Guilford Press.

Siegel DJ. (1996). Cognition, memory and dissociation. *Child Adole Psych Clin of North Am.* 5:509–536.

Sroufe LA, Fox N, Pancake V. (1983). Attachment and dependency in developmental perspective. *Child Dev.* 55:17–29.

Sullivan MA, Saylor CF, Foster KY. (1991). Post-hurricane adjustment of preschoolers and their families. *Adv Behav Res Ther.* 13:163–171.

Terr L. (1979). Children of Chowchilla. *Psychoanalytic Study Child.* 34:547–623.

Terr L. (1988). What happens to the early memories of trauma—a study of 25 children under age five at the time of documented traumatic events. *Am J Child Adolesce Psychiatry.* 27:96–104.

Terr L. (1990). *Too Scared to Cry: Psychic Trauma in Childhood.* New York: Harper & Row.

van der Kolk BA. (1994). The body keeps the score: memory and the evolving psychobiology of post traumatic stress. *Harvard Rev Psychiatry.* 1(5):253–265.

Wolmer L, Laor, N, Gerson, A, et al. (2000). The mother-child dyad facing trauma: A developmental outlook. *J Nerv Ment Dis.* 188(7):409–415.

Yule W. (1994). Posttraumatic stress disorder. In: Rutter M, Hersov L, eds. *Child and Adolescent Psychiatry: Modern Approaches.* London: Blackwell Sciences Ltd.

13

Treatment of Children Exposed to Trauma

Elissa J. Brown, Ava Albrecht, Jennifer McQuaid, Dinohra M. Munoz-Silva, and Raul R. Silva

Every day, children across the world are exposed to traumatic events, including sexual abuse, physical abuse, domestic violence, motor vehicle collisions, community violence, disasters, and war. These children exhibit a wide variety of emotional and behavioral problems, including posttraumatic stress disorder (PTSD). Although the rates of PTSD vary across studies, the majority of children exposed to traumatic events report symptoms of reexperiencing, avoidance, and arousal. Generalized anxiety, separation anxiety, depressive disorders, and disruptive behavior disorders are additional reactions common among children exposed to trauma (Brown, 2003).

Given the variability in the nature and severity of children's responses to trauma, it is not surprising that our understanding of efficacious treatment has only recently materialized. Studies have been conducted on both psychosocial and pharmacological interventions. Strong evidence has emerged for the efficacy of cognitive behavioral therapy (CBT) for the treatment of PTSD and other trauma-related symptoms. The research on pharmacological interventions in adults has identified effective options. For children, alternatives are less developed, though equally important findings are beginning to surface.

This chapter examines the treatment outcome studies of psychosocial and pharmacological treatment of children's

PTSD. We review the theoretical argument for CBT before presenting the literature on the efficacy of CBT and other psychosocial interventions. Mediators and moderators of treatment outcome are discussed. We then present the treatment outcome studies of psychopharmacological interventions. Clinical implications and research recommendations are presented.

Theoretical Argument for Trauma-Specific CBT

In his bio-informational theory of emotions, Lang (1977, 1979) hypothesized that an emotional image is a cognitive schema containing information about the stimulus, its meaning, and responses to the stimulus. Foa and Kozak (1986) extended this work to trauma, arguing that schemas related to fear must include information that the stimuli or responses are dangerous. They referred to this combination of stimulus, meaning, and responses related to fear as the *fear network*. What distinguishes PTSD from other anxiety disorders (in which the fear network is more circumscribed) is that the trauma is a psychological, physical, or moral violation that disrupts previous concepts of safety (Herman, 1992; Janoff-Bulman, 1992). In terms of schema, numerous stimuli and responses in the victim's daily life that previously signaled safety are now associated with danger.

Resick and Schnicke (1992, 1993) have extended this work beyond the sole emotion of fear. They argue that intrusive recollections and avoidance may be activated by other strong emotions such as anger, humiliation, and guilt. Drawing from cognitive theory, they argue that these strong emotional reactions to trauma may arise from conflicts between prior schemata and the current event (Resick & Schnicke, 1993). For example, people believe in a "just world," in which good things happen to good people and bad things happen to bad people (Lerner & Miller, 1978). In traumatic circumstances, a conflict emerges because the new information ("I have been abused.") is inconsistent with preexisting beliefs ("I am a good kid." and "Abuse doesn't happen to good kids.").

Hollon and Garber (1988) suggested that when a person is exposed to schema-discrepant information (such as occurs in cases of maltreatment), the result is assimilation, accommodation, or over-accommodation. With assimilation, the victim-survivor alters conception of the event (e.g., "Maybe it wasn't really abuse."). Flashbacks and other intrusive memories may be attempts at integration when assimilation fails and when memories are triggered through stimuli in the environment. Over-accommodation involves altering existing schema to such an extreme that the new schema are maladaptive (e.g., "No adults can ever be trusted."). Alternatively, *healthy accommodation* involves changing the existing schemata to incorporate the discrepant information (e.g., "Sometimes bad things happen to good people."). The promotion of healthy accommodation is one goal of cognitive behavioral therapy.

Exposure therapy (conducted gradually or via flooding) and cognitive restructuring are the core elements of cognitive behavioral therapy. According to Foa and colleagues (1989), exposure to the traumatic memory and associated fear network alters the memory such that threat cues are reevaluated in the absence of aversive consequences and in a setting that allows for habituation. Resick and Schnicke (1992) argued that activation of the network may result in decreases in perceptions of danger, but it may not alter emotional reactions other than fear. For emotions such as shame or anger, patients need the direct confrontation of conflicts, misattributions, and expectations. In addition to eliciting memories of the event (through exposure therapy), they recommend directly confronting conflicts and maladaptive cognitive structures (through cognitive restructuring). Thus, trauma-specific cognitive behavioral therapy typically includes a combination of exposure therapy and cognitive restructuring, with additional coping skills (e.g., stress inoculation training) designed to help patients cope with their physiological responses to the trauma memory (including during exposure therapy).

Efficacy of Trauma-Specific CBT

Due to awareness of the prevalence of trauma among children and the subsequent development of PTSD and other sequelae, the treatment outcome literature grew significantly in the 1990s. A review of studies revealed that all of the randomized clinical trials were published from 1996 to 2003. Prior to these additions to the literature, a number of quasi-experimental or multiple baseline designs were conducted. These studies provide interesting preliminary information and a foundation on which to build. The following is a brief review of studies of psychosocial interventions for children exposed to trauma. Although the focus of this chapter is children's PTSD, we chose to include all studies of trauma-related psychopathology in order to address the variability in children's symptom picture following traumatic events.

The majority of the investigations conducted to date have been of CBT for victims of child sexual abuse (CSA). The first group of these used quasi-experimental designs. In the first study of a standard treatment protocol for CSA-related PTSD, Deblinger and associates (1990) found significant reductions in PTSD, general anxiety, and depression for 19 girls receiving 12 sessions of CBT. Because this was preliminary research, there was no control group, and participants ranged in age from 3 to 16. Using a multiple baseline design across time and focusing on a narrower age bracket (only preschoolers), Stauffer and Deblinger (1996) investigated the efficacy of concurrent CBT for 19 preschool CSA victims and their non-offending mothers. No significant changes became evident from baseline to pretreatment, whereas significant pre–post gains were seen on measures of parental psychopathology, parenting practices, and children's sexual behavior problems. These gains were maintained at the 3-

month follow-up assessment. Farrell and colleagues (1998) also conducted a multiple baseline design investigation of CBT for CSA victims with PTSD. The three (of four) children with clinically significant symptoms at baseline reported decreases in PTSD, depression, and anxiety symptoms during treatment.

In the only quasi-experimental design with a waitlist control group, McGain and McKinzey (1995) evaluated treatment conducted with 30 school-age girls who had experienced CSA within the past year. After treatment, about one-third of the 15 treated girls were exhibiting behavioral problems, whereas more than two-thirds of the 15 controls continued to exhibit behavior problems. Conclusions are limited because the treatment was not standardized, assignment to group was not randomized, and investigators did not conduct a time by treatment interaction analysis.

Another limitation of this quasi-experimental research is that CSA was the only trauma for which treatments were developed and evaluated. However, Swenson and Brown (1999) conducted a preliminary study of CBT designed to address sequelae specific to school-age, child physical abuse (CPA) victims. This first attempt to provide CBT to victims of another type of trauma, CPA, demonstrated its effectiveness at decreasing trauma symptoms in this group of children as well.

Three recent quasi-experimental investigations have extended previous work by designing focused interventions for children exposed to disaster and war. Goenjian and colleagues (1997) examined the efficacy of a brief trauma/grief-focused therapy for early adolescents exposed to the 1988 earthquake in Armenia. Eighteen months after the earthquake, schools were randomly assigned to a treatment or a no-treatment-control group. They found that the 35 treated children improved on PTSD symptoms and did not change on symptoms of depression, whereas the 29 untreated children reported more symptoms of PTSD and depression at posttreatment than they had at pretreatment. Because many of the treated children remained symptomatic at posttreatment, the authors concluded that 4½ hours of classroom group sessions might have been inadequate.

Layne and associates (2001) conducted an open trial of a trauma/grief protocol (psychoeducation, skill-building exercises, and group process activities) for 55 war-exposed Bosnian adolescents. The participating children reported decreases over time in posttraumatic stress, complicated grief, and depressive symptoms. Nevertheless, about half of the children showed no improvement. Study limitations include the absence of a psychotherapy control group, completion of the entire treatment protocol by less than half of the participants, lack of parent or teacher reports on the children, absence of treatment process measures, and lack of follow-up evaluation.

March and colleagues (1998) used a multiple baseline design across setting and time to evaluate 18 weekly sessions of CBT for children exposed to a fire. Like Goenjian and colleagues (1997), March and colleagues (1998) conducted school-based treatment. The authors excluded children with chronic abuse-related PTSD, severe conduct problems, or limited social problem-solving skills. The 14 children (ages 10–15) with mild to moderately severe PTSD, anxiety, and depression at pretreatment experienced significant pre–post reductions. At posttreatment, 57% of the children no longer met criteria for PTSD and, at 6-month follow-up, 86% no longer met criteria for PTSD.

Many of the limitations of the aforementioned studies have been addressed by eight recently completed randomized clinical trials, five of which were conducted with CSA victims, one of which was conducted with CPA victims, and two of which were conducted with one set of children exposed to a disaster. Cohen and Mannarino (1996a) compared *abuse-specific* CBT to a non-specific supportive treatment for preschool-age victims of CSA, and found that only children who received the abuse-specific treatment showed reductions in parent-reported internalizing and externalizing behavior problems. A 1-year follow-up study

(Cohen & Mannarino, 1997) revealed continued improvements for the children who received CBT and no significant changes for those who received non-specific supportive therapy. In an examination of mediators of outcome, Cohen and Mannarino (1996b) found that caregivers' response to the abuse was predictive of improvements in children's social competence and behavior problems, revealing the potential importance of caregiver participation in treatment.

Cohen and Mannarino (1998) extended their work to school-age children by comparing CBT to nondirective supportive therapy with 7 to 14-year-old children and their caregivers. More children in the CBT condition experienced clinically significant improvement on depression, behavior problems, and social competence than in the nondirective supportive therapy condition. Nevertheless, the differences between treatment groups were less than those found in the preschool studies. The authors propose two plausible explanations for this finding: (1) the children were less symptomatic at pretreatment than in the preschool study; and (2) the school-age children were more likely than preschoolers to bring up abuse during nondirective supportive therapy, limiting the differences between the two conditions.

In another investigation of school-age victims of CSA, Celano and colleagues (1996) compared structured (designed to address maladaptive abuse-related cognitions) to unstructured, supportive individual psychotherapy conducted with school-age children and their caregivers. The participants were primarily from low-income, African-American families and none had received treatment prior to the study. There were no significant differences across treatment conditions on measures of children's symptoms, but the structured psychotherapy was associated with significant increases in caregivers' support of their children and decreases in caregivers' self-blame and expectations of undue negative consequences of the abuse on their children.

Like Celano and colleagues (1996), Berliner and Saunders (1996) designed a treatment for CSA victims to address abuse-specific symptomatology. The authors compared CBT (parallel groups for children and caregivers) with and without gradual exposure. There were no significant differences between the groups on the degree of reduction in fear, anxiety, depression, behavior problems, and inappropriate sexual behaviors. Like Cohen and Mannarino (1998), Berliner and Saunders (1996) attributed their findings to the lack of clinically significant symptom levels at pretreatment, indicating perhaps that exposure therapy is more important for children with more severe symptomatology.

To date, the only randomized clinical trial of CBT completed with children exposed to a traumatic event other than CSA is Kolko's (1996b) study of child physical abuse (CPA). Like Berliner and Saunders (1996), Kolko (1996b) compared two well regarded alternative approaches, CBT and family therapy (FT). Both CBT and FT provided skills training to children and their caregivers. These active treatments were compared to a treatment-as-usual condition. Improvements were found for both active treatments on children's internalizing and externalizing symptoms, child-to-parent aggression, parental distress, abuse risk, and family cohesion and conflict. Participants involved in FT exhibited greater reductions in parent-reported violent behavior toward children and family conflict, whereas children receiving CBT reported fewer problems with peers and continued reduction in drug use from post-treatment to 1-year follow-up. This suggests that, while both CBT and FT emphasized direct and comparable child and parent participation in order to promote improvements in functioning (Kolko, 1996b), the reciprocal aspect of family therapy may promote greater change in this area. A strength of this investigation is the repeated assessment of numerous areas of functioning: psychiatric symptoms, social support, parenting style, parental psychopathology, family relationships, abuse incidents, and treatment characteristics and obstacles. Unfortunately, this study provides little guidance regarding the treatment of PTSD because, in spite of its focus on a veritable traumatic incident, CPA, only 2 participants (of 47) met criteria for the disorder.

Like many of the other randomized clinical trials, Kolko's study (1996b) provides support for the notion that caregivers should participate in the treatment of children exposed to trauma. Taking the next step, Deblinger and colleagues (1996) compared the efficacy of CBT as a function of treatment participants (i.e., CSA victim or non-offending caregivers). Ninety 7 to 13-year-old children who met full or partial criteria for PTSD subsequent to CSA were randomly assigned to one of four conditions of participants in the therapy: (1) child only, (2) non-offending caregiver only, (3) both child and caregiver, or (4) community referral control sample. Deblinger and colleagues (1996) found that children who were randomly assigned to CBT in which they directly participated evidenced greater reductions in PTSD symptoms than children in the community referral control sample. Children assigned to CBT in which their parents directly participated showed greater reductions in depression and externalizing behaviors than children in the community referral control sample.

In 2002, two randomized controlled trials were conducted to evaluate psychosocial interventions for children exposed to a disaster who showed evidence of PTSD (Chemtob, Nakashima, & Carlson, 2002; Chemtob, Nakashima, & Hamada, 2002). Chemtob, Nakashima, and Hamada examined an intervention that included 4 weeks of a protocol involving themes addressed through play, art, and talk therapy. Using a randomized lagged-groups design, children ages 6 to 12 were randomly assigned to one of three treatment waves of this protocol. Within each treatment wave, participants were randomly assigned to group versus individual therapy. Interestingly, although there were no differences in symptom reduction between conditions, attrition rates were higher among individual versus group therapy participants.

Symptoms of PTSD decreased for children in treatment compared to those on the waiting list.

Chemtob, Nakashima, and Carlson followed this study with an investigation of eye movement desensitization and reprocessing (EMDR) treatment for 32 of the children who continued to meet PTSD criteria 1 year after the earlier study. Again, a randomized lagged-groups design was used, with only two treatment waves. The children received three sessions of EMDR. Children in both waves of EMDR showed significant decreases in symptoms of PTSD, general anxiety, and depression. Although both of these studies were limited by the lack of a therapy placebo, they provide important initial evidence for the value of short-term psychodynamic interventions for disaster-related PTSD.

In summary, cognitive behavioral approaches to the treatment of PTSD, anxiety, depression, and other trauma-related symptoms have been quite efficacious with children exposed to various forms of trauma. The data suggest the importance of focusing directly on the traumatic event and including both children and their caregivers (Friedrich, 1996). These conclusions are strengthened by the fact that further studies included larger sample sizes, administered assessments to children and their caregivers, examined psychiatric symptoms and social competence, and monitored treatment integrity and parental satisfaction.

The CBT Rationale: Making a Practical Argument for Families and Therapists

The empirical support for CBT is strong. Nevertheless, convincing families to buy into the treatment approach can be a challenge. Providing an acceptable rationale to therapists and patients is critical. To address this issue, we now describe the reasons why CBT is not only scientifically based, but also clinically appropriate and feasible with children exposed to trauma (Addis & Carpenter, 2000; Verduyn & Calam, 1999).

With cognitive behavioral therapy, attention is given to a diversity of symptoms using a model that addresses cognitive, physiological, and behavioral responses to trauma cues. Thus, the aforementioned diversity of children's responses to trauma exposure (e.g., maladaptive cognitions, hyperarousal, and behavior problems) is addressed within a single treatment modality.

Within the cognitive response set, two of the most unsettling cognitive distortions reported by trauma survivors are perceived uncontrollability and unpredictability of their surroundings. One of the ways in which CBT provides a sense of control and predictability is by making the rationale and strategies for implementing treatment explicit to patients. For example, prior to relaxation training, the therapist describes the flight-or-fight reaction, with an explanation of the way in which relaxation reduces anxiety by decreasing muscle tension. The therapist and client then work collaboratively to choose a method of relaxation training (e.g., progressive muscle relaxation versus visualization). In addition to the client's mastery of the chosen coping skill, this collaboration empowers the patient, reestablishing a sense of control.

Cognitive behavioral therapy also addresses the developmental differences among children exposed to trauma (i.e., due to age, time elapsed since the trauma occurred, cognitive development). Coping techniques are designed to incorporate developmental level into the empirically-supported model. For example, when teaching relaxation, a simple, two-step procedure (e.g., acting like a "tin soldier," then a "wet noodle") is used with younger children, whereas progressive muscle relaxation is used with teenagers. Additionally, coping skills are portable techniques that can be used in multiple settings in which children's symptoms arise (e.g., classroom, home, car). This aspect of CBT enables children to generalize their therapeutic gains. Because some children who are exposed to trauma are asymptomatic immediately following the trauma but report symptoms later in their development (i.e., sleeper effect), participation in CBT immediately following trauma exposure may prevent the development of later psychopathology.

Lastly, in spite of common beliefs regarding certain types of trauma (e.g., child maltreatment), children exposed to trauma are socioeconomically, racially, and ethnically diverse. Given these demographics and the finding that African-American girls may be particularly vulnerable to emotional problems following a trauma, the feasibility of CBT with people of color is critical. The active, directive, and structured nature of CBT appears to be effective with and acceptable to people of color (Verduyn & Calam, 1999).

Factors Related to Treatment Outcome

Recent studies have investigated variables associated with outcome, predictors of treatment response, and various treatment components that may impact outcome. Gaining a greater understanding of the characteristics of the trauma (e.g., severity), family factors (e.g., cohesion, parental support of child), and treatment components (e.g., participation of children or parents) that impact outcome is critical to maximizing treatment efficacy, acceptability, and feasibility.

Variables Associated with Outcome

As an extension of their randomized clinical trials with both preschoolers and school-age children, Cohen and Mannarino (1996b, 2000) examined correlates of outcome Both studies looked at demographic variables, abuse related variables (i.e., number of abusive episodes, type of abuse), parental emotional responses to their children being abused, levels of family cohesion and adaptability, and levels of parental support for and blame of their children regarding the abuse. In their study of preschoolers

(1996b), parents' emotional responses to the abuse were associated with children's parent-reported behavior problems, whereas in their study of school-age children (2000), parents' emotional responses were associated with children's self-reported internalizing symptoms (i.e., anxiety, depression) following treatment. This distinction might be due to methodological (e.g., parent-report on preschoolers versus self-report by school-age children) or developmental differences (e.g., children at different ages responding in different ways to parents' distress). Nevertheless, the findings highlight the importance of parental functioning. Similarly, the degree to which rules and boundaries shift in families was associated with social skills deficits and behavior problems in preschoolers, and associated with children's anxiety and posttraumatic stress symptoms in school-age children.

In addition to the aforementioned variables, school-age children's attributions and perceptions related to the abuse incident were examined following treatment (Cohen & Mannarino, 2000). Children's lack of interpersonal trust, self-blame for negative events, lack of perceived credibility, and perception of being different from their peers were strongly associated with symptoms of anxiety, depression, and anger. This set of results indicates that children's attributions related to the abuse may be important correlates of internalizing and externalizing problems.

Predictors of Outcome

Based on Kolko's (1996b) randomized clinical trial comparing CBT, FT, and routine community care for physically abused children and their caregivers, Kolko and Brown (1998) examined potential moderators of treatment outcome to determine whether demographic, child, parent, and family features prior to treatment were associated with differential improvement following the intervention. For children who viewed the world as very dangerous prior to treatment (compared to those who did not), their parents showed less improvement in violent behavior toward children, abuse risk, and use of force. Perhaps these children's views reflect the degree to which abusive behavior is incorporated into the family structure, making it resistant to change. In contrast, parents of children high (versus low) on self-blame for the abuse evidenced greater improvements on parental anger. In this case, children's blaming themselves may remove responsibility from the parent and result in decreased resentment and anger. Parents of children who scored high on global assessment of functioning showed more improvement in violent behavior toward their child. With treatment, these parents may have been able to recognize (potentially, for the first time) the effect their behavior has on their children.

Additionally, analyses from Kolko's (1996a, 1996b) treatment outcome study suggest the importance of monitoring treatment course. Reports of high-risk behaviors such as parental anger, physical discipline, physical force, and family problems were collected from children and their caregivers at the start of each weekly session over 19 weeks of treatment. Child reports of parental anger, physical discipline, and physical force within the first four sessions were associated with parental anger, physical discipline, and physical force in the last four sessions of treatment. Early parent reports of family problems, physical discipline, and physical force predicted late reports of the same.

Clinical Implications of Research on the Efficacy of CBT

By understanding correlates and predictors of treatment response, several clinical implications can be drawn. The first is that parents should be key participants in the intervention process. Each of the studies cited above provides evidence attesting to the valuable role they play in their child's response to treatment. A second implication drawn from the research is that one must take a developmental perspective when considering intervention design. In the preschool years, the association of a parent's emotional reaction to their child's abuse—which incorporates responses such as fear, guilt, anger, embarrassment, and feeling upset—suggests that working with parents on their own experience of their child's sexual abuse may play a particularly important role in treatment outcome at this age. While preschoolers are more likely to be impacted by the emotional reactions of their parents, the importance of this factor for 7 to 14-year-old children decreases, and a child's individual attribution style begins to play a more prominent role. Interventions for this age group may be highly effective if they choose to allow children ways in which they can examine their perceptions, reorganize their attribution style, and improve their own emotional functioning. Additionally, interventions with children at this age should involve treatment components designed so that their parents are able to improve their parenting practices and their overall functioning, increase their support for their children, and decrease their level of blame towards the child around the abuse incident.

A third conclusion which can be drawn from the studies reviewed in this chapter is that more research on predictors of children's response to treatment is necessary. After examining the literature, a large gap was evident, with only studies of treatment for child physical and sexual abuse providing empirical evidence of predictors. The research on children's response to treatment following exposure to other trauma—disaster related, war related, automotive injuries, and domestic violence—would benefit from advances in this area.

Argument for Psychopharmacological Interventions

The use of pharmacotherapy in children and adolescents for the treatment of posttraumatic stress disorder has not been extensively studied. A literature review shows scant research on this subject that consists mostly of open trials and case studies, as well as literature reviews. At this point, pharmacological interventions are primarily considered to be adjunctive to psychosocial treatment modalities (Cohen, 1998), including CBT, family therapy, hypnosis, and EMDR. There are several overviews on the treatment of PTSD in children and adolescents (Perrin et al., 2000; Marmar et al., 1993; Pynoos et al., 1993) in which pharmacotherapy is considered to have a secondary role in the treatment of PTSD, to control intolerable and debilitating symptoms or treat comorbid conditions. Unlike psychosocial interventions, pharmacotherapy appears to be guided by specific target symptoms rather than the disorder itself. Below is a description of the different studies that may guide choice of a medication for PTSD. Table 1 (p. 274) summarizes these findings.

Psychopharmacological Interventions

Early studies of the efficacy of psychopharmacological interventions focused on the treatment of nightmares and other reexperiencing symptoms that are particularly troubling for children with PTSD. An open study by Famularo and associates (1988) looked at the use of propanolol in the treatment of acute PTSD in 11 children ages 6 to 12 years. Propanolol was studied due to evidence that it reduced behavioral explosiveness and nightmares in combat-related symptoms of veterans. Children were reevaluated to confirm a diagnosis of PTSD following referral to the study. Baseline physical exam and laboratory studies were performed. There were no comorbid psychiatric conditions. An inventory of symptoms was completed and each child was rated on a measure of PTSD symptom severity. An ABA design was utilized. Starting dosage of propanolol was 0.8 mg/kg daily in three divided doses. The dose was gradually increased over a 2-week period to a maximum of 2.5 mg/kg daily. The medication was given for 4 weeks and then tapered over the 5th week. Children received concomitant psychotherapy. No other medications were used. Blood pressure and pulse was monitored twice weekly. The PTSD inventory was completed during treatment and 3 weeks after the medication was discontinued. Results revealed a significant pre–post improvement on PTSD severity. Adverse effects included sedation and mildly lowered blood pressure and pulse, but no child required discontinuation of medicine due to side effects. The tendency toward relapse after medication discontinuation suggested that propanolol was beneficial in the treatment of acute PTSD only during its use.

Given the side effects of propanolol, later research on the treatment of reexperiencing symptoms in children evaluated alternative medications. Loof and colleagues (1995) reported results of the treatment of 12 girls and 16 boys (ages 8 to 17) with a diagnosis of PTSD with carbamazepine during hospitalization in a state hospital. The 28 participants had histories of chronic sexual abuse and had symptoms of intrusive thoughts, flashbacks, hypnogogic phenomena, and nightmares. More than half of the subjects had comorbid conditions. The initial starting dosage of carbamazepine was 100 mg twice per day and titrated up every 4 to 7 days. Carbamazepine was dosed (300 to 1,200 mg/day) to a serum level of 10.0 to 11.5 mcg/mL. There were no adverse drug reactions to the carbamazepine. Four of the patients with comorbid attention deficit hyperactivity disorder (ADHD) also had methylphenidate or clonidine added. Four depressed patients were also treated with antidepressants (selective serotonin reuptake inhibitors [SSRIs] or a tricyclic). The authors found that 22 out of the 28 patients became asymptomatic with the remaining 6 being significantly improved (with rare abuse-related nightmares).

In a similar examination of an alternative medication for children's nightmares, Horrigan (1996) described the use of clonidine and guanfacine in the treatment of nightmares in a

TABLE 1.
Psychopharmacological Intervention Studies in Children and Adolescents with Traumatic Stress Disorders

Author/Year	Agent/Dose/Level	Trauma/Diagnosis	Sample Size/Age	Result	Side Effects	Design
Famulara et al (1988)	Propanolol 0.8 mg/kg/d to 2.5 mg/kg/d	Acute PTSD	n = 11 6–12 y/o	Significant ↓ pre & post PTSD severity	Sedation mild ↓ blood pressure	Open ABA
Loof et al (1995)	Carbamazepine 200–1200 mg/d serum 10.0–11/5 Mcg/ml	PTSD, sexual abuse	n = 28 8–17 y/o	22/28 Asymtomatic	None	Open
Harmon & Riggs (1996)	Clonidine 0.05–0.2 mg/d	PTSD, physical or sexual abuse & neglect	n = 7 3 – 6 y/o	↓ Aggression, ↓ hyperarousal, ↓ sleep problems	Sedation (transient) ↓ blood pressure	Open
Horrigan (1996)	Guanfacine 0.5 mg hs	Chronic PTSD, nightmares, physical abuse, domestic violence	n = 1 7 y/o	Nightmares resolved	None	Open

TABLE 1. *continued*

Robert et al. (1999)	Imipramine 1 mg/kg–100 mg/d versus 25 mg/kg–500 mg/d	Acute stress disorder, burns	n = 25 2–19 y/o	83% Response	None	Random† doubleblind
Seedat et al (2001)	Citalopram 20 mg/d	PTSD	n = 8 12–18 y/o	38% ↓ PTSD sysmptoms	Mild	Open 12 wk
Seedat et al. (2002)	Citalopram 20–40 mg/d	PTSD	n = 24 10–18 y/o versus n = 14 25–25 y/o	66% Responded 54% ↓ PTSD severity versus 64% responded 39% ↓ PTSD severity	Most mild	Open 8 wk

†random assignment of patients
hs hour of sleep
↓ decrease
ASD acute stress disorder
BP blood pressure
CBZ Carbamazepine
d day

7–year-old girl diagnosed with chronic PTSD. The patient had a history of physical abuse and exposure to domestic violence. She had remained symptomatic following 3 months of psychotherapy, at which point clonidine 0.05 mg at hour of sleep was introduced. This medication was initially helpful in reducing the nightmares, but breakthrough nightmares began after 3 weeks. A change to guanfacine 0.5 mg at hour of sleep was made due to its longer half-life relative to clonidine. The nightmares resolved and remained suppressed for the subsequent 7 weeks. The medication was well tolerated and there were no adverse effects reported.

Although Horrigan (1996) found clonidine problematic in the treatment of nightmares, Harmon and Riggs (1996) reported success with clonidine for symptoms of aggression, hyperarousal, and sleep disturbances. The investigators conducted an open trial of clonidine in 7 preschool children diagnosed with PTSD resulting from severe maltreatment. The children ranged in age from 3 to 6 years and were receiving psychosocial treatment at a day hospital. Medication was provided for those children whose symptoms of hyperarousal, impulsivity, and aggression remained severe after 1 month in the day hospital. Children were physically healthy with no neurological impairments. Starting dosage of clonidine was 0.05 mg in the morning and if well tolerated a second dose was added of 0.05 mg at the hour of sleep. The average range of dose was 0.1 mg at the hour of sleep to 0.05 mg bid and 0.1 mg at the hour of sleep. Two of the children were also being treated with imipramine for depression. One boy with severe PTSD was already on clonidine at the time of admission. Most children experienced transient sedation for the first week. In addition, blood pressure levels declined in 10% of the sample. No other side effects were reported. The clonidine patch was utilized in all seven subjects in an effort to avoid the initial sedating effects and was found to be well tolerated with less sedation and greater compliance with treatment. Two subjects developed local irritation that was transient, one boy continued to pull off his patch, and one boy developed a severe poststreptococcal glomerulonephritis with hypertension—the parents had abruptly discontinued the patch prior to hospitalization. This abrupt discontinuation was thought possibly contributory to the elevated blood pressure. Target symptoms, assessed weekly, were rated as moderately to greatly improved with clonidine treatment by both teachers and physicians. This study did not use standardized symptom-assessment scales and results were based on subjective clinical impressions. Nevertheless, clonidine was deemed to be effective in reducing symptoms of aggression, hyperarousal, and sleep disturbances in children with PTSD. In addition, the parents and clinicians were of the opinion that the medication was necessary to enable the child to benefit from psychosocial treatments.

Instead of focusing on a single PTSD symptom cluster, recent studies of psychopharmacological interventions have evaluated the efficacy of medications for all three clusters of PTSD symptoms. Seedat and colleagues conducted a 12-week open trial on the use of citalopram in adolescents with PTSD. The authors hypothesized that SSRIs may relieve intrusive, avoidant, and hyperarousal symptoms, as well as treat comorbid conditions. Based on support for this hypothesis from research on adults, Seedat's group conducted a trial of citalopram with eight adolescents (mean age = 14.8 years). Participants were diagnosed with moderate to severe PTSD. Comorbid anxiety or mood disorders were permitted as long as they did not precede the PTSD diagnosis. Six of the adolescents met criteria for mild major depression and one for panic disorder. They were given 20 mg of citalopram and administered a diagnostic measure of PTSD every 2 weeks over a period of 12 weeks. Seven of the adolescents completed the study and all seven responded to citalopram, rated by clinicians as "much improved" or "very much improved" on PTSD. There was a 38% reduction in PTSD symptoms. The citalopram was well tolerated with mild adverse effects reported, the most common being sweating, nausea, headache, and fatigue. Five of the six with major depression no longer met criteria for this at the end of study, although they continued to have depressive symptoms.

Seedat and associates (2002) continued their examination of citalopram in another open trial comparing response to treatment in children, adolescents, and adults with PTSD. The authors conducted an 8-week trial that contrasted 24 children and adolescents whose ages ranged from 10 to 18 years (mean = 14.3 years) to 14 adults whose ages ranged from 20 to 52 years (mean = 33.5 years). The sample from Seedat and colleagues' 2001 study was included in the group of children/adolescents. Biweekly assessments included an age-appropriate diagnostic interview and PTSD symptoms scales. Mean duration of PTSD symptoms was 10.96 months in children and 38.4 months in adults. Subjects who met criteria for bipolar, psychotic disorder, substance abuse, or organic disorder in the preceding 6 months were excluded. Comorbid mood and anxious disorders were excluded only if they preceded the diagnosis of PTSD. Twelve children and 6 adults met criteria for a depressive disorder. One adolescent met criteria for panic disorder. Patients previously treated with citalopram were excluded. There was a 2-week washout period for all subjects. Concomitant pharmacotherapy or psychotherapy was not permitted during this trial, but supportive counseling was provided by the treating clinician. Two children had been treated with amitriptyline and imipramine for one month previously, and seven had been treated with supportive therapy. Two adults had been treated with sertraline and fluoxetine for 6 months and two with amitriptyline for 3 months. Participants were prescribed 20 to 40 mg of citalopram daily. Mean dose of citalopram in adults was 27.9 mg versus 20 mg in children and adolescents. In the child and adolescent group, 16 were responders, 5 were minimally improved, and 3 were mini-

mally worse on the PTSD symptom measure, with a 54% reduction in PTSD severity. In the adult group, 9 were classified as
responders, 4 were minimally improved, and 1 minimally worse,
with a 39% reduction in PTSD severity. There were no significant differences between the two age groups, except for greater
improvement on hyperarousal cluster symptoms in children and
adolescents at week 8. Duration of symptoms, mode of onset, and
presence of comorbidity did not impact treatment outcome for
either age group. Five children and 3 adults were lost to follow-
up. Two children withdrew due to adverse effects of nosebleed
and skin rash. Most side effects were mild and self-remitting,
including drowsiness, headache, nausea, sweating, yawning,
insomnia, dizziness, tremor, and increased appetite. One adolescent experienced akathisia of moderate severity, which resolved
without intervention after 3 weeks.

In the only randomized controlled trial of medication treatment, Robert and associates (1999) evaluated the efficacy of
imipramine versus chloral hydrate in 25 children (ages 2–19) suffering from acute stress disorder (ASD) following burn injuries
(on 45% of their body surface). Chloral hydrate was selected as
one intervention because symptoms of ASD were noted to be
most pronounced during sleep and chloral hydrate was often used
to facilitate sleep in these patients. Children presenting with
ASD symptoms at time of admission for burn injuries were
recruited for the study if these symptoms had persisted for at least
48 hours. The assessment, a structured interview scale, was
administered prior to treatment and three times during treatment. Number and intensity of symptoms were documented by
parents, children, and nurses. If symptoms were decreased by
50% or more, a patient was considered improved, otherwise the
patient was considered a nonresponder. If a nonresponder, the
patient was reevaluated and treated. Imipramine and
desipramine levels were measured midway through the treatment
week. If the blood level exceeded 300 nanograms/mL, the med-

ication was discontinued. Baseline EKG and rhythm strips were obtained at 3 days and after 1 week for all subjects. The electro-cardiogram guidelines used were: 1) the P-R interval on the EKG was not to exceed 0.21 seconds, and 2) the QRS interval on the EKG was not to exceed 0.02 seconds more than the baseline interval. The pharmacist randomly assigned the children to one of the two conditions, imipramine or chloral hydrate for 7 days. Using a double blind design, medications were provided in fla-vored syrup. The dose of imipramine was 1mg/kg and adminis-tered nightly (maximum dose was 100 mg). In all cases, the imipramine/desipramine serum levels were less than 40 nanograms/mL. Chloral hydrate was dosed at 25 mg/kg (maximum dose of 500 mg) nightly. Other medications included acetaminophen or morphine solution for pain, diphenhydramine or hydroxyzine for itching, lorazepam for anxiety, and midazolam for procedural pain. Imipramine (with 83% responders) was more effective than chloral hydrate (with 38% responders) in relieving ASD symptoms. Upon completion, most participants agreed to continue treatment. The typical course of pharma-cotherapy lasted 6 months without relapse. The eight partici-pants who did not respond to chloral hydrate were subsequently given imipramine, to which seven of those children responded. The one remaining nonresponder was then given both imipra-mine and fluoxetine due to mood-related symptoms with no success. No negative side effects of the medications were detected.

Clinical Implications of Research on Pharmacological Interventions

In summary, research on the use of medication as treatment for PTSD is emerging and encouraging. Studies have moved from the treatment of a single symptom, nightmares, to the reexperiencing cluster, to the diagnoses of PTSD and ASD. The latest investigations are strengthened by the use of medications without impairing side effects. The availability of medications without side effects significantly increases the feasibility and acceptability of pharmacological interventions.

In clinical practice, children with PTSD are often considered for medication when the results of other psychotherapeutic interventions are less then optimal (Donnelly & Amaya-Jackson, 2002). Additionally, they feel pharmacotherapy can be a useful adjunct in helping children with some of the more disabling symptoms that impact on functioning.

Medication choice is complicated by the presence of a comorbid condition (e.g., depression, anxiety). Unfortunately, comorbidity is often the rule and not the exception in everyday clinical practice. Furthermore, PTSD frequently is not the primary reason for mental health referrals in these children. Based on the two most recent open studies employing SSRIs in children with PTSD, their use, especially in those patients with comorbid depression, should be strongly considered. This approach has also been supported by others (Putnam & Hulsmann, 2002). Donnelly and Amaya-Jackson (2002) have stated that in cases like this, agents such as the SSRIs should be considered the first line medication option in children. Based on the results of the studies we have reviewed previously, other classes of medication should be considered as well, depending on the target symptoms (e.g., nightmares, hyperarousal).

When one initiates any psychopharmacologic agent, elements of informed consent need to be addressed. Issues related to the onset of action need to be reviewed carefully in order to establish realistic expectations and avoid premature frustration and discontinuation of potentially useful agents. This is especially important with some of the SSRIs that are associated with delays in onset of action.

The issue of duration of treatment for children and adolescents with PTSD is more complicated. Systematic research is lacking and thus can not help physicians in guiding their treatment planning. Putnam and Hulsmann (2002) suggested that responders with acute forms should continue the agent for at least 6 months following remission, while continued treatment for periods not less than 12 months is indicated for those with chronic forms of the disorder.

Finally, the clinician may wish to refer to the treatment practice parameters established for this particular condition (Cohen, 1998).

Conclusions and Research Recommendations

The literature reviewed in this chapter clearly reveals that there has been much advancement over the past decade in our understanding of the treatment of children's PTSD. Psychosocial interventions, especially CBT, have been successful in the treatment of trauma-related symptoms with preschoolers, elementary school age children, and adolescents. Nevertheless, a subset of these youth treated with CBT remain symptomatic. Further research on mediators and moderators of treatment outcome might improve our understanding of this subset and the potential need for additional treatment components. Additionally, there is a subset of children who are unable to enter psychosocial treatment due to their severe symptomatology (e.g., suicidality, agoraphobia). To address the needs of these children, a combined intervention of pharmacological and psychosocial interventions may be warranted. To date, there has been no empirical investigation of a combined treatment. Common practice is to consider medication when symptoms are debilitating or unresponsive to psychosocial treatment modalities. There may be a more central role for medication, especially given the complexity of the symptom picture of traumatized youth. Future research that compares psychosocial and pharmacological treatments may be interesting. More telling might be a study that combines the interventions and examines the order in which they are implemented (i.e., would a larger group of children be more amenable to CBT if there most impairing psychiatric symptoms were addressed?). By using more sophisticated research designs, the next phase in the study of mental health interventions for children's PTSD could be critical in maximizing the likelihood of successful outcomes.

References

Addis ME, Carpenter KM. (2000). The treatment rationale in cognitive behavioral therapy: psychological mechanisms and clinical guidelines. *Cognitive Behav Pract.* 7(2):147–156.

Berliner L, Saunders BE. (1996). Treating fear and anxiety in sexually abused children: results of a controlled 2-year follow-up study. *Child Maltreatment.* 1:294–309.

Brown EJ. (2003). Child physical abuse: risk for psychopathology and efficacy of interventions. *Curr Psychiatry Rep.* 5(2):87–94.

Celano M, Hazzard A, Webb C, McCall C. (1996). Treatment of traumagenic beliefs among sexually abused girls and their mothers: an evaluation study. *J Abnorm Child Psychol.* 24:1–17.

Chemtob CM, Nakashima J, Carlson JG. (2002). Brief treatment for elementary school children with disaster-related posttraumatic stress disorder: a field study. *J Clin Psychol.* 58(1):99–112.

Chemtob CM, Nakashima JP, Hamada RS. (2002). Psychosocial intervention for postdisaster trauma symptoms in elementary school children. *Arch Pediatr Adolesc Med.* 156:211–216.

Cohen J. (1998). Practice parameters for the assessment and treatment of children and adolescents with posttraumatic stress disorder. *J Am Acad Child Adolesc Psychiatry.* 37(S):4S–26S.

Cohen JA, Mannarino AP. (1996a). A treatment outcome study for sexually abused preschool children: initial findings. *J Am Acad Child Adolesc Psychiatry.* 35:42–50.

Cohen JA, Mannarino AP. (1996b). Factors that mediate treatment outcome of sexually abused preschool children. *J Am Acad Child Adolesc Psychiatry.* 35:1402–1410.

Cohen JA, Mannarino AP. (1997). A treatment study for sexually abused preschool children: outcome during a one-year follow-up. *J Am Acad Child Adolesc Psychiatry.* 36(9):1228–1235.

Cohen JA, Mannarino AP. (1998). Interventions for sexually abused children: initial treatment outcome findings. *Child Maltreatment.* 3(1):17–26.

Cohen JA, Mannarino AP. (2000). Predictors of treatment outcome in sexually abused children. *Child Abuse Neglect.* 24(7):983–994.

Deblinger E, Lippmann J, Steer R. (1996). Sexually abused children suffering posttraumatic stress symptoms: initial treatment outcome findings. *Child Maltreatment.* 1:310–321.

Deblinger E, McLeer SV, Henry D. (1990). Cognitive behavioral therapy for sexually abused children suffering from post-traumatic stress: preliminary findings. *J Am Acad Child Adolesc Psychiatry.* 29(5):747–752.

Donnelly CL, Amaya-Jackson L. (2002). Post-traumatic stress disorder in children and adolescents: epidemiology, diagnosis and treatment options. *Paediatric Drugs.* 4(3):159–70.

Famularo R, Kinscherff R, Fenton T. (1988). Propanolol treatment for childhood posttraumatic stress disorder, acute type. *Am J Disorders Children.* 142:1244–1247.

Farrell SP, Haims AA, Davies D. (1998). Cognitive behavioral interventions for sexually abused children exhibiting PTSD symptomatology. *Behavior Ther.* 29:241–255.

Foa, EB, Kozak MJ. (1986). Emotional processing of fear: exposure to corrective information. *Psychological Bull.* 99:20–35.

Foa EB, Steketee G, Rothbaum BO. (1989). Behavioral/cognitive conceptualizations of post-traumatic stress disorder. *Beh Ther.* 20:155–176.

Friedrich WN. (1996). An integrated model of psychotherapy for abused children. In: Briere J, Berliner L, Bulkley J, Jenny C, Reid T, eds. *The APSAC Handbook on Child Maltreatment.* Thousand Oaks, Calif: Sage Publications; 104–118.

Goenjian AK, Karayna I, Pynoos RS, et al. (1997). Outcome psychotherapy among early adolescents after trauma. *Am J Psychiatry.* 154:536–542.

Harmon R, Riggs P. (1996). Clonidine for posttraumatic stress disorder in preschool children. *J Am Acad Child Adolesc Psychiatry.* 35:1247–1249.

Herman JL. (1992). *Trauma and Recovery*. New York: Basic Books.

Hollon SD, Garber J. (1988). Cognitive therapy. In: Abramson, LY, ed. *Social Cognition and Clinical Psychology: A Synthesis*. New York: Guilford; 204–253.

Horrigan J. (1996). Guanfacine for PTSD nightmares [letter]. *J Am Acad Child Adolesc Psychiatry*. 35:975–976.

Janoff-Bulman R. (1992). *Shattered Assumptions*. New York: Free Press.

Kolko DJ. (1996a). Clinical monitoring of treatment course in child physical abuse: psychometric characteristics and treatment comparisons. *Child Abuse Neglect*. 20:23–43.

Kolko DJ. (1996b). Individual cognitive behavioral treatment and family therapy for physically abused children and their offending parents: a comparison of clinical outcomes. *Child Maltreatment*. 1:322–342.

Kolko DJ, Brown EJ. (1998, July). *Individual cognitive behavioral therapy and family therapy for physical abuse: what characteristics influence clinical outcome?* Seminar presented at: Annual Meeting of the American Professional Society on the Abuse of Children; Chicago, Ill.

Lang PJ. (1977). Imagery in therapy: an information processing analysis of fear. *Behav Ther*. 8:862–886.

Lang PJ. (1979). A bio-informational theory of emotional imagery. *Psychophysiology*. 16:495–512.

Layne CM, Pynoos RS, Saltzman WR, et al. (2001). Trauma/grief-focused group psychotherapy: school-based postwar intervention with traumatized Bosnian adolescents. *Group Dynamics. Theory, Research, and Practice*. 5:277–290.

Lerner MJ, Miller DT. (1978). Just world research and the attribution process: looking back and ahead. *Psychological Bull*. 85:1030–1051.

Loof D, Grimley P, Kuller F, Martin A, Shonfeld L. (1995). Carbamazepine for PTSD [letter]. *J Am Acad Child Adolesc Psychiatry*. 34:703.

March JS, Amaya-Jackson L, Murray MC, Schulte A. (1998). Cognitive-behavioral psychotherapy for children and adolescents with posttraumatic stress disorder after a single-incident stressor. *J Am Acad Child Adolesc Psychiatry*. 37:585–593.

Marmar CR, Foy D, Kagan B, Pynoos RS. (1993). An integrated approach for treating posttraumatic stress. In: Pynoos R, ed. *Posttraumatic Stress Disorder: A Clinical Review*. Luterville, Md: Sidran Press; 239–271.

McGain B, McKinzey RK. (1995). The efficacy of group treatment in sexually abused girls. *Child Abuse Neglect.* 19(9):1157–1169.

Perrin S, Smith P, Yule W. (2000). Practitioner review: the assessment and treatment of post-traumatic stress disorder in children and adolescents. *J Child Psychol Psychiatry.* 41(3):277–289.

Putnam FW, Hulsmann JE. (2002). Pharmacotherapy for survivors of childhood trauma. *Seminars Clin Neuropsychiatry.* 7(2):129–136.

Pynoos RS, Nader K. (1993). Issues in the treatment of posttraumatic stress in children and adolescents. In: Wilson JP, Raphael B, eds. *International Handbook of Traumatic Stress Syndromes.* New York: Plenum Press; 535–549.

Resick PA, Schnicke MK. (1992). Cognitive processing therapy for sexual assault victims. *J Consult Clin Psychol.* 60:748–756.

Resick PA, Schnicke MK. (1993). *Cognitive Processing Therapy for Rape Victims: A Treatment Manual.* Newbury Park, Calif: Sage Publications.

Robert R, Blakeney P, Villarreal C, Rosenberg L, Meyer W. (1999). Imipramine treatment in pediatric burn patients with symptoms of acute stress disorder: a pilot study. *J Am Acad Child Adolesc Psychiatry.* 38:873–882.

Seedat S, Lockhat R, Kaminer D, Zungu-Dirwayi N, Stein DJ. (2001). An open trial of citalopram in adolescents with post-traumatic stress disorder. *Int Clin Psychopharmacology.* 16:21–25.

Seedat S, Stein D, Ziervogel C, et al. (2002). Comparison of response to a selective serotonin reuptake inhibitor in children, adolescents, and adults with posttraumatic stress disorder. *J Child Adolesc Psychopharmacology.* 12:37–46.

Stauffer LB, Deblinger E. (1996). Cognitive behavioral groups for nonoffending mothers and their young sexually abused children: a preliminary treatment outcome study. *Child Maltreatment.* 1:65–76.

Swenson CC, Brown EJ. (1999). Cognitive-behavioral group treatment for physically abused children. *Cognitive Behav Pract.* 6:212–220.

Verduyn C, Calam R. (1999). Cognitive behavioral interventions with maltreated children and adolescents. *Child Abuse Neglect.* 23(2):197–207.

14

Clinical Cases of Child and Adolescent PTSD

Richard A. Oberfield and Anastasia E. Yasik

This chapter presents case examples of children and adolescents who experienced a variety of traumatic incidents. Staff members at a large metropolitan hospital referred individuals who had experienced, witnessed, or confronted an event that involved actual or threatened death or serious injury, or a threat to their personal physical integrity or the physical integrity of others. Clinics that referred patients included those that provide medical care, such as a pediatric emergency room, adolescent medical unit, and pediatric orthopedic clinic. Similarly, staff from clinics that provide psychiatric or social work services on an outpatient basis referred patients (e.g., pediatric consultation-liaison psychiatry clinic, pediatric crime victim's program). All cases were referred after presenting to the hospital for physical or psychological sequellae of the traumatic event. The ethnic composition of the children and adolescents referred was 53% Hispanic, 19% African American, 13% white, 9% Asian, and 6% other.

These youths were referred for evaluation to determine the effects of their traumatic experiences on their social, emotional, and cognitive functioning. Ten percent of these patients experienced sexual assaults and 30% experienced physical assaults. About 10% of the individuals referred had been shot at or actually wounded during a shooting. Motor vehicle accident victims comprised 21% of the cases evaluated. The remaining cases experienced hand injuries (12%), dog attacks (7%), smoke inhalation (5%), and other traumas (5%).

A team of clinicians interviewed the patients using both structured and unstructured clinical interviews to determine the presence of posttraumatic stress disorder (PTSD) and significant comorbid conditions such as major depression, attention deficit hyperactivity disorder (ADHD), conduct disorder, and substance dependence. Each child or adolescent was evaluated using a standard assessment protocol that included a number of self-report measures (e.g., Children's Depression Inventory [CDI], Kovacs, 1992; Revised Children's Manifest Anxiety Scale [RCMAS], Reynolds & Richmond, 1985; Junior Eysenck Personality Inventory [JEPI], Eysenck, 1963; Piers-Harris Children's Self-Concept Scale [PHCSCS], Piers, 1984) and measures of cognitive functioning (e.g., Wechsler Intelligence Scale of Intelligence-III [WISC-III]; Wechsler, 1991). In addition, parents rated their child's current affective and behavioral functioning on parent checklists.

Based on information obtained via structured (e.g., Children's PTSD Inventory, Saigh, 1998; Diagnostic Interview for Children and Adolescents—Revised [DICA-R] Reich et al., 1994) and unstructured interviews, we present a review of the symptoms of these children and adolescents. A brief summary of the most striking psychological assessment data will also be offered. Consideration for important risk factors exemplified by the various cases will be noted.

Physical Assault Cases

The first patient, a 14-year-old white male, was the victim of a physical assault as well as a witness to his stepfather being assaulted by a group of men. His father was pinned down by the assailants and stabbed in the chest. As the patient witnessed this assault he attempted to get help. The assailants, however, punched him in the stomach and threatened that they would harm his family if the police were contacted. Since the attack, the patient has complained of stomach pains and vomiting. Prior to this incident, these assailants frequently threatened the patient and his family. Furthermore, these assailants previously assaulted him by punching him, slapping him, and elbowing him in the back.

Whereas the patient was referred for a psychological evaluation two months after the assault, he also reported experiencing ongoing bullying from other children in his neighborhood. Given the severity and duration of these traumatic experiences, he was at risk for persisting difficulties dealing with the traumatic events he experienced. At the time of the evaluation, the patient endorsed 16 out of 17 *Diagnostic and Statistical Manual of Mental Disorders, Fourth Edition (DSM-IV)* symptoms for PTSD during the clinical interviews. Consistent with the epidemiological review of the literature (Saigh et al., 1999), he also presented with comorbid major depression. Specifically, he endorsed symptoms such as depressed mood, diminished interest, insomnia, fatigue, inappropriate guilt, and a diminished ability to think or concentrate.

The patient's presentation included several reexperiencing symptoms. For example, he reported having bad dreams about the attack as well as frightening dreams without recognizable content. These dreams were so vivid that he would often awaken and vomit. Similar physiological reactivity as well as psychological reactivity was also noted in the form of heart racing, a nervous stomach, and crying when exposed to traumatic reminders. He also attempted to distance himself from these events by avoiding thoughts, conversations, people, or places that would remind him of the assault. Furthermore, he reported detachment or estrangement from others, stating that: "I don't talk a lot. Before I used to love talking to people. . . . My friends don't know what happened." A sense of foreshortened future was also noted, coupled with a fear that the assailants might attack him again.

The patient perceived that his stepfather was also having difficulties dealing with the assault. His stepfather was having problems at work and was often very frustrated. The patient consequently attempted to behave himself and not to argue with his parents or to cause any problems at home. This attentiveness to his stepfather's difficulties in dealing with the incident is consistent with literature that has suggested that as parental symptoms of PTSD increase, the child's symptoms also increase (Koplewicz et al., 1994; McFarlane, 1987; Sack et al., 1994; Saigh et al., 1999).

On the RCMAS, his total score was at the 81st percentile and on the Worry subscale he scored at the 95th percentile. Self-report on the CDI was also elevated, with a total CDI score in the very much above average range. Consistent with his desire to please his parents and to be a well-behaved child it is of interest that the patient scored in the "very much above average" range on all subscales (e.g., Negative Mood, Ineffectiveness, Anhedonia, Negative Self-Esteem) of the CDI except the Interpersonal Problems subscale for which he attained a score in the slightly above average range. This may suggest a need to get along with others and not to cause difficulties for his family. On the Children's Self-Concept Scale he reported a negative self-perception in many areas including behavior, intellectual/school status, physical appearance, anxiety, popularity, and happiness/satisfaction. This suggests that the patient tends to internalize his feelings regarding the attack and to devalue his own personal identity as a result.

Our next patient was a 13-year-, 8-month-old African-American female referred by a hospital social worker. She reported that an older adolescent female assaulted her one month prior to the interview. She came to the interview with a brace on her right hand from being injured during the altercation. The patient reported, "She threw her bag at me. She was hitting me on the head and I told her to stop and she didn't listen. I got angry with her then and we got into a fight. She threw it at me and I tried to block it and twisted my finger."

The patient endorsed situational reactivity. She reported, "I wasn't thinking or feeling anything, just anger." She also described reexperiencing the event via upsetting thoughts (e.g., "sometimes I wonder if it will happen again") and becoming emotionally upset upon exposure to traumatic reminders such as the location of the fight or seeing the girl at school. This patient also endorsed physiological reactivity (e.g., racing heart) upon exposure to traumatic reminders.

Acknowledgement of a number of avoidance and numbing symptoms was also apparent. She reported trying not to think or talk about it or have feelings about it, and staying away from people or places that reminded her of what happened. She also indicated she was less interested in things that had been of interest to her prior to the incident. "I used to love basketball with my friends, now I just don't want to and also can't throw the ball because I shoot with my right hand." Furthermore, she added that it had become difficult since the incident to show others how she feels.

During the interview, our patient described having symptoms of increased arousal, demonstrating more irritability (e.g., "Sometimes I feel like I want to kill the girl.") She had also become very careful and watchful in her life and expressed significant subjective feelings of distress: "Just angry. It's like something inside me that you haven't finished it. That I have to fight her. You know when something inside tells you, you haven't finished a job. You have to do it again right." She stated that her grades had gone down since the fight, but had not experienced problems with her parents or teachers.

In sum, this patient endorsed three reexperiencing, three avoidance and numbing, and two increased arousal symptoms. In view of these symptoms, and as her reactivity had been present for less than three months, a diagnosis of acute PTSD was given. Despite her symptom presentation, there was not significant anxiety or depressive symptoms as per self-report data. Similarly, her mother did not indicate clinically significant emotional or behavioral difficulties. As the literature suggests, the magnitude of PTSD tends to decrease over time (Koplewicz et al., 1994; Sack et al., 1993; Saigh et al., 1999). There was a relatively short duration between the trauma and clinical interview, and a reevaluation was recommended to determine the persistence of symptoms over time.

The next physical assault case involves a 14-year-, 3-month-old male, referred by a psychologist who had seen him as part of a school evaluation. He was held back in the 6th grade because he failed all academic subjects. The reason for referral to our project was that the patient had been physically assaulted as well as witnessing his parents being severely assaulted. As noted by Saigh and associates (1997) academic impairments are often associated with the development of PTSD. Despite average Verbal IQ on the WISC-III (VIQ = 91) and prior academic performance of As and Bs, he had not been able to function since the time of the assault.

Upon clinical interview, he stated, "My mother got stabbed in the head. And my father got his chest cut open. They hit me in the face. They punched me until I was black and blue." The mother's injuries (i.e., stabbed in right arm, fractured skull) required that she be hospitalized for almost 4 weeks. The father was also hospitalized for 2 weeks. The patient received medical attention in the hospital emergency room. Despite the severity of these acts, no one in the family received any type of mental health follow-up services.

Structured clinical interviews revealed the presence of 15 out of 17 *DSM-IV* symptoms of PTSD. Within the reexperiencing symptom cluster, he reported having upsetting thoughts about what happened, having flashbacks, having bad dreams (with and without recognizable content), a sense of reliving the traumatic event, and physiological reactivity to traumatic reminders. He avoided thinking about the attack and avoided people that reminded him of the assault. Psychogenic amnesia was also evident, as he reported being unable to remember important aspects of the trauma.

In addition to these symptoms, the patient acknowledged clinically significant impairment in social, academic, and family domains. For example, it was hard for him to get along with peers and he reported that he had "fights and stuff like that. They talk about me and I get into a fight." When asked about his family situation he reported having more difficulties getting along with his siblings and reported hitting his brothers and sisters.

These symptoms were noted as beginning "right after" the incident, suggesting that if he had also experienced dissociative symptoms (e.g., depersonalization, derealization, being in a daze, emotional numbing) "right after" the trauma, he would have qualified for a diagnosis of acute stress disorder at that time. If, however, symptom presentation did not occur until 6 months after the assault, a diagnosis of delayed onset PTSD would have been considered. At the time he was evaluated, a diagnosis of chronic PTSD was made, as the problems reported have lasted longer than 3 months. In fact, his symptoms persisted for 2 years, during which time he had not received any treatment.

The psychological evaluation revealed anxiety symptoms as the primary complaint. For example, on the RCMAS he scored at or above the 98th percentile on the physiological, worry and oversensitivity, and social concerns/concentration subscales. Although he did not meet diagnostic criteria for major depression as determined by the DICA-R, clinically significant levels of depressive symptoms were revealed on the CDI (total score, 94th percentile). Consistent with adult PTSD literature suggesting elevated levels of neuroticism associated with PTSD (Breslau et al., 1991), his score on the Neuroticism scale of the JEPI was above average. In contrast, his score on the Extraversion scale of the JEPI was below average.

The last physical assault case to be discussed is that of a 13-year-, 4-month-old Hispanic adolescent male who had been assaulted by three males when he stopped at a store on his way home from school. Upon leaving the store, he was followed by three young men who entered his building. These men entered the elevator right behind him and the patient became suspicious. As he left the elevator, one of the youths grabbed him from the back and the other hit him. The boy avoided being robbed by fighting them off, he explained. Throughout the interview, he repeated that he "didn't want to be too paranoid" during the event.

The patient reported being very upset when the assault occurred and said that he felt there was nothing he could do to stop it from happening. He endorsed some reexperiencing symptoms, including increased heart rate upon seeing kids like the ones who assaulted him. He also reported avoidance and numbing symptoms such as trying to avoid places that remind him of the event. In terms of increased arousal, he has become more careful and watchful. He denied significant distress and said his grades had actually improved since the incident. Despite the severity of this trauma, this case did not meet criteria for PTSD. Furthermore, self-report measures of anxiety and depression were within normal limits. Parent report of affective and behavioral problems was also within the average range. His benign psychological functioning may be related to his perception of having a very cohesive and supportive family that helped him through this experience.

Sexual Assault Cases

This patient, a 16-year-, 2-month-old white adolescent male, was referred by a social worker from the crime victims program of the hospital after being raped 3 years prior to the interview. He had filed charges against the male perpetrator, who had a prior record of rape at gunpoint, and identified the perpetrator in a police lineup.

The patient explained that he went to use a restroom at a store and was followed by an older male who raped him inside the restroom. Testing for HIV was conducted as part of the medical follow-up. He explained, "I was raped 3 years ago. I was walking down the block. This guy, about age 20, I used to see around stopped me. We went to the store. I went to the restroom and he followed me. There was a back door to the bathroom. He pushed me and turned off the lights. He started to kiss me. He pushed me inside another door and I said, 'no.' He tried to take off my clothes. He raped me. He was cursing at me."

The patient endorsed symptoms of situational reactivity: he said he had been scared, did not understand what was happening at the time, and did not feel that he could do anything to stop it from happening. He also described re-experiencing the event: he reported having upsetting thoughts and flashbacks of what happened, having bad dreams with and without recognizable content (e.g., "til this day I still dream about it"). He also reported being very upset at exposure to traumatic reminders, and elevated heart rate and stomach discomfort when he thinks about it. For example, he indicated that "I tremble a bit and get a little nervous."

He also described avoidance and numbing responses: trying not to think, talk, or have feelings about what happened. He avoids people, places, and things that remind him of what happened (e.g., "In my school, there's a kid who looks like him. They wanted me to sit next to him and I refused."). He also feels different from his classmates ("I feel just different. Feel like I'm the only boy in school who has been in this situation."). He also described difficulty expressing his feelings ("Very difficult to express my feelings. Don't like to talk about it. People may think I'm gay."). He also acknowledged a sense of a foreshortened future, reporting that he did not anticipate having a normal life span.

The patient also described symptoms of increased arousal: he reported sleep disturbance ("problems going to sleep in the beginning. Not as bad as it used to be."). He had also felt chronically angry and irritable, often yelling at people. Furthermore, he had become very careful and vigilant.

When asked about specific distress, he replied that he had been more upset after the incident. Specifically, he stated, "Before I never got upset. Now I get easily upset, every little thing bothers me. Like my brother. I take out my anger on him." He explained that his school grades were getting worse: "I was a good student in elementary school. I've gone down. This year has been worse. Before I was getting a lot of A's. Now I'm failing three classes." The patient also reported having problems with family. He stated, "I fight about stupid stuff. I don't know why I'm like that. It's not really me."

Based on this information, the patient was diagnosed with chronic PTSD. He had endorsed a total of 13 out of 17 PTSD symptoms. Although some depressive features were present, the patient did not evidence major depressive disorder as determined by clinical interview and administration of the DICA-R. On self-report measures, significant negative affect was indicated. His scores on the RCMAS total and subscale scores (physiological, worry/oversensitivity, and social concerns/concentration) were all above the 87th percentile. Whereas his overall score on the CDI was within the average range, he scored at the 95th percentile on the CDI subscale that assesses negative mood. Along these same lines, he reported a low self-concept. Consistent with the clinical interview, self-report measures also revealed significant feelings of anger and a tendency to express his anger verbally towards other. Similarly, parent report indicated elevated levels of withdrawn, anxious, and depressive features.

The next patient, a 17-year-, 6-month-old female, was referred after a sexual assault that occurred one month earlier. At the age of 7 years, the patient had been molested by 2 adult males who lived in the same apartment building. The perpetrators were sent to prison but were subsequently released. One of the assailants abducted the patient at age 16 as she left a bus. He raped her in the back of an alley and indicated that this was "payback" for having implicated him years earlier. She reported that the assailant, who was not found after the second incident, threatened the patient and her family.

The adolescent reported, "I was going to school to get a card for summer school. I turned and I see somebody covering my mouth and he pulled me in the alley. He was yelling and cursing at me that it was my fault that he went to jail. He moved my panties so he could touch me. When he stopped he ran out so I started to walk home."

When asked about the incident at age 7, she explained, "When I was 7 years old I stayed at home by myself while my mom was working. I was nervous when the bell rang but I went out because I thought it was my mother. They were at the door. I had on a skirt that day. They fondled me. They threatened my family." She added that she got away by telling one of them there were things on the stove and running into the apartment.

The time between the trauma and the assessment was 1 month and 10 days. Given this and the fact that the patient endorsed 14 symptoms of PTSD, a diagnosis of acute PTSD was made. Although her self-report measures indicated depressive affect slightly above average, clinical interviews did not suggest the presence of major depressive disorder. With regard to PTSD symptomotology, she endorsed feeling very scared and upset when this happened to her. In addition, she acknowledged a number of re-experiencing symptoms including: upsetting thoughts and pictures popping into her head, bad dreams with and without recognizable content, feeling as if the bad experience was happening again, becoming upset when something reminds her of it, and physiological reactivity (sweaty hands, heart racing, bad feeling in stomach) to traumatic cues. The avoidance and numbing symptoms that she endorsed included trying not to think about or have feelings about what happened and trying to stay away from places that remind her of it (e.g., "don't go there anymore," "don't go by myself anymore"). She also indicated that she experienced increased irritability (angry, yelling at people), had become very careful and watchful, and experienced a startle response. Although the patient reported significant distress related to interpersonal functioning (e.g., "I get angry about anything now. I talk back to my father and fight with my sister a lot."), she also reported that this experience had not affected her school work as she had been on summer vacation.

The total score on the RCMAS was above normal limits. On the RCMAS Physiological Anxiety and Social Concerns/Concentration subscales she scored above the 90th percentile. Specifically, her self-report on the CDI indicated feelings of negative self-esteem that were much above average and feelings of anhedonia that were slightly above average. Her self-reports indicate above average neuroticism but average extraversion. She reported a negative self-concept with regard to her physical appearance, popularity, and happiness and satisfaction with her life. This level of affective distress was also confirmed by her mother who reported that the patient evidenced clinically significant levels of conduct problems, learning problems, psychosomatic symptoms, impulsive-hyperactive behaviors, and anxiety on the Conners' Parent Rating Scale.

Accident-Related Cases

An 16-year-, 5-month-old Hispanic male had been referred due to an accident with a hand saw at his place of work. This accident resulted in loss of two fingers to the patient's dominant hand. After the accident, he carried his own fingers to the hospital ER. He described the accident as follows: "I went to work as usual. I was doing something and then my supervisor told me to do something else. I was not sure. A piece of wood kicked out at me and I fell forward on the saw and hit my head. I took my fingers and went to the hospital." The accident had occurred less than 3 months before the interview, and he still was wearing bandages. Upon questioning regarding previous traumatic experiences, he related that a friend had died of a stabbing in front of his school.

On interview, the patient denied that he had suffered situational reactivity (e.g., "I didn't have any feeling, was just thinking of my hand."). He did endorse reexperiencing the event, with upsetting thoughts; flashbacks of the event that arose spontaneously in his head; having bad dreams about what had happened; getting upset when he goes to the spot where it happened; and having sweaty hands when he sees or thinks about people, places, or things that remind him of the accident. The patient also described avoidance and numbing feelings: trying not to think about it, trying not to talk about it, and being less interested in doing things he had previously enjoyed. He also described a foreshortened future, including not being certain of an occupation he could count on.

The patient also reported symptoms of increased arousal: insomnia, becoming angry easily, getting into fights, having difficulty paying attention in class or to carefully listen, and becoming very careful and vigilant. He also described becoming more easily upset (e.g., "Everybody's just trying to be so nice. I tend to get angry when people try to be nice just because of this. Basically, my father and my sisters."). He added that he has not been attending school and has had more communication problems with his father since the accident.

The patient's symptoms were present for less than 3 months after the incident, and a diagnosis of acute PTSD was noted. On self-report measures, he endorsed symptoms suggesting elevated levels of anxiety, particularly physiological anxiety. In addition, he reported significant interpersonal problems on the CDI.

The next accident-related case involved a 10-year-, 4-month-old white female who was referred by her pediatrician after she had been involved in an accident 1 year before. While she was walking from school with her mother, there was an explosion involving a manhole cover and she was thrown off her feet and inhaled a great deal of smoke. She was taken to a nearby hospital and examined medically, but had no physical injury. After that time, she became unable to sleep alone, woke up frightened during the night, and stopped participating in activities at school.

The patient explained, "It was 3 o'clock and my mom and I and 3 other kids were crossing the street when this big top [manhole cover] flew up. Then we stepped on it, it flew up like a flying saucer. My mother wanted to vomit but she couldn't. My throat was hurting. The other girls, their throats were hurting too. We came to the hospital to get oxygen." On interview, she endorsed situational reactivity, and said she was frightened when the incident occurred.

The patient acknowledged re-experiencing symptoms such as flashbacks of the explosion, bad dreams, and rapid heartbeat when she is exposed to traumatic reminders.

She also reported avoidance and numbing symptoms including the following: she tried to stay away from places reminiscent of the accident, had difficulty remembering parts of the experience, has become less interested in previously enjoyable activities, has had difficulty expressing her feelings, and has vacillated about her future plans based upon the accident. She also complained about difficulty falling asleep, and has become more careful and watchful generally. She also reported significant distress and empathy with accident victims. The patient explained that "when somebody else gets hurt I don't laugh at them. I feel a little bit more nervous. Feel like I'm gonna fall on the [subway] tracks, so I hold on to my mom's hand." Her parents reported significant impairment in school functioning.

Within this context, a diagnosis of chronic PTSD was given as she endorsed three re-experiencing, five avoidance and numbing, and two increased arousal symptoms. Whereas child report indicated average levels of anxiety and depression, parent report indicated clinically significant internalizing symptoms. Her mother reported on the Conners' Parent Rating Scale that the patient evidenced behaviors suggestive of elevated psychosomatic symptoms, anxiety, and learning problems. This highlights the need to obtain multiple sources of information when evaluating young people.

The next patient, a 14-year-, 9-month-old Hispanic female, was crossing the street on her way to music lessons when she was struck by a car that ran a stop light and hit a lightpost that fell onto her. As a result of this accident, she stayed out of school for 4 months and required surgery on her back. Although the patient was an excellent student who received all As prior to the accident, upon returning to school she had difficulties catching up with the work. Referred by her pediatrician one year after the accident, she presented with symptoms warranting a diagnosis of chronic PTSD. She endorsed nine symptoms of PTSD. A clear example of avoidance behavior displayed by the patient was that she would take a different route to her lessons to avoid the intersection of the accident.

It was apparent from the structured and unstructured clinical interviews that symptoms of PTSD and her removal from school for several months have negatively impacted both her academic and social functioning. Specifically, she reported, "my mind wanders off" and "I think about it at school. Sometimes during class." With regard to her friends, she stated that "I feel like I missed a lot. If they talk about stuff from last year, I don't know what they are talking about," and that "I don't get along as well with my friends as I used to. I don't know if it was due to my accident. But this began happening after my accident."

Attempted Abduction Case

The last patient, an 8-year-, 11-month-old African-American female, was referred for an evaluation 3 weeks after an attempted abduction. The patient reported, "The man was in a blue car. He told me to get in the car, that my father sent him to get me. But my father had told me never to go with someone like that. I don't remember it all now." When questioned about the presence of situational reactivity (e.g., feelings of helplessness), she reported that "when I saw it [the man in the van] I freezed." Not only did she find the event itself traumatic, but she also stated "when they [the police] showed me pictures of the man, since that day too I couldn't sleep because I saw a lot of pictures."

Structured clinical interviews revealed the presence of 14 symptoms of PTSD, warranting a diagnosis of acute PTSD. She acknowledged thinking about the man at night, having flashbacks, and reliving the experience during the day. Nightmares in which she was actually abducted occurred with relative frequency. The patient's mother reported that she often awoke at night screaming and crying. She also endorsed physiological reactivity to traumatic reminders (e.g., "once I couldn't breath"). When asked about her perceptions of the future, the patient stated, "I haven't thought about it yet. All I think about is the man." As this experience occurred at the end of the academic year, her academic performance was not immediately impacted. Nevertheless, she reported symptoms likely to interfere with academic progress when school resumed for the fall term. For example, she reported that she finds it hard to concentrate and that she cannot listen to others because she is constantly thinking of the man.

Self-reports revealed depressive symptoms in the very much above average range on the CDI. In contrast, measures of anxiety and neuroticism were within the average range. Stressing the importance of obtaining multiple sources of information when assessing traumatized youth (Saigh & Yasik, 2002), parent reports revealed considerable internalizing problems for the patient. Her mother endorsed behaviors suggesting clinically significant withdrawal, somatic complaints, anxiety, depression, and attention problems.

Conclusion

It is apparent that PTSD may develop in children and adolescents exposed to a broad variety of traumatic events. As was apparent in the cases presented, children and adolescents with PTSD vary widely in their presentation. A comprehensive evaluation that draws information from a variety of sources (e.g., parents, teachers, child) and covers a wide range of functioning is critical to understanding the presenting problems. Diagnostic interviewing should serve not only to establish the presence or absence of PTSD but should also serve to identify comorbid conditions that are frequently present. Psychological assessment should address not only affective and behavioral functioning but also consider implications for cognitive and academic functioning. An accurate and thorough assessment is critical in identifying key issues to be addressed in treatment planning.

References

Breslau N, Davis G, Andreski P, Peterson E. (1991). Traumatic events and posttraumatic stress disorder in an urban population of young adults. *Arch Gen Psychiatry*. 48, 216–222.

Eysenck, SB. (1963). *Junior Eysenck Personality Inventory*. San Diego, Calif: Educational and Industrial Testing Service and Human Services.

Harris EV, Harris DB. (1984). *Piers-Harris Children's Self-Concept Scale*. Los Angeles, Calif: Western Psychological Services.

Koplewicz HS, Vogel JM, Solanto MV, et al. (1994, October). *Child and parent response to the World Trade Center bombing*. Poster presented at: Annual Meeting of the American Academy of Child and Adolescent Psychiatry. New York.

Kovacs M. (1992). *The Children's Depression Inventory*. North Tonowanda, NY: Multi-Health Systems.

McFarlane AC. (1987). Posttraumatic phenomena in a longitudinal study of children following a national disaster. *J Am Academy Child Adolesc Psychiatry*. 26:764–769.

Piers EV. (1984). *Piers-Harris Children's Self-Concept Scale: Revised Manual*. Los Angeles: Wesden Psychological Services.

Reich W, Leacock N, Shanfeld C. (1994). *Diagnostic Interview for Children and Adolescents—Revised*. St. Louis, Mo: Washington University.

Reynolds CR, Richmond BO. (1985). *Revised Children's Manifest Anxiety Scale Manual*. Los Angeles, Calif: Western Psychological Services.

Sack WH, Clarke G, Him C, et al. (1993). A six year follow-up of Cambodian adolescents. *J Am Acad Child Adolesc Psychiatry*. 32:3–15.

Sack WH, McSharry S, Clarke GN, et al. (1994). The Khmer adolescent project, I. Epidemiological findings in two generations of Cambodian refugees. *J Nerv Ment Dis*. 182:387–395.

Saigh PA. (1998). *Children's PTSD Inventory (DSM-IV Version)*. Privately printed.

Saigh PA, Mroueh M, Bremner JD. (1997). Academic impairments among traumatized adolescents. *Behav Res Ther*. 35:429–436.

Saigh PA, Yasik AE. (2002). Diagnosing child-adolescent posttraumatic stress disorder. In: Brock SE, Lazarus PJ, eds. *Best Practices in School Crisis Prevention and Intervention*. Bethesda, Md: National Association of School Psychologists.

Saigh PA, Yasik AE, Sack W, Koplewicz H. (1999). Child-adolescent posttraumatic stress disorder: Prevalance, comorbidity, and risk factors. In: Saigh PA, Bremner JD, eds. *Posttraumatic Stress Disorder: A Comprehensive Text*. Needham Heights, Mass: Allyn & Bacon; 19–43.

Wechsler D. (1991). *Wecshler Intelligence Scale for Children—Third Edition*. San Antonio, Tex: The Psychological Corporation.

15

PTSD in Children and Adolescents Following War

John Fayyad, Elie Karam, Aimée Nasser Karam, Caroline Cordahi Tabet, Zeina Mneimneh, and Michela Bou Ghosn

According to UNICEF's "The State of the World's Children Report" in 2000, more than 2 million children have been killed and more than 6 million have been injured or disabled in armed conflicts in the decade since the adoption of the Convention on the Rights of the Child in 1990. It is also estimated that more than 10 million children in the decade of the 90s have been "psychologically traumatized" by wars. In Africa alone, over 30 wars have erupted since 1970, mostly within countries and states. These wars accounted for more than half of all war-related deaths worldwide in 1996. In developing countries, more than half of war related deaths are those of women and children who are not participants in the fighting. In addition to death and injuries, wars wreak destruction of property, resulting in displacement of entire communities, economic hardships, famine, states of siege, and separation from family. Children can be further victimized during war conditions by imprisonment, kidnapping, torture, and sexual assault (Westermeyer & Wahmanholm 1996). Even after war zones turn peaceful, landmines are left behind by invading armies upon their withdrawal, and it is estimated that 8,000 to 10,000 children become landmine victims every year (UNICEF, 2000). More than one million children were orphaned during armed conflicts between 1986 and 1996 (Unicef, 2000), and hundreds of thousands were used as child soldiers. While these astounding figures reveal the magnitude of trauma affecting children directly, one can only begin to imagine the many millions more who are indirectly affected but who are not counted among the victims.

Needless to say, war is a form of trauma that may be extreme for some individuals and, like other traumatic events, can therefore lead to psychopathology in affected children. This psychopathology may take the form of posttraumatic stress disorder (PTSD) among many other psychiatric conditions that may appear following trauma (Arroyo & Eth, 1996). Unlike well circumscribed traumatic events such as motor vehicle accidents, industrial disasters, or hurricanes, wars encompass many other events that are potentially traumatogenic on their own. Furthermore, wars may become protracted, waxing and waning in their severity. Because of the heterogeneous nature of war, measuring its exposure and relating it to subsequent development of PTSD poses problems of its own. While numerous studies describe PTSD symptoms in children and adolescents in their communities after war in various countries (Laor et al., 1996; Thabet & Vostanis, 1999; Nader et al., 1993; Husain et al., 1998; Macksoud & Aber, 1996; Smith et al., 2001; Karam et al., 2000, Goldstein et al., 1997; Ahmad et al., 2000; Weisenberg et al., 1993; Laor et al., 2001; Allwood et al., 2002), the course of PTSD in affected individuals was examined in only a few (see below). Thus, whether symptoms abate by themselves or require treatment has received very little attention. In this chapter, we will review and discuss findings from the recent literature and from our own study of Lebanese children and adolescents traumatized by war. We will address issues pertaining to measurement of exposure to war trauma and its relationship to PTSD. We will examine the prevalence of PTSD in children and adolescents after war and what we know about its outcome over time. To this effect we will restrict our discussion to studies of children and adolescents who are representative of their communities. This therefore excludes studies of refugees who have relocated to other countries. The reader is referred to the seminal prospective studies of Cambodian refugees by Kinzie and colleagues (1989) and Sack and associates (1993) and to several other excellent papers for additional insight on these special populations (Westermeyer & Wahmanholm, 1996; Sack, 1998; Mollica et al., 1997; Realmuto et al., 1992). In addition, we will examine what we know about risk and protective factors for PTSD after war and whether it is meaningful to identify subjects with subsyndromic PTSD and comorbid conditions. Since children who are orphaned during war are traumatized twofold, we will examine this special at-risk subgroup and the interplay of trauma and grief. Finally, as the issue of whether and when to intervene with psychological programmes continues to garner controversy (Pupavac, 2002; Summerfield, 1999), we will discuss our experience with group treatment community intervention and its outcome.

Measurement of Exposure to War in Children and Adolescents

The issue of causality in mental health has come a long way with the adoption of the descriptive, medical model put forth by the professional community starting in the early 1970s and spearheaded by Washington University and its famous Feighner Criteria (Feighner et al., 1972). The decision to describe symptoms first and then secondly to look for possible life event causality has shaped today's psychiatric and psychological research and practice. Two tracks of research were born from this. The first one was the classification of disorders leading to the successive *DSMs (Diagnostic and Statistical Manual of Mental Disorders) (III, III-R, IV,* and soon *V)* and *International Classifications of Diseases (ICDs).* These are all offspring of the famous *Criteria for Research* (Woodruff et al., 1974) that has become the "initiation" book in our department. The second track was the assessment of life events, reaching its sophisticated and meticulous approach with Brown and Harris (1978). Thus strides were made to describe the symptomatology and to describe a part of the possible social etiological (or precipitant) factors.

War events are a subgroup of life events that have received relatively little attention in the published literature since all wars occurred far away from countries where the modern change in mental health research has sprung in the last 30 years (O'Toole et al., 1996; Engel et al., 2000). This has changed recently with wars taking place in the backyards of Europe (Bosnia, Chechnya, etc.) and in the heart of the United States (the terrorist attacks of 9-11-01. Thus, whereas research on war trauma in the West focused on its own military combatants coming back from the remote areas where wars were fought (Vietnam, Persian Gulf), other wars are hitting close and civilian casualties have come to the foreground. In parallel, quite a bit of research on war and mental health was sprouting in the non-Western countries (Thabet & Vostanis, 1999; De Jong et al., 2001; Karam et al., 1997a) and more recently children and adolescents have become the focus of this research (Thabet, 1999; Nader, 1993; Goldstein et al., 1997; Allwood et al., 2002; Rousseau et al., 1999; Dyregov et al., 1996; Clark et al., 1993; Almqvist & Brandell-Forsberg, 1997). This is probably because of the parallel advances in the field of child and adolescent psychiatry, and because of the potentially long-term sequelae of war trauma occurring during crucial phases of human growth, affecting areas traditionally thought of as being a haven of safety devoted to ensure proper build-up of personality and acquisition of the adult survival tools, including education.

Our group created an instrument in 1989, the War Events Questionnaire (WEQ), designed to measure exposure to war events from both the objective and subjective angles. We insisted on both aspects to avoid the circular conclusions that had plagued mental health research: by assessing only the sub-jective reactions to war, one falls into the tautology of judging the reaction to an event based on the reaction itself (Karam et al., 1999). Thus the WEQ primarily addresses a series of war events and divides them into two broad categories: the individ-ual and the collective ones. In short, individual events refer to house damage, physical injury, and kidnapping, whereas collec-tive ones refer to shelter, displacement, and water and food shortages. These two categories of stressful war-related events differ broadly in their concept. The first category covers more life-threatening and circumscribed (time-limited) events whereas the second category covers events less acute and less severe in their threat to life.

An innovative aspect of the WEQ is the "witnessing" feature. Thus not only are individuals asked about the occur-rence of a specific event, but they are asked too about the degrees of the "how" of their experience: participants are specifically asked if they were in the house when it was destroyed, whether very close to it or far, if they were physically close to their friend or neighbor when he or she was killed or injured. Thus with assigning proper weights (left open to be adjusted by the wit-nesses of individual wars), it is possible to construct a total "war events score" while keeping the possibility of measuring specific war events (kidnapping, etc.). The instrument allows researchers to have a subjective "score" on the negative impact of each and every war event.

When assessing war exposure in children and adolescents, researchers often resort to a variety of approaches that try to maximize objectivity by taking into consideration the unique characteristics of these developmental stages. For instance, Allwood and colleagues opted to read aloud the items of their measure of exposure (a list of war events) to their sample of 6- to-16-year-old Bosnian children when they assessed them in the midst of wartime. Thabet and Vostanis modified the Gaza Traumatic Event checklist to add four new items that included different sensory types of exposure to traumatic experiences, such as auditory, visual, or olfactory experiences. Servan-Schreiber and colleagues (1998) observed that 8- to-17-year-old Tibetan children were initially very reluctant to talk to interviewers, but the situation became better when an interview was preceded by a 30-minute group introductory session in each home with all the children that had arrived from Tibet in that home. In the same vein, Nader and Pynoos have highlighted the importance of establishing rapport with children before interviewing them about their traumatic experiences. In their extensive research with traumatized children, they established rapport by having the child draw a picture and tell a story about it. The interviewer's genuine interest in the picture and story have been observed to help build a comfortable relationship between the interviewer and the child.

The issue of measurement of war events in children is complicated further by the difficulties inherent in recall in younger age groups and with the ethical problems related to stirring up painful memories in the very young. Many, including our group, have opted for measurement of these by the parents as we have observed that children in most war zones still live with their parents or with an adult (Karam et al., 2000; Karam et al., 1997; Rousseau et al., 1999; Almqvist & Brandell-Forsberg, 1997; Cordahi, 2002; Karam et al., 1997). Obviously, the subjective experience of the child (i.e., what he or she perceives as life threatening), in the case of selecting the specific events in PTSD, might be totally different, and this is one of the challenges facing this field. This is why we proceeded by going over all possible war events in our countries and we didn't select a priori for further analysis the ones that induced greater subjective trauma.

Another issue in the assessment of war events is measuring its specifics (Allwood et al., 2002). For example torture might be a pivotal war event in some wars (De Jong et al., 2001) whereas beating is important to look for in others (Thabet & Vostanis, 1999). Another issue is displacement, which might be temporary, protracted, or permanent (Paardekooper et al., 1999). Furthermore, displacement can turn into a refugee status or resettlement. Thus, we have paid attention in our research to the environment into which the child or adolescent has been moved (familiar? with relatives?) and with whom he or she move (did he or she leave a family member behind?) (Karam et al., 2000; Karam et al., 1997a, 1997b; Cordahi, 2002).

On the other hand, the importance of war-specific research has increased the need for more comprehensive war events measurement instruments, putting at risk the quality and quantity of details that could be obtained in interviews where war events are only a small part of a long interview, the latter factor being key in compromising the quality of data obtained from nonclinical, epidemiological samples, especially in children. We have seen that firsthand in one of our studies on the Cana orphans (Cordahi, 2002), as it had been difficult to keep children focused on interviewing, due to a "What do I care" attitude.

Another issue is that of the interference of the traumatic reaction on the recall of exposure to war events: Does the emergence of PTSD, or one of its specific clusters, i.e., intrusive recollection, make it more likely to recall event *a* or event *b* (King, 2000)? Should one measure PTSD and other possibly long-term reactions including *disorders of extreme stress not otherwise specified* (DESNOS; Ford, 1999) to all war events or only to the worst, since there is ample evidence nowadays about the cumulative effects of trauma (Allwood et al., 2002; Breslau et al., 1999)? More so, it has also become apparent in our prospective studies with children that other potentially negative life events (domestic violence, abuse, etc.) have been found important in predicting psychopathology in our understanding of the possible interplay between the "peace" and the "war" stressful events. Thus, it is important to take into consideration all nonwar stressors as well.

These are huge challenges, especially when adding the issues of inter-rater and test-retest reliability of measurements and the difficulties inherent in the documentation of life events. There is also the well-known possibility of reconstruction by children of memories passed on by adults, as evidenced in the possible pitfalls of repeated interviews with children and recall of adverse events (Gudjonsson, 1993).

How Prevalent is PTSD Following War?

Posttraumatic stress disorder is not the only psychosocial outcome to expect after war. As Jensen and Shaw (1993) pointed out in their review of children and war, other psychopathological outcomes such as depressive and anxiety reactions may occur, and wartime conditions may also impact values and attitudes of children and their families. Indeed it would be quite reductionistic to assume that PTSD is the only measurable psychosocial consequence of war. With this caveat in mind, and since this chapter's only focus is PTSD, we will discuss findings related to PTSD itself, knowing full well that if we were to discuss the full psychosocial impact of war, other outcomes would have to be addressed as well.

The reported rates of PTSD in children and adolescents following natural disasters range from 2.9% following Hurricane Andrew (Garrison et al., 1995) to 95% following the 1988 earthquake in Armenia (Goenjian et al., 1995). Similarly, the rates of PTSD vary from one war study to another, ranging from 19.1% following SCUD missile attacks in Israel (Weisenberg et al., 1993) to 94% during the war in Bosnia (Goldstein et al., 1997). An interplay of several factors contributes to this variability, namely the instrument used to measure PTSD, whether dysfunction is required as a criterion, and the severity of exposure to war events.

In 1993, Weisenberg and colleagues measured PTSD in a sample of Israeli children exposed to SCUD missile attacks 3 weeks after the end of the Persian Gulf War in 1991. A group of 492 children and adolescents was randomly selected from grades 5, 7 and 10. They were administered the Stress Reaction Questionnaire which consists of items from the Child PTSD Reaction Index with additional items added by the authors to cover *DSM-III-R* criteria for PTSD not covered by the index. During the war and over 6 weeks, the subjects and their families experienced the missile attacks while taking shelter with gas masks on in a sealed room sometimes for hours before and after missile impact. When it was certain that no chemical or biological agents were present, subjects were allowed to leave the sealed room. Of 492 subjects 94 (19.1%) developed PTSD.

Nader and colleagues (1993) reported PTSD in a sample of 51 Kuwaiti children and adolescents ages 8 to 21 years interviewed 4 months after the invasion of Kuwait. Using a 10-item exposure questionnaire, 35% of the subjects reported witnessing the death or injury of someone, 65% seeing dead bodies, 57% experiencing the threat of death, and 24% being injured themselves. Utilizing the Child PTSD Reaction Index, 70% of the subjects had a PTSD score of at least moderate severity. None of the subjects scored in the very severe range. There was a positive correlation between overall exposure and severity of PTSD. When exposure was analyzed further, it was the "witnessing" factor that best predicted the reaction index score.

Goldstein and colleagues (1997) reported on a sample of 357 Bosnian children ages 6 to 12 years living in 25 collective centers for displaced persons. Subjects were still exposed to shelling during the study. Two thirds of them had a significant person killed, 40% witnessed the death or violent injury of parents or siblings, and 59% experienced victimization at the hands of military forces. To measure PTSD, the authors used the Sead Picture Survey Tool, a cartoon-based interview modified from a similar National Institute of Mental Health (NIMH) instrument designed to measure distress symptoms following violence exposure in a USA community. This instrument was administered to groups of 12 or less. The interviewer read a script detailing the war-related feeling or behavior depicted in the illustration. Children marked an answer if they experienced the feeling or behavior in question and how frequently they did. According to this instrument, 94% of the children met *DSM-IV* criteria for PTSD. The authors do not indicate whether any measurement of dysfunction took place, and it is assumed that none did, possibly inflating the prevalence of PTSD.

Thabet and Vostanis (1999) reported PTSD symptoms in a sample of 239 children ages 6 to 11 years from the Gaza Strip, Palestine. They were randomly selected from 97 elementary schools in the five districts of Gaza, and the study was conducted following a peace accord. The authors used the Gaza Traumatic Event Checklist consisting of 21 items of various traumatic events experienced by the children, most importantly witnessing the beating of a close relative or a friend (56.5%), witnessing the killing of a close relative or a friend (19.2%), tear gas inhalation (56.1%), witnessing the breaking of a relative's or friend's limbs (19.3%), and witnessing house demolition (17.5%). To measure PTSD, the Child PTSD Reaction Index was used, with 40.9% of the subjects scoring in the moderate to severe range. Only 27.5% of the children were classified as potential cases of mental health disorder according to their parents' ratings on the Rutter A2 questionnaire. No measure of global function of the child was taken. The total number of traumatic events predicted severity of the PTSD score. Among the traumatic events, experiencing tear gas and witnessing the killing or beating of a relative or a friend best predicted PTSD scores in the moderate and severe ranges.

Ahmad and colleagues (2000) measured PTSD in a sample of 45 Kurdish children and adolescents, ages 7 through 17 years, randomly selected from two camps for families who survived the "Anfal" Iraqi military campaign in 1988 against the Kurds in northern Iraq. The interviews took place in 1993. Using the Harvard Trauma Questionnaire (HTQ) it was reported that in addition to raids, shelling, and arrests the subjects experienced, 20% were also tortured, 17.7% came close to death, and more than half had a family member or a friend die. To measure PTSD the authors constructed the Posttraumatic Stress Symptoms in Children scale (PTSS-C) based on *DSM-III-R* criteria. Taking the PTSD Reaction Index as a criterion, the PTSS-C showed 96% sensitivity and 100% specificity. According to the PTSS-C, 87% of the sample had PTSD, and the higher the HTQ score, the higher the PTSS-C score. Interestingly, the authors note that subjects with high symptoms scores were functioning well overall, their symptoms not interfering with school attendance or job performance, as most of them had to work to support their families.

Husain and colleagues (1998) and Allwood and colleagues (2002) reported PTSD symptoms in a sample of 791 Bosnian children and adolescents, ages 7 through 15 years, drawn from all 10 schools within one school district in Sarajevo. The war was ongoing when the study was undertaken. Using the War Experiences Questionnaire, the subjects reported experiencing direct sniper fire (85%), losing a family member (66%), and food deprivation (26%), among other war events. To measure PTSD, the authors used both an interviewer-based Child PTSD-Reaction Index and a self-rated Impact of Events Scale. Information was pooled from both instruments to conform to *DSM-IV* criteria, revealing that 41% of the sample scored in the clinically significant range of PTSD. To qualify the relationship of exposure to PTSD, the sample was divided into four groups depending on the presence or absence of direct violence exposure and nonviolent exposure to deprivation and relocation. As anticipated, subjects who had experienced both types of exposure had the highest PTSD rates. However, when the group with direct violence only and that with deprivation/relocation only were compared, no significant differences in rates of PTSD were found, raising the possibility that exposure to nonviolent deprivation/relocation confers an equal risk to develop PTSD. The authors acknowledged the unknown psychometric properties of the War Experiences Questionnaire.

Our group investigated PTSD in a sample of 386 Lebanese children and adolescents exposed to the Grapes of Wrath military operation in South Lebanon in 1996. Karam (1992) had started the research, which has come to be known as the "Lebanon War Studies," about 2 decades ago (1992). These studies initially focused on adults and then included children and adolescents. All the coauthors of this chapter have participated in various capacities in this active ongoing research on children and adolescents. During the Grapes of Wrath campaign, families in their homes or in shelters were exposed to shelling and bombardment by tanks, airplanes, and warships. This operation lasted for 15 days, resulting in hundreds of fatalities, thousands of casualties, substantial destruction of property, and massive displacement of entire communities. The sample was randomly selected from 25 schools representing the region. Subjects' age ranged from 6 to 19 years. Using the WEQ (Karam et al., 1999) to measure exposure, 15.8% of the sample reported the house damage of a very close person and 18.9% their own homes. Injury of a very close person was reported by 7.8% of the subjects. Sections from the Diagnostic Interview for Children and Adolescents—Revised (DICA-R) were administered to both parents and children and adolescents. In addition to PTSD, the diagnoses of major depressive disorder (MDD), separation anxiety disorder (SAD), and overanxious disorder (OAD) were assessed as well. A symptom was considered present if it was endorsed by either parent or subject. The presence of dysfunction was required to make the criteria compatible with *DSM-IV*. Data collection took place 3 weeks after the cease fire and over a period of 3 weeks. The prevalence of PTSD was 24.1%. There was a substantial level of comorbidity between PTSD and MDD, SAD, and OAD.

In order to measure the child's or adolescent's war exposure, we needed to take into consideration the type of war event, the person affected, and the witnessing of that event. The WEQ was designed to measure these different aspects by assigning different numerical weights to the severity of the war event and the degree of witnessing it. A summary measure, the *log war* score, could then be calculated indicating the individual's overall degree of exposure.

To examine the relationship between war exposure and PTSD in our sample, we first used this continuous summary measure. A marginal relationship was found in the bivariate analysis: subjects with PTSD had a mean log war of 2.19 (±3.13) while those with no disorder had a mean of 1.52 (±2.66), p = 0.066. However, this marginal relationship disappeared after controlling for demographics (age and gender) and psychosocial stressors that were found to be significant in the bivariate analysis. In order to explore the relationship between war exposure and PTSD further, we decided to use war exposure as a categorical variable: being not exposed at all, being informed about the event, and actually witnessing the event. This indeed allowed us to find a stronger relationship with PTSD where subjects who witnessed the war event had significantly higher rates of PTSD when compared to those who were not exposed (OR = 2.47, p = 0.011). Moreover, no significant difference was found between those who were told about the war event and those who were not exposed (OR = 1.07, p = 0.8236). When controlling for the other variables, the effect of witnessing the war event (OR = 2.07, p = 0.0561) remained more important than being told about the event (OR = 0.996, p = 0.9901) in predicting PTSD, but the relationship was only marginal. Interestingly, we did find a significant relationship between

WEQ scores and the diagnosis of MDD. Thus when examining war exposure in its relationship to PTSD, it is quite essential to measure the witnessing of the war event, because it might be much more important that the fact of being exposed per se.

Our study is an exception among war studies in children and adolescents in its measurement of PTSD as a full categorical diagnosis and as opposed to continuous score on a rating scale. While this makes the PTSD diagnosis more clinically relevant and better defined, it may have limited our capacity to measure severity and its relationship to war exposure. Additionally, as Smith and colleagues (2001) found in their paper on Bosnian children and early adolescents exposed to war, it was the intrusion subscale on the Impact of Events Scale-Revised that best correlated with children's reports of exposure. It is therefore plausible that should we divide PTSD symptoms into their three component clusters, we might find a significant relationship with one or two of the clusters but not all three. Additional studies are needed to fine tune the relationship between the type of war exposure and the type of PTSD symptoms that may emerge.

What Besides Exposure Predicts PTSD After War?

The majority of war studies in children and adolescents found no differences in the rates of PTSD between boys and girls. While the literature on non-war traumatic events reported mixed results regarding the relationship of age to PTSD, several of the war studies we reviewed documented higher rates of PTSD in adolescents compared to children (Nader et al., 1993; Goldstein et al., 1997; Ahmad et al., 2000; Weisenberg et al., 1993). This may be partly explained by the fact that in chronic war conditions (as in most of the wars examined in the literature), adolescents have been exposed to a greater number of traumatic events by virtue of having lived a longer time.

The child's coping style was examined by Weisenberg and colleagues (1993), finding that those who used denial and emotion-focused coping had less risk of developing PTSD than those who used problem solving coping. Mothers' reactions and coping were also found to be significant predictors of posttraumatic symptoms in a sample of Israeli preschoolers exposed to SCUD missile attacks and displacement (Laor et al., 1996). Similarly, mothers' psychological health came second to war exposure in predicting Impact of Events Scale scores in a sample of Bosnian children (Smith et al., 2001). In our study of Lebanese children exposed to war, two significant predictors of PTSD turned out to be a child's fear of being beaten and financial problems, two of the psychosocial stressors measured in the DICA-R. More attention needs to be given in the literature to the psychosocial/familial stressors as predictors of psychopathology in conjunction with traumatic events, as they may be interrelated.

While community support in the form of material supplies and rebuilding is known to play a helpful role following mass trauma and natural disasters, community support can take on different dimensions during and following wars. This support may be political, religious, or ideological, each a powerful factor that by itself is sufficient to ignite the spark of war or be a harbinger of peace. As war-exposed children and adolescents become more aware of the political realities around them, they are likely to want to "take sides" or "make a stand," and by doing so find themselves immersed in a group solidarity through which they may accept or justify their personal losses as being for the "common good." The mental health literature has just started to examine the role these issues play. Ziv and colleagues (1974) reported that children exposed to shelling showed higher levels of patriotism than unexposed children. Punamaki and colleagues (1996) reported that higher levels of patriotism and political commitment protected children against development of psychopathology. Similarly, religious beliefs, active community involvement, helping others, and "a sense of participating in a nation's struggle against an oppressor" protected Tibetan children against the development of PTSD and minimized the impact of trauma and loss (Servan-Schreiber et al., 1998). While we did not formally measure it in our study of Lebanese children, the effects of community factors were clearly palpable in a nationwide outpouring of material and moral support to families in the bombarded areas in south Lebanon and the southwest Bekaa Valley. Indeed the entire country's mood following the war became one of solidarity. Families in destroyed villages were frequently regarded more as heroes and less as victims of war. Such genuine support on every level is something to take into account when constructing models that foster our understanding of pathways leading to PTSD. While accounts of children as political activists and associated theoretical constructs, abound in the sociologic and popular literature (Cairns, 1996), this issue has yet to be studied extensively in the psychology/medical literature as a factor in the development of PTSD.

Does Television Viewing Play a Role in PTSD?

Following the invasion of Kuwait, Nader and colleagues (1993) reported that 65% of their subjects had also seen images of violence, death, and grotesque mutilation displayed repeatedly on television. This television exposure added significantly to the Child PTSD Reaction Index scores, even after the effects of other types of exposure were controlled. Even in times of peace, television viewing has been reported to result in PTSD symptoms in the cases of two boys of age 10 who independently developed severe PTSD following watching a show titled "Ghostwatch" on Halloween in Great Britain in 1994 (Simons & Silveira, 1994). Pfefferbaum and colleagues (2001) reported that television exposure to the 1995 Oklahoma City bombing was associated with posttraumatic stress symptoms in a sample of over 2000 middle-school students 7 weeks after the incident. Even among children with no physical or emotional exposure, the degree of television exposure was apparently related to posttraumatic stress symptomatology. In a recent letter to the editor, Duggal and associates (2002) reported a case of an 11-year-old boy who developed PTSD along with major depression after watching on television the images of airplanes crashing into the World Trade Centers and their buildings and their collapse. As Pfefferbaum and colleagues suggested, it is possible that increased television viewing by children after disasters may itself be a sign of distress itself and future research needs to address this issue.

Regardless of the fact that some of those who developed PTSD after television viewing may have had preexisting signs of anxiety, the fact remains that repeated broadcasting of horrific images of mutilation and body parts during peacetime and times of war can contribute to children's overall traumatic exposure. While some children may not be affected, or their anxiety is appropriately contained by parents supervising the viewing, other children's emotional resources may be overly taxed by violent imagery overwhelming their defenses, resulting in PTSD or other anxiety disorders. Networking with media outlets may be an important step for child mental health professionals to intervene after wars and disasters. This may prevent spreading or magnifying the exposure, particularly to those who are not already physically or emotionally exposed. Needless to say, sensitizing parents to the need of monitoring their children's television viewing of news events cannot be overemphasized.

The Course of PTSD Following War: Spontaneous Remission?

While the majority of prospective studies of children and adolescents following natural disasters report that PTSD symptoms generally decrease with time, the literature on the course of war-related PTSD is dichotomously divided depending on the sample selected for investigation. The longitudinal studies on PTSD in children and adolescents following wars have used samples of either refugees who relocated to another country (Westermeyer & Wahmanholm, 1996; Kinzie et al., 1989; Sack et al., 1993; Mollica et al., 1997; Realmuto et al., 1992) or a population of children and adolescents randomly sampled from their community and interviewed in their country (Laor et al., 2001; Schwarzwald et al., 1994; Thabet & Vostanis, 2000). The outcomes of these two types of samples go in opposite directions: in samples of refugees, PTSD symptoms seem to persist for years whereas in community samples, they diminish with time. While many hypotheses can be offered to explain the differences (e.g., the refugees' experiencing and witnessing atrocities and torture in concentration camps, spending years as detainees, experiencing additional hardships after escaping) it remains that samples depicted in the refugee studies represent only a small portion of the populations exposed to war the world over, and findings from these studies do not readily generalize. War exposure can be mild for some children (depending on the nature and magnitude of war events) or extreme, as is the case for the refugees described above. We will therefore review the three war-related studies of samples that are representative of their communities and discuss our findings from our prospective study of Lebanese children exposed to war.

Schwarzwald and colleagues (1994) followed a sample of 326 Israeli children and adolescents from grades 5 (age 11), 7 (age 13), and 10 (age 16) randomly selected from schools in a region hit by SCUD missiles during the Gulf War. The authors used the Stress Reaction Questionnaire (SRQ; an adaptation of the Child PTSD Reaction Index with items added to permit coverage of all DSM-III-R criteria for PTSD) 1 month after exposure and a year later. They calculated the Global Symptom Score (GSS), which is the sum of the scores for each item in the SRQ. They also diagnosed PTSD categorically based on whether subjects fulfilled *DSM-III-R* criteria or not. Inspection of the GSS scores revealed a "marked drop" in mean scores for all three grades. The rate of PTSD decreased from 22.1% at baseline to 12.0% one year later. The reduction in the stress reaction was greater among the older than the younger children. Subjects whose houses were hit reported significantly greater levels of stress 1 year later than subjects whose houses were not hit. No parental measures of the child's PTSD were taken.

Thabet and Vostanis (2000) followed a sample of 234 Palestinian children ages 6 to 11 years from the Gaza Strip exposed to war events as detailed earlier in this chapter. The Child PTSD Reaction Index was self-rated by the subjects at baseline and 1 year later. At both times, the Rutter A2 and B2 questionnaires were filled by parents and teachers respectively. The proportion of children with moderate to severe PTSD reactions significantly decreased from 40.6% to 10.0% a year later. The Rutter parent and teacher ratings of "caseness" also decreased (parents from 26.9% to 20.9% and teachers from 43.6% to 31.8%). Moderate to severe PTSD reactions 1 year later were best predicted by the total number of traumas experienced by the child at the initial assessment and by caseness on the teacher Rutter scales at the initial assessment. No parental ratings of PTSD were obtained. The fact that there was a higher number of "caseness" on the Rutter scales than PTSD cases probably indicates the children may have had psychiatric diagnoses other than PTSD (e.g., internalizing or externalizing disorders).

Laor and colleagues (2001) followed a sample of 81 Israeli preschoolers ages 3 to 5 years for a period of 5 years. They were directly exposed to SCUD missile attacks, initially interviewed 6 months after the ceasefire, then again at 30 months and 5 years later. The study was also designed to measure the impact of a mother's functioning on a child's symptoms. The child measures included the Child Behaviour Checklist, the Preschool Children's Assessment of Stress Scale and the Child PTSD Reaction Index. Over a period of 5 years, children's externalizing and general stress symptoms showed a significant decrease regardless of gender or age. Upon examining PTSD clusters in this sample, the authors found that while arousal symptoms significantly decreased, there was a significant increase in avoidance. Mothers with the poorest functioning had children with the most symptoms whereas those with the best functioning had children with the least symptoms. The severity category of PTSD for a third of the children progressed from doubtful or mild to moderate or severe in the period between 30 months and 5 years, and this was partly explained by poor psychological functioning in the mother. Residentially displaced children exhibited more symptoms than residentially stable ones.

We followed prospectively a subsample (N = 143) of representatively selected Lebanese children and adolescents described earlier in the chapter who were exposed to war (Karam et al., 2000) and reevaluated them one year later. The DICA-R was administered to the subjects and their parents. We were surprised to see that the prevalence of PTSD had dropped from 24.1% at Phase I to 1.2% at Phase II. We then examined the prevalence of PTSD clusters (reexperiencing, avoidance, and arousal) as defined by DSM-IV and required the criterion of dysfunction due to these symptoms to be present. The prevalence of reexperiencing (which requires only one symptom to be present) had decreased from 35.2% at baseline to 14% one year later. Avoidance (which requires three symptoms to be present) decreased from 28.2% to 4.2% and arousal (which requires two symptoms to be present) decreased from 34.2% to 12.6%. 11.9% (N = 17) of the subjects at Phase II met criteria for two or more PTSD clusters with associated dysfunction. Eleven subjects had two clusters only and six had all three clusters but did not meet the required duration of 4 weeks. This implied that one year later there were children and adolescents still suffering from PTSD symptoms but who were subsyndromic for the *DSM-IV* full disorder. Upon examining their diagnostic status at Phase I 1 year earlier, we found that 10 out of the 17 had had full PTSD, 1 had all three clusters without the duration of 4 weeks, 1 had two clusters, and 5 had not met any of the PTSD clusters at Phase I. Additionally, there was a direct relationship between the number of PTSD clusters the subjects met at Phase II and the logwar score from the WEQ (logwar no cluster 1.45, logwar one cluster 3.61, logwar two or more clusters 5.03, p = 0.0000). Interestingly, all subjects who had SAD at Phase II had PTSD, which was comorbid with another anxiety disorder or depression at Phase I.

Our findings illustrated that while the majority of subjects with PTSD improved with time alone, a significant number continued to manifest partial symptoms, and some developed new onset of symptoms that were not reported at the initial evaluation (i.e., delayed onset PTSD). This finding of delayed onset of PTSD symptoms is analogous to Laor and colleagues (2001) reporting of worsening of the PTSD category on the Child PTSD Reaction Index in some subjects from doubtful/mild at 30 months to moderate/severe at 5 years of follow-up and similar to Schwarzwald and colleagues' (1994) report of delayed PTSD (14.58% for 5th grade and 2.53% for the older grades) found a year later.

We can therefore conclude from the results of the above four prospective studies of children and adolescents exposed to war that PTSD, whether measured categorically or on a continuum, decreases spontaneously in at least half of the subjects. Some children and adolescents continue to have either full or partial symptoms and have delayed onset of full or partial symptoms as well. The persistence (or the emergence) of PTSD symptoms seems to be related to the severity of the exposure or maintained by family factors (mother's dysfunction or familial psychosocial stressors).

Orphaned by War: Greater Risk of PTSD?

There are few studies about the effect of parental death and bereavement on children and adolescents during war. Non-war bereavement studies have mainly examined the impact of parental death from the perspective of depression (Weller et al., 1991; Zvizdic & Butollo, 2001), well-being and cognitive functioning (Wolff & Fesseha, 1998; Morah et al., 1998), emotional distress and disruptive behaviors (Wolff et al., 1994; Wolff & Fesseha, 1999), and general prognosis (Birtchnell & Kennard, 1984; Liotti et al., 2000). None of these studies explored possible post traumatic stress disorder symptomatology in bereaved children.

The concept of "traumatic grief" started with researchers at Pittsburg University (Prigerson et al., 1995) when they created the Inventory of Complicated Grief, and used it first with a group of elders who lost their spouses. Since 1995, this concept has been applied to other samples, including physically abused and neglected adolescents with substance abuse or dependence (Gerador, 2001) and adolescents exposed to a peer's suicide (N. Melhem, personal communication). This relatively new concept of traumatic grief highlights the need for specificity in child and adolescent psychiatric research and outcome studies, particularly about orphans assumed to be traumatized because of the sudden nature of their parent's death.

Criterion A of *DSM-IV* PTSD diagnosis defines trauma as follows: (1) The experience, witness or confrontation with one or more events that involved actual or threatened death, or serious injury, or a threat to the physical integrity of self or others. (2) The person's response involved intense fear, helplessness or horror (APA, 1994). This definition of trauma is not—cannot be—as rigorous and as objective as we are used to in the *DSM-IV* conceptualization of disorders. At a first level, any researcher would generally agree that war, a human-made disaster, or sudden death, an unexpected irreversible event, fulfills criterion A(1) and probably criterion A (2). However, this latter criterion is not always systematically checked. Indeed, many thinkers (Jensen & Shaw, 1993; Garmezy & Rutter, 1985; Yule, 2000; Berman, 2001) have highlighted the fact that in some situations, shelling might become somehow a routine part of the individual's and family's lives, provided that no specific war traumatic events impact them directly.

In the Lebanese experience, from a sociological point of view, there have been several reports of such phenomena, describing war times as not necessarily traumatic. These war situations may have been depressing or anxiety-provoking, but nevertheless had the unexpected positive effect of consolidating families, friendships, and neighborhood bonds, soliciting families' creative coping strategies to survive (by networking to find ways to maintain resources for food, water, electric light), and finding positive occupations for children who continued studying in small groups and playing in underground shelters. These shared community activities serve an even more important role when displacement takes place.

This issue is of major importance if one wants to draw at least approximate conclusions about orphans of war. Among the studies that explored the mental health of war orphans, only a few have described "cumulative traumatic war experiences, without assuming that war equals trauma (Karam, 1999). If for war-orphaned children, war was not really a traumatic event, and if they personally did not experience both criteria A(1) and A (2) described in *DSM-IV*, then it is possible that war-orphaned children might represent a group that is similar to any group of nontraumatized bereaved children (keeping in mind their high risk for developing symptoms other than "traumatic" per se).

To our knowledge, few studies looked in depth at the issue of children witnessing the death of their parent or meeting criterion A(2) of PTSD. Melville and Lykes (1992) assessed

Guatemalan Indian children aged 8 to 16 years who experienced the loss of immediate family members and witnessed violent deaths. The assessment took place 5 years after this twofold trauma. These children reportedly still suffered from severe fears and many uncertainties. Whether they lived in orphanages or in refugee camps in Mexico, the children seemed to hold onto the severe specific PTSD symptom of a sense of foreshortened future. One can see how specifically that PTSD symptom may block some of the natural grief defense mechanisms that usually occur after a painful loss, such as becoming progressively able to forsee new future emotional investments as possible. Similarly, from a psychoanalytical point of view, the sense of estrangement due to PTSD may make the mourning process extremely complicated (Lebovici, 1994). The symptoms of posttraumatic stress disorder and bereavement are intensified when they are both present simultaneously. According to theories of self-formation, attachment theories, and the development-of-self concepts, it can be expected that the psychic work of building the self through identification processes are particularly weakened when parents are missing in a child's life. The sense of estrangement, that specific DSM-IV PTSD symptom, makes it hard for the child to build new bonds with potential caring figures (teacher, uncle or aunt, step parent, older sibling).

Other studies also looked at children who truly experienced a twofold trauma of traumatic war and traumatic sudden death. Husain and colleagues (1998) assessed 791 children and adolescents aged 7 to 15 during war in Sarajevo, using the PTSD-RI and the IES, combined into a "DSMIV-PTSD Scale." They found that war orphans were much more traumatized that nonorphans of the same war. On the other hand, Bachar and colleagues (1997) assessed the differential effect between 23 war-bereaved adolescents and 19 bereaved adolescents due to road accidents. They found that the war-bereaved individuals were much less traumatized than controls. Although this study has many limitations (heterogeneous war events, retrospective assessment of adolescents who became adults 2 to 10 years later; heterogeneity in the group of deceased relatives mixing parents, siblings, grand parents, aunts, uncles), it pinpoints the need for future qualitative research about how the meaning bereaved children and adolescents attached to death can affect the mental health outcome.

Indeed, having a parent die as a hero or for a "noble" cause in war times might be a protective factor, contributing to the child or adolescent's resilience. Unlike other experiences of sudden traumatic death of a parent, in war conditions the orphan's grief does not remain hidden and is even sometimes highlighted for political endeavors. This sociopolitical artifact might be "curing" the PTSD symptoms of avoidance, by coincidentally inducing therapeutic mechanisms such as reexposure, sharing pain, and creating an atmosphere of compassion towards the bereaved families. Such a social time for ventilation of feelings is itself a manifestation of natural support. As we described in an earlier paper (Karam et al., 2001), children and adolescents who became orphans witnessing their parents' death during the war of April 1996 in Lebanon were grouped together in a childcare program (keeping each child within his or her surviving extended family) by a sociopolitical organization, which ended up giving them a new heroic identity and a sense of belonging to a kind of new larger "family."

Elizur and Kaffman (1982) studied posttraumatic stress symptoms in war orphans aged 2 to 10 years controlling for psychiatric history prior to the October 1973 Yom Kippur War and found that 40% of children showed evidence of pathological bereavement and traumatic symptoms. There was no mention of a control group in this article. In another article (1983), the same authors concluded that the degree of severity of bereavement in war times, and the vulnerability of children over time, are determined by their baseline PTSD condition, the quality of the surviving parent's response, and the availability of social support.

Indeed, several studies (Smith et al., 2001; Laor et al., 2001; Scherer et al, 1996) have replicated the finding that the relationship of the child with the surviving parent, the child's perception of the mother's psychological well-being, and the mother's psychiatric functioning, are major determinants of the prognosis of posttraumatic symptoms. It is worth mentioning that to our knowledge, there are no studies that explored the specific impact of deceased mothers and surviving fathers during war times on the child's mental health.

In our study on Lebanese war orphans, Cordahi and colleagues (2002a) followed a group of school-aged children who were exposed to war-trauma in south Lebanon and who where orphaned in the shelling of a United Nations (UN) shelter in April 1996, where they lost at least one parent, and in 40% of the cases at least one sibling as well. These children were first evaluated 1 year after the traumatic event, and then at yearly intervals. Narratives of each child's experience of that April episode of war and the extent to which each witnessed his or her parent's death were taken through clinical interviews. They met PTSD criterion A for a twofold trauma.

The study was conceived to report the prevalence of psychopathology in this group of traumatized war orphans prospectively, and also to create a longterm multidisciplinary naturalistic intervention program to help these children develop optimally into adulthood. Psychosocial risk and protective factors were also explored. The study, also called "The Child Care Program," included assessment based on in-depth clinical interviews, as well as on a series of standardized tests and scales that were administered to both children and their surviving parents. Instruments included the Diagnostic Interview for Children and

Adolescent-Revised (DICA-R; Welner et al., 1987), a fluid reasoning subtest from the Woodcock Johnson Psycho-Educational Battery-Revised (WJ-R; Woodcock & Johnson, 1989, 1990), the Parental Bonding Instrument (PBI; Arrindell et al., 1998), the Beck Anxiety (BAI) and Depression (BDI) Inventories (Beck & Steer, 1990; Beck et al.; 1996) and the Impact of Events Scale (IES; Weiss, 1996).

The Child Care Program was conceptualized along four dimensions: educational, pediatric (physical health), psychiatric/psychological (including child, surviving parent, and family well-being), and economic. Treatment was naturalistic: moderate to severe cases were enrolled in individual therapy, while others were followed by a social worker in coordination with a clinical psychologist. Yearly therapeutic summer camps were organized for the orphan group. Detailed description and results can be found elsewhere (Cordahi et al., 2002a, 2002b).

To summarize our findings from this study, comparing orphan versus non-orphan war-exposed children in their rates of PTSD 1 year later indicates a significantly lower prevalence (1.6%) in the non-orphan group versus orphans (20.7%). In addition, orphans of war assessed 1 year later displayed a high prevalence of other comorbid disorders such as depression, separation anxiety disorder, overanxious disorder, and behavioral disorders. In this high-risk group, during the second and third years, the prevalence of PTSD decreased significantly and stabilized at 8% and 6%, respectively. It is after the 4th year that only 1.4% of the 69 war orphans (Phase IV) still displayed full PTSD, a rate that was reached by non-orphan traumatized children of the same group in a 1 year's time. These results are concordant with Elizur and Kaffman's (1982, 1983) results on the 25 orphans of the Yom Kippur War. Both studies are prospective over 4 years, the reported prevalences are quite similar, and they follow the same pattern of decrease in prevalence over time. It is worth mentioning that in our study of the Lebanese, this course of PTSD was probably positively affected by the extensive availability of psychological and family support, financial help, as well as educational and medical follow-up to ensure to all orphans optimal development.

Some risk and protective factors were studied in correlation with the outcome of PTSD in that same group of Lebanese war orphans (Cordahi et al., 2002a, 2002b). Results show that both boys and girls were equally traumatized whether it was 1 or 2 years later. There was a trend for adolescents to show more PTSD reactions than children at 1 year, but not 2 years later. Interestingly, children's and adolescents' reactions to sudden parental death in war times is different depending on the gender of the deceased parent: the loss of a mother seems to induce significantly more PTSD reactions, while the loss of a father induces significantly more SAD reactions. In other words, in the situation of a violent parental death in war times, the absence of a mother seems to create a traumatized climate in the child's life that is sustained over 2 years (statistical significance holds for phases I and II). The absence of the father in the same conditions seems to create instead a kind of pathological attachment of the child to his surviving mother during the first year (statistical significance holds only for Phase I).

This finding raises the importance of studying how the nature of parental bonding with mothers and fathers may affect the child's reaction to traumatic grief when losing one of them. In fact, our preliminary results on the Prenatal Bonding Instrument (PBI) scores indicate that a perceived controlling, overprotective mother is a risk factor for developing depression after trauma, while a perceived caring mother, encouraging the autonomy of her child, is a protective factor for depression and overanxious disorders after trauma. Our results are also statistically significant with regards to the fact that the more the deceased

parent is perceived as having been overprotective and controlling, the more likely the child or adolescent is to display PTSD
as opposed to the other disorders measured.

On the other hand, it appears that a perceived caring stepmother, is not enough to be protective of any disorder including
PTSD. In fact, it seems that on the contrary, a perceived caring
stepmother is a significant risk factor for child/adolescent dysthymia. This finding may seem strange but it goes along with
Lebovici's (1994) and Melville and Lykes's (1992) discussions on
how a child's sense of estrangement and foreshortened future
may prevent the child from being able to reinvest emotionally in
new potential parental figures. When this new figure (in this case
the stepmother) is positive and caring, it seems to sink the child
into "nostalgic feelings" that we may have diagnosed as dysthymia following *DSM-IV* criteria.

Concerning surviving parents, a marginally significant relationship was found between parental psychopathology and posttraumatic disorders in children. Similarly, only a trend was found
for a relationship between the child's IQ and trauma-related psychopathology. Qualitatively, there seems to be a greater concentration of children and adolescents with disorders in the
low-average IQ group compared to other categories. These findings may need further analysis or replication in other studies, as
our numbers in each cell were probably too small for statistical
significance. In the studies of Wolff and colleagues (1994, 1999)
the authors found that war-traumatized orphans who lost both
parents and were living in orphanages, despite their severe emotional distress, did cognitively the same if not better than war-
traumatized non-orphans living with at least one surviving
parent.

There is consensus in the available literature that orphans of
war are at a high risk for developing psychopathology. There is
not enough information, though about how significantly traumatic should the loss or the war episode be. There is a need for

more emphasis while assessing orphans of war regarding their degree of exposure, their degree of witnessing violence, and the "traumatic significance" of the stress induced by war and by parental death. If criteria A (1) and (2) of the *DSM-IV* PTSD is confirmed by the child, than maybe one can safely call any disorder that the child develops after the event of criterion A, "posttraumatic." In Phase V of our study we included the "Inventory of Complicated Grief" (Prigerson et al., 1995), which assesses the concept of traumatic grief. More research in that same direction is needed to further confirm traumatic grief as a possibly distinct diagnostic entity. Since family and social support seem to be significant protective factors in the reported literature, there seems to be a need to assess the impact of the death of siblings in addition to that of parents.

It is difficult to study large enough numbers of war orphans to satisfy the statistics or to find appropriate control groups or to control for confounding variables within the same war-orphan group. In our study, children and adolescents were treated naturalistically, which makes our sample not ideally homogeneous for scientific research. Some variables (IQ, parental psychopathology) were assessed without bringing out clear-cut answers (only trends were found), maybe because of the small numbers in cells. However it is reassuring to see very similar findings between Elizur and Kaffman's study (1982) on the orphans traumatized by the Yom Kippur War and the Lebanese war orphans in terms of duration of posttraumatic stress reactions and patterns of improvement over time.

The challenge in our study was to assess the effects of a twofold trauma (war and bereavement) using clinical interviews and well-established structured instruments and to simultaneously conceptualize an individualized intervention plan that could address the needs of this high-risk population. The uniqueness of this intervention program lay in the fact that treatment was continuously based on ongoing empirical research findings.

Is Community Group Intervention Helpful?

Theoretical models for group therapy of children and adolescents following natural or human-made disasters have been proposed in the last 2 decades, providing guidelines for psychological first-aid (Pynoos & Nader, 1988) and steps in intervention (Dyregrov & Mitchell, 1992; Vernberg & Vogel, 1993). Some mainly descriptive accounts of community or school-based interventions have been reported in the literature (Blom, 1986; Rigamer, 1986, Klingman, 1987), and a few authors studied outcome of community-based treatment following natural disasters (Galante & Foa, 1986; Goenjian et al., 1997), bus accidents (Stallard & Law, 1993), and single incident stressors (March et al., 1998) finding improvement in PTSD symptoms in the treated groups. Methodological shortcomings such as absence of control groups (Stallard & Law, 1993; March et al., 1998), and small sample size (Stallard & Law, 1993; Snodgrass et al., 1993) in these studies limit their generalizability. The only war-related treatment outcome study of children and adolescents in the literature that we surveyed is limited to 11 Vietnamese refugees who were interviewed 8 to 14 years after war exposure (Snodgrass et al., 1993).

In parallel to the sample of Lebanese children and adolescents described earlier in this chapter, our group undertook the task of a school-based intervention targeting all 2,500 students of six public schools located in six villages designated by the Lebanese ministry of education as the most heavily exposed. The treatment delivered to these children was inspired from the model of Pynoos and Nader (1988) and modified to fit the specific context of war. It consisted of a combination of cognitive behavioral strategies, debriefing, and stress inoculation training. It was delivered by 68 fulltime teachers from the six selected schools chosen by their school principals for their reliability, assertiveness, and knowledge of their students. The teachers were trained and supervised to follow a step-by-step therapy manual and were asked to document their interventions daily (Karam, 2002). Therapy sessions took place in the classroom daily for 30 minutes each, over the course of 12 school days.

Out of the 2,500 treated students, a sample of 103 children and adolescents was randomly selected. Subjects and their parents were interviewed before treatment (Phase I) and re-interviewed 1 year later (Phase II) using the sections of the DICA-R indicated earlier in the chapter. The WEQ (Karam et al., 1999) was administered to parents. This sample comprised the "therapy group" (TG). Three mental health experts rated the teachers' manuals after the completion of the intervention. They rated according to the specificity with which the training instructions were followed in administering the intervention. This led to the division of TG into 2 groups: Specific Therapy Group (TG-S, N = 51) and Non Specific Therapy Group (TG-NS, N = 52). The TG-NS group thus became a natural control group, serving to control for nonspecific factors common to most psychotherapies (e.g., empathy and support of therapist).

The mean age of TG subjects was 11.79 ± 2.58 years with 56% at 12 years or younger and 52.6% males. A full 90% of the subjects were displaced and a third of their homes were damaged or destroyed (40% witnessed it). Just 15% of the subjects knew a close person who was injured (30% of that group witnessed it) (Karam et al., 2000). The prevalence of PTSD in the TG group at Phase I was 27.6% and there was substantial comorbidity with the other measured disorders (MDD, SAD, and OAD). At Phase II however there was only one case of PTSD in the TG-NS group and none in the TG-S. Since we could not demonstrate any difference between the two groups in the prevalence of PTSD of phase II we reexamined the subjects at Phase II with respect to the three clusters at the core of the PTSD diagnosis: reexperiencing, avoidance, and arousal. We required that subjects had dysfunction as a result of their PTSD symtomatology. We found that nearly 20% of all subjects in both treatment groups at Phase II met criteria for all three PTSD clusters with dysfunction but with removing the duration criteria of 4 weeks. This implied that a significant number of children and adolescents suffered from dysfunction related to PTSD symptoms but for a duration of less than 4 weeks. Although the two treatment groups did not differ significantly at Phase I with respect to the prevalence of the three PTSD clusters (TG-S 29.5%, TG-NS 44.7%, p = 0.136), there were significantly more subjects with three PTSD clusters in TG-S at phase II (TG-S 35.6%, TG-NS 8.3% p = 0.001). When examining the profile of the subjects in TG-S who had three PTSD clusters at Phase II, we discovered that 70% of them came from a single classroom (grade 3) in one particular school. That classroom happened to have received specific therapy and to have, at the same time, the highest war score on the WEQ of all the sample. A reanalysis of the data excluding subjects in this classroom made outcomes similar in both therapy groups.

Even though we could not demonstrate a significant effect of therapy regarding the outcome of the prevalence of disorders, we think that we were not able, through the instruments we have used, to measure some other possibly significant parameters more subtle to measure. The lack of demonstrably significant effects of therapy regarding the outcome of the prevalence of disorders may be attributable to the instruments inability to measure changes such as: changes in the way of thinking, in conceptualizing danger, processing rumors, dealing with emotions such as fear, sadness, loss, or uncertainty, projection of one's self into the future, and avoidance of particular situations.

We believe that should we have to reevaluate significant progress in children's or adolescents' quality of life as well as their resilience to trauma, details such as automatic thoughts, beliefs, and schemata of thinking would have to be measured. This would allow us to evaluate parameters that could inform us about the well-being of an individual, his or her strengths, resilience to events, the capacity for useful modulation of thoughts, coping strategies, and the capacity to deal with several emotions and managing them (anxiety, procrastination, insecurity). We could also measure remaining vulnerabilities and difficulties in those same domains. Our instruments were limited to assessing disorders only as clusters of symptoms, therefore inappropriate for examining details concerning the cognitive, emotional, and social rooting at the heart of anxiety and what maintains it.

In summary, the goal of this emergency intervention was to prevent and minimize the severity of clinical psychological manifestations resulting from traumatic war events. Several components of the stress inoculation training were emphasized throughout our intervention, particularly skills promoting and encouraging communication. Cognitive restructuring aiming at guiding the student's process of thinking, modifying his or her dysfunctional attitudes and beliefs, reducing harm from stress, shaping strategies of adaptation, and directing and reinforcing exploration and use of new possibilities were also important components used in the intervention.

Some positive effects of our therapeutic intervention could be observed through the following: communication between students and teachers became more focused and fruitful, the role of teachers was maximized to make it more efficient and directed towards specific students' needs while in a critical period of their lives, teachers allowed and facilitated the process of normalization, and symptoms of sadness, anxiety, and trauma were noticeably reduced. Working through common feelings and emotions as well as shared painful and extreme situations may have consolidated a sense of social bonding.

The debriefing experience, although questioned as a useful technique (Pupavac, 2002; Summerfield, 1999; Bisson & Deahl, 1994), was conducted in a structured, well-guided manner and manipulated towards finding alternatives for pain and despair. We insisted on open discussions and disclosures around a specific subject, well-processed and accurately reformulated by the teachers to reach appropriate closure before the end of a given session. When it was difficult to accomplish such a task in one session, the same issue was reopened in the course of the following session until reaching the desired goal.

Although we are not sure how efficient our intervention was in reducing the prevalence of the considered disorders (at times we would think it led to the opposite), we strongly believe that it is essential to view childhood and adolescence—as developmental periods—from a lifespan perspective. Both current risk and protective factors, as well as the history of their dynamic transactions and how they could influence the evolving individual over the course of development, are parameters to be considered in this part of our discussion. Therefore, in such a particular context where war and its associated adversities seem all-encompassing, we face a group of high-risk youth exposed to multiple interacting risk factors. Preventive efforts aiming to identify processes that contribute to positive adaptation despite profound adversities would be essential to promote in the lives of high-risk children and adolescents in general. Increasing number of protective factors or resources may facilitate resilient outcomes in children and adolescents at this stage of life, where possibilities are still open, because this stage constitutes a significant transitional period in development with the consequent emergence of new behavioral organization. From this perspective, our intervention provides a possible opportunity for prevention. Recent reviews have concluded that not all maltreated individuals are equally affected by their traumatic experiences (Cicchetti & Toth, 1995; Cicchetti & Rogosch, 2002). So from a developmental psychopathology perspective, our work could have meaning in terms of prevention and being a reliable source of "multifinality" emerging from a specific shared social adversity (the war). However, we might have needed a longer prevention program geared towards assisting such a high-risk youth community across successive periods in order to be effective in combating the heavy weight of multiple risk factors.

Many questions remain unanswered: What should be the duration of intervention and How should we decide to stop? Emergency interventions seem to be somehow useful but how long should they be maintained to prevent the installment of a chronic PTSD or negative affectivity? What do we mean by improvement and what kinds of improvement do we wish to attain in the aftermath of traumatic events? How to measure such improvement? A significant effort is to be put into answering these questions. Our measurements clearly do not point to a favorable effect of intervention; maybe the positive effects lie somewhere else as outlined above.

Developmental psychology and psychopathology which take into consideration several parameters across scientific disciplines at multiple levels of analysis and multiple domains would enhance our understanding and help us identify and emphasize the critical variables prone to be involved in the various trajectories taken by different individuals. In the light of this perspective, we can better direct our work in terms of effective prevention and treatment.

Conclusion

As the previous century drew to a close, many wars in many countries had ravaged the world, taking their heavy toll on families and children. If the first 3 years of this century are any indication for what is yet to come, we must brace ourselves for more wars, not only in the developing world but possibly in regions that were previously considered immune. Whether it is full-blown war or isolated acts of terrorism, children will be exposed to violence whether in person or from a distance viewed with unimaginable macabre and gory detail on television.

We have seen that war exposure can result in significant numbers of children and adolescents with PTSD either as the sole disorder or comorbid with other disorders such as major depressive disorder (MDD), separation anxiety disorder (SAD), and overanxious disorder (OAD). All studies reviewed found a direct relationship between PTSD and war exposure, but it is the specific experience of witnessing the war trauma that is traumatogenic. It seems insufficient to simply be there in the midst of bombing to develop PTSD. However, the case is not that clear-cut for children and adolescents with specific risk factors that predispose them to be more prone to develop PTSD or for PTSD to last longer. Indeed, relational issues pertaining to the child's or adolescent's parents seem to exert an effect in both directions: these issues can complicate outcomes or facilitate recovery and adjustment. We found this to be particularly true in the case of orphans bereaved during war. For this special population even witnessing trauma was insufficient as a predictor: the meaning ascribed to parental death seemed paramount in the phases that followed acute bereavement.

With war being a social phenomenon first, it is conceivable that while this negative external stressor can be powerful enough to induce mental health disorders, social support may also gather momentum in the aftermath of war trauma to become a positive force that can play a role in remission of disorders. Indeed, studies that examined the effect of posttrauma social support seem to suggest a potentially pivotal role in outcome of children and adolescents. Clearly, more elaborate and prospective research designs are needed to investigate this further.

Our reading of the literature of prospective studies of children and war and our own community studies suggests that while large numbers of children and adolescents appear to be afflicted with PTSD (or other mental health disorders) during or after war exposure, the majority of subjects seem to improve over the course of at least 1 year. While on the surface this may appear reassuring, a closer look reveals that while many subjects do not meet full criteria for PTSD anymore, they are subsyndromic for this disorder and they have dysfunction associated with these symptoms. Thus whether PTSD is measured categorically or dimensionally, the current criteria cannot be relied upon solely to distinguish those with treatment needs from those who are adjusting well. Similarly, the current PTSD criteria were insufficient in measuring the child's or adolescent's posttraumatic disorder when parental death was an integral part of the war event. Exciting research in the field of traumatic grief can hopefully shed light on these issues and perhaps describe in one disorder a fuller and more complete picture of child's psychopathology than a combination of two or more comorbid but separate disorders.

The fact that there appears to be a spontaneous remission of PTSD after war raises interesting questions pertaining to intervention. Is it necessary to intervene on a mass community level shortly after war (or disasters) or is it wiser to wait until at least several months pass in order to target only individuals with symptoms severe enough to interfere with their lives? The literature and our prospective study of an epidemiologic sample of children and adolescents suggests the latter approach. If a postwar intervention is planned, should it include everyone who was exposed (as is done with debriefing) or only those who continue to exhibit psychopathology several months later? Our controlled group community study could not demonstrate a long term (i.e., 1 year later) effect of the intervention. However, we had disorders and psychopathology as outcome. War, in the broadest sense, affects more than the individual child's psyche. At stake are the children's families, their education, their peer relations, and their homes. Millions of dollars are spent on psychological intervention programs following wars and disasters. Our survey of the literature and our data suggests that a closer look at their efficacy and long term outcome is warranted before they become routine measures to implement. We do not know if equally positive outcomes can be achieved by a social program of rebuilding and restoring normalcy to war zones without a psychotherapeutic component built in. Can a social intervention cure PTSD or posttraumatic depression and anxiety the same way psychotherapy does? It would be morally, ethically, and scientifically challenging to design such a study, but these are crucial questions that need to be addressed by mental health researchers and policy makers alike.

What is it like for a child or adolescent to experience war events? What effect does it have to be constantly aggressed upon and have one's safety and stability constantly violated? What messages do children receive by watching war atrocities committed against other children while no one seems to be able to intervene? Sad as it may seem, wars are likely to flare up for many more years to come and PTSD will remain at the fore of childhood disorders. Eighty percent of the world's children reside in developing countries, where most wars are taking place. These are also the countries where child mental health training and services are most lacking (Fayyad et al., 2001). Child mental health professionals need to take leading roles, locally in their respective cultures as well as internationally, to help bridge gaps in our knowledge about wars and psychopathology, as well as cost-effective interventions.

The research done in Lebanon to which this chapter refers was supported by the Institute for Development of Research and Applied Care (IDRAC), Lebanon, the Lebanese Ministry of Interior, UNICEF, the Dutch Foreign Ministry, the Hariri Foundation, and the Lebanese Research Council.

The authors wish to acknowledge the following individuals for their contribution to the field work that took place in 1996 and 1997 for the study on children and war: Nadine Melhem PhD, MPH, Viviane Zebouni MA, Ghazi Kayyali MPH, Philip Yabroudi MA, Nisrine Rachidi MPH, and Hani Dimasi MPH.

Finally the authors are indebted to the efforts of Ms. Caroline Ayvazian and Ms. Zeina Kozah for their support in the completion of the manuscript.

References

Ahmad A, Sofi MA, Sundelin-Wahlsten V, Von Knorring AL. (2000). Posttraumatic stress disorder in children after the military operation "Anfal" in Iraqi Kurdistan. *Eur Child Adolesc Psychiatry.* 9(4):235–243.

Allwood MA, Bell-Dolan D, Husain SA. (2002). Children's trauma and adjustment reactions to violent and nonviolent war experiences. *J Am Acad Child Adolesc Psychiatry.* 41(4):450–457.

Almqvist K, Brandell-Forsberg M. (1997). Refugee children in Sweden: posttraumatic stress disorder in Iranian preschool children exposed to organized violence. *Child Abuse Neglect.* 21(4):351–366.

American Psychiatric Association. (1994). *Diagnostic and Statistical Manual of Mental Disorders* (4th ed.) Washington, DC: American Psychiatric Association.

Arrindell WA, Gerlsma C, Vandereycken W, Hageman WJJM, Daeseleire T. (1998). Convergent validity of the dimensions underlying the parental bonding instrument (PBI) and the EMBU. *Personality Individual Differences.* 24(3):341–350.

Arroyo W, Eth S. (1996). Post-traumatic stress disorder and other stress reactions. In: Apfel RJ and Simon B, eds. *Minefields in their Hearts.* New Haven, Conn: Yale University Press; 52–74.

Bachar E, Canetti L, Bonne O, Denour AK, Shalev AY. (1997). Psychological well being and rating of psychiatric symptoms in bereaved Israeli adolescents: differential effect of war versus accident-related bereavement. *J Nerv Mental Dis.* 185(6):402–406.

Beck AT, Steer RA. (1990). *Beck Anxiety Inventory: Manual.* San Antonio, Tex: Harcourt Brace.

Beck AT, Steer RA, Brown GK. (1996). *Beck Depression Inventory: Manual* (2nd ed). San Antonio, Tex: Harcourt Brace.

Berman H. (2001). Children and war: current understanding and future directions. *Public Health Nursing.* 18(4):243–252.

Birtchnell J, Kennard J. (1984). How do the experiences of the early separated early bereaved differ, and to what extent do such differences affect outcome? *Soc Psychiatry.* 19(4):163–171.

Bisson JI, Deahl MP. (1994). Psychological debriefing and prevention of post-traumatic stress; more research is needed. *Br J Psychiatry*. 165:717–720.

Blom GE. (1986). A school disaster-intervention and research aspects. *J Am Acad Child Adolesc Psychiatry*. 25(3):336–345.

Breslau N, Chilcoat H, Kessler R, Davis G. (1999). Previous exposure to trauma and PTSD effects of subsequent trauma: results from the Detroit area survey of trauma. *Am J Psychiatry*. 156(6):902–907.

Brown GW, Harris T. (1978). *Social Origin of Depression: A Study on Psychiatric Disorders in Women*. New York: Free Press.

Cairns E. (1996). Children as political activists. In: Cairns E, ed. *Children and Political Violence*. Oxford, UK: Blackwell Publishers; 107–137.

Cicchetti D, Rogosch FA. (2002). A developmental psychopathology perspective on adolescence. *J Consult Clinical Psychology*. 70 (1):6–20.

Cicchetti D, Toth SL. (1995). A developmental psychopathology perspective on child abuse and neglect. *J Am Acad Child Adolesc Psychiatry*. 34:541–565.

Clark G, Sack W H, Goff B. (1993). Three forms of stress in Cambodian adolescent refugees. *J Abnormal Child Psychology*. 21:65–77.

Cordahi C, Karam E G, Nehmeh G, Fayyad J, Melhem N, Rashidi N. (2002a). Les orphelins de la guerre: expérience Libanaise et méthodologie d'un suivi prospectif. *Revue Francophone du Stress et du Trauma*. 2(4):1–9.

Cordahi C, Karam EG, Nehmeh G, Fayyad J, Melhem N, Rashidi N. (2002b). Les orphelins de la guerre: vulnérabilité et résilience. *Revue Médicale Libanaise*. Janvier:11–16.

De Jong JVM, Komproe IH, Van Ommeren M, et al. (2001). Lifetime events and posttraumatic stress disorder in 4 post-conflict settings. *J Am Med Ass*. 286(5):555–562.

Duggal HS, Berezkin G, John V. (2002). PTSD and TV viewing of World Trade Center. *J Am Acad Child Adolesc Psychiatry*. 41(5):494–495.

Dyregov A, Kuterovac G, Barath A. (1996). Factor analysis of the impact of events scale with children in war. *Scandinavian J Psychology*. 37:339–350.

Dyregrov A, Mitchell JT. (1992). Work with traumatized children—psychological effects and coping strategies. *J Traumatic Stress*. 5 (1): 5–17.

Elizur E, Kaffman M. (1982). Children's bereavement reactions following death of the father: II. *J Am Acad Child Adolesc Psychiatry.* 21(5):471–480.

Elizur E, Kaffman M. (1983). Factors influencing the severity of childhood bereavement reactions. *Am J Orthopsychiatry.* 53(4):668–676.

Engel CC Jr, Liu C, McCarthy B D, Miller R F, Ursano R. (2000). Relationship of physical symptoms to posttraumatic stress disorder among veterans seeking care for Gulf War-related health concerns. *Psychosomatic Med.* 62:739–745.

Fayyad JA, Jahshan CS, Karam EG. (2001). Systems development of child mental health services in developing countries. *Child Adolesc Psychiat Clin N Am.* 10(4):745–762.

Feighner JP, Robins E, Guze SB, Woodruff RA, Winokur G, Munoz R. (1972). Diagnostic criteria for use in psychiatric research. *Arch Gen Psychiatry.* 26:57–63.

Ford JD. (1999). Disorders of extreme stress following war-zone military trauma: associated features of posttraumatic stress disorder or comorbid but distinct syndromes? *J Consult Clinical Psychology.* 67(1):3–12.

Galante R, Foa D. (1986). An epidemiological study of psychic trauma and treatment effectiveness for children after a natural disaster. *J Am Acad Child Adolesc Psychiatry.* 25(3):357–363.

Garmezy N, Rutter M. (1985). Acute Reactions to Stress. In: Rutter M, Hersov L, eds. *Basic Handbook of Child Psychiatry.* New York: Basic Books; 270–283.

Garrison CZ, Bryant ES, Addy CL, Spurrier PG, Freedy JR, Kilpatrick DG. (1995). Posttraumatic stress disorder in adolescents after Hurricane Andrew. *J Am Acad Child Adolesc Psychiatry.* 34(9):1193–1201.

Gerardot D. (2001). *Traumatic Grief in the Chemically Abusing/Dependent Adolescent in Treatment.* Dissertation Abstracts International. 62 (3–13), Sep 2001, 1574, US: Univ Microfilms International.

Goenjian AK, Karayan I, Pynoos RS, et al. (1997). Outcome of psychotherapy among early adolescents after trauma. *Am J Psychiatry.* 154:536–542.

Goenjian AK, Pynoos RS, Steinberg AM, et al. (1995). Psychiatric comorbidity in children after the 1988 earthquake in Armenia. *J Am Acad Child Adolesc Psychiatry.* 34(9):1194–1184.

Goldstein RD, Wampler NS, Wise PH. (1997). War experiences and distress symptoms of Bosnian children. *Pediatrics*. 100(5):873–878.

Gudjonsson G. (1993). *The Psychology of Interrogations, Confessions and Testimony*. West Sussex, UK: Wiley.

Husain SA, Nair J, Holcomb W, Reid JC, Vargas V, Nair SS. (1998). Stress reactions of children and adolescents in war and siege donditions. *Am J Psychiatry*. 155:1718–1719.

Jensen PS, Shaw J. (1993). Children as victims of war: current knowledge and future research needs. *J Am Acad Child Adolesc Psychiatry*. 32 (4):697–708.

Karam EG. (1992). Depression et guerres du Liban: methodologie d'une recherche. *Annales de Psychologie et des Sciences de l'Education*. (Université St. Joseph, Beyrouth). 99–106.

Karam EG, Al Atrash R, Saliba S, Melhem N, Howard D. (1999). The War Events Questionnaire. *Soc Psychiatry Psychiatric Epidemiology*. 34(5):265–274.

Karam EG, Karam AN, Cordahi C, et al. (2000). *Community group treatment and outcome of war trauma in children*. Presented at: 47th Annual Meeting of the American Academy of Child and Adolescent Psychiatry. New York.

Karam EG, Karam AN, Cordahi C, et al. (2001, December). *Trauma and wars: outcome of treatment interventions and a large scale prospective study*. Presented at: Association de Langue Française pour l'Etude du Stress et du Trauma (ALFEST) Congress. Paris, France.

Karam AN, Karam EG, Zbouni B, Yabroudi P, Cordahi C, Fayyad J. (2002). Traumatismes et guerres: prévention psychologique à large echelle. *Revue Francophone du Stress et du Trauma*. 2(3):169–177.

Karam EG, Melhem N, Karam AN, et al. (1997a). Acute responses to war trauma in children and adolescents: the Lebanon Wars. *Traumatic stress points. News for The International Society for Traumatic Stress Studies (ISTSS)*. 11(3):1, 7.

Karam EG, Melhem N, Karam AN, et al. (1997b). *War and Mental Health: Children and the Grapes of Wrath, Updated Report*. Beirut: UNICEF.

King DW, King LA, Erikson DJ, Huang MT, Sharkansky E J, Wolf J (2000). Posttraumatic stress disorder and retrospectively reported stressor exposure: a longitudinal prediction model. *J Abnormal Psychology*. 109(4):624–633.

Kinzie JD, Sack W, Angell R, Clarke G, Ben R. (1989). A three-year follow-up on Cambodian young people traumatized as children. *J Am Acad Child Adolesc Psychiatry*. 28(4):501–504.

Klingman A. (1987). A school-based emergency crisis intervention in a mass school disaster. *Professional Psychology: Res Practice*. 18(6):604–612.

Laor N, Wolmer L, Cohen DJ. (2001). Mothers' functioning and children's symptoms 5 years after a SCUD missile attack. *Am J Psychiatry*. 158(7):1020–1026.

Laor N, Wolmer L, Mayes LC, et al. (1996). Israeli preschoolers under SCUD missile attacks: a developmental perspective on risk-modifying factors. *Arch Gen Psychiatry*. 53:416–423.

Lebovici S. (1994). Le travail de deuil chez l'enfant. In: *Monographie de la Revue Française de Psychanalyse*. Paris: PUF; 73–93.

Liotti G, Pasquini P, Italian Group for the Study of Dissociation. (2000). Predictive factors for borderline personality disorder: patient's early traumatic experiences and losses suffered by the attachment figures. *Acta Psychiatrica Scandinavia*. 102:282–289.

Macksoud MS, Aber JL. (1996). The war experiences and psychosocial development of children in Lebanon. *Child Dev*. 67:70–88.

March JS, Amaya-Jackson L, Murray MC, Shulte A. (1998). Cognitive-behavioral psychotherapy for children and adolescents with PTSD after a single-incident stressor. *J Am Acad Child Adolesc Psychiatry*. 37(6):585–593.

Melville MB, Lykes MB. (1992). Guatemalan Indian children and the socio-cultural effects of government-sponsored terrorism. *Soc Science Med*. 34(5):533–548.

Mollica RF, Poole C, Murray CC, Tor S. (1997). Effects of war trauma on Cambodian refugee adolescents' functional health and mental health status. *J Am Acad Child Adolescent Psychiatry*. 36(8):1098–1106.

Morah E, Mebrathv S, Sebhatuk. (1998). Evaluation of the orphan reunification project in Eritrea. *Evaluation and Program Planning*. 21(4):437–448.

Nader KO, Pynoos RS. (1991). Play and drawing as tools for interviewing traumatized children. In: Schaeffer C, Gitlan K, Sandgrund A, eds. *Play, Diagnosis, and Assessment*. New York: Wiley; 375–389.

Nader KO, Pynoos RS, Fairbanks LA, Al-Ajeel M, Al-Asfour A. (1993). A preliminary study of PTSD and grief among the children of Kuwait following the Gulf crisis. *Br J Clin Psychol.* 32:407–416.

O'Toole BI, Marshall RP, Grayson DA, et al. (1996). The Australian Vietnam veterans health study: III. Psychological health of Australian Vietnam veterans and its relationship to combat. *Int J Epidemiology.* 25(2):331–340.

Paardekooper B, De Jong JT, Hermanns JM. (1999). The psychological impact of war and the refugee situation on South Sudanese children in refugee camps in Northern Uganda: an exploratory study. *J Child Psychol Psychiatry.* 40(4):529–536.

Pfefferbaum B, Nixon SJ, Tivis RD, et al. (2001). Television exposure in children after a aerrorist attack. *Psychiatry.* 64(3):202–211.

Prigerson HG, Maciejewski PK, Reynolds CF, et al. (1995). Inventory of Complicated Grief: a scale to measure maladaptive symptoms of loss. *Psychiatry Res.* 59(1–2):65–79.

Punamaki RL. (1996). Can ideological commitment protect children's psychological wellbeing in situations of political violence? *Child Dev.* 67:55–69.

Pupavac V. (2002). Afghanistan: The risks of international psychosocial risk management. *Health in Emergencies* (World Health Organization). 12:1–2.

Pynoos RS, Nader K. (1988). Psychological first aid and treatment approach to children exposed to community violence: research implications. *J Traumatic Stress.* 1(4):445–473.

Realmuto GM, Masten A, Carole LF, Hubbard J, Groteluschem A, Chlun B. (1992). Adolescent survivors of massive childhood trauma in Cambodia: life events and current symptoms. *J Traumatic Stress.* 5(4):589–599.

Rigamer EF. (1986). Psychological management of children in a national crisis. *J Am Acad Child Adolesc Psychiatry.* 25:364–369

Rousseau C, Drapeau A, Plartt R. (1999). Family trauma and its association with emotional and behavioral problems and social adjustment in adolescent Cambodian refugees. *Child Abuse Neglect.* 23(12):1263–1273.

Sack WH. (1998). Multiple forms of stress in refugee and immigrant children. *Child and Adolesc Psychiat Clin N Am.* 7(1):153–168.

Sack WH, Clarke GN, Tim C, et al. (1993). A 6-year follow-up study of Cambodian refugee adolescents traumatized as children. *J Am Acad Child Adolescent Psychiatry*. 32(2):431–437.

Scherer DG, Melloh T, Buyck D, Anderson C, Foster A. (1996). Relation between children's perception of maternal mental illness and children's psychological adjustment. *J Clin Child Psychology*. 25(2):156–169.

Schwarzwald J, Weisenberg M, Solomon Z, Waysman M. (1994). Stress reactions of school-age children to the bombardment by SCUD missiles: a 1-year follow-up. *J Traumatic Stress*. 7(4):657–667.

Servan-Schreiber D, Lelin B, Birmaher B. (1998). Prevalence of posttraumatic stress disorder and major depressive disorder in Tibetan refugee children. *J Am Acad Child Adolesc Psychiatry*. 37(8):874–879.

Simons B, Silveira WR. (1994). Post-traumatic stress disorder in children after television programmes. *Br Med Journal*. 308:389–390.

Smith P, Perrin S, Yule W, Rabe-Hesketh S. (2001). War exposure and maternal reactions in the psychological adjustment of children from Bosnia-Herzegovina. *J Child Psychol Psychiatry*. 42(3):395–404.

Snodgrass LL, Yamamoto J, Frederick C, et al. (1993). Vietnamese refugees with PTSD symptomatology: intervention via a coping skills model. *J Traumatic Stress*. 6(4):569–575.

Stallard P, Law F. (1993). Screening and psychological debriefing of adolescent survivors of life-threatenning events. *Br J Psychiatry*. 163:660–665.

Summerfield D. (1999). A critique of seven assumptions behind psychological prauma programmes in war-affected areas. *Soc Science Med*. 48:1449–1462.

Thabet AA, Vostanis P. (2000). Post-traumatic stress reactions in children of war: a longitudinal study. *Child Abuse Neglect*. 24(2):291–298.

Thabet AAM, Vostanis P. (1999). Post-traumatic stress reactions in children of war. *J Child Psychol Psychiatry*. 40(3):385–391.

UNICEF. (2000). *The State of the World's Children Report*. New York: UNICEF.

Vernberg EM, Vogel JM. (1993). Task force report, Part 2: Interventions with children after disasters. *J Clin Child Psychology*. 22(4):485–498.

Weisenberg M, Shwarzwald J, Waysman M, Solomon Z, Klingman A. (1993). Coping of school-age children in the sealed room during SCUD missile bombarment and postwar stress reactions. *J Consult Clin Psychology*. 61 (3):462–467.

Weiss D. (1996). Psychometric review of the impact of events scale-revised. In: Stamm BH, ed., *Measurement of Stress, Trauma, and Adaptation*. Lutherville, Md: Sidran Press; 186–188.

Weller EB, Weller RA, Fristad MA, Bowes JM. (1991). Depression in recently bereaved prepubertal children. *Am J Psychiatry*. 146(11):1536–1540.

Welner Z, Reich W, Herjanic B, Jung KG, Amado H. (1987). Reliability, validity and parent-child agreement studies of the diagnostic interview for children and adolescents (DICA). *J Am Acad Child Adolesc Psychiatry*. 26:649–653.

Westermeyer J, Wahmanholm, K. (1996). Refugee children: In: Apfel RJ and Simon B, eds. *Minefields in their Hearts*. New Haven, Conn: Yale University Press; 75–103.

Wolff PH, Fesseha G. (1998). The orphans of Eritrea: are orphanages part of the problem or of the solution? *Am J Psychiatry*. 155(10):1319–1324.

Wolff PH, Fesseha G. (1999). The orphans of Eritrea: a five year follow-up study. *J Child Psychol Psychiatry*. 40(8):1231–1237.

Wolff PH, Tesfani B, Egasso H, Aradom T. (1994). The orphans of Eritrea: a comparison study. *J Child Psychol Psychiatry*. 36(4):633–644.

Woodcock RW, Johnson MB. (1989, 1990). *Woodcock-Johnson Psychoeducational Battery-Revised*. Itasca, Ill: Riverside Publishing.

Woodruff RA, Goodwin D, Guze SB. (1974). *Psychiatric Diagnosis*. New York: Oxford University Press.

Yule W. (2000). From pogroms to "ethnic cleansing:" meeting the needs of war-affected children. *J Child Psychol Psychiatry*. 41(6):695–702.

Ziv A, Kruglanski AW, Shulman S. (1974). Children's psychological reactions to wartime stress. *J Pers Soc Psychol*. 30(1):24–30.

Zvizdic S, Butollo W. (2001). Related loss of one's father and persistant depressive reactions in early adolescents. *European Psychologist*. 6(3):204–214.

Index